Environmental Certification for Organisations and Produc

Environmental certification is an effective tool for managing the environmental impact of companies, leveraging their competitive capabilities, and ensuring their compliance with environmental principles. A growing number of countries across the world are adopting this practice and the growth of new environmental standards – with different scopes, aims, and roles – calls for a clear and updated systematisation of the issue.

This book provides a comprehensive, up-to-date overview of the different environmental certification tools. As well as examining practical methods of implementing the standards for each type of certification, the book discusses their added value from a corporate management perspective. In identifying the most important requirements and standards for the issuing of environmental certification of both products and processes, the book demonstrates how companies can use operational methods to develop an environmental management system or a product certification in practice.

Balancing a complete theoretical presentation of the issue with an operational perspective, the book supports the adoption and implementation of environmental certification tools. It will be a valuable resource for professionals as well as students and scholars of environmental management, sustainable business, and corporate social responsibility.

Tiberio Daddi is Assistant Professor at the Institute of Management at the Sant'Anna School of Advanced Studies, Italy.

Fabio Iraldo is Associate Professor at the Institute of Management at the Sant'Anna School of Advanced Studies and Research Director at Bocconi University, Italy.

Francesco Testa is Associate Professor at the Institute of Management at the Sant'Anna School of Advanced Studies, Italy.

Routledge Research in Sustainability and Business

Environmental Certification for Organisations and Products
Management approaches and operational tools
Edited by Tiberio Daddi, Fabio Iraldo and Francesco Testa

Formerly restricted to accounting audits, certification practices have grown exponentially in recent years, notably in the area of environmental management. Written by experienced scholars and practitioners with a deep understanding of environmental certification, this book provides an enlightening, instructive and well documented synthesis of this little-known field.

*Olivier Boiral, Université Laval, director of the Canada
Research Chair in Sustainable Development Management
Standards – Canada*

All readers will find in this book much to stimulate their thinking on environmental management. Its contents, the variety of benefits coming from the adoption of enviromental initiatives, are explored, and the practices and tools available are shown to the reader in a very practical way.

*Víctor Vázquez, Head of Environmental Department, Andalusian
Institute of Technology – IAT – Spain*

The book not only offers a comprehensive overview of the existing environmental management practices and certification schemes but also successfully serves as a deep interpretation and understanding of the standards requirements and the necessary steps for their adoption and implementation, constituting itself into an excellent educational material for academics and practitioners.

*Aida Szilagyi, chair of National Centre for Sustainable
Consumption and Production (NCSPC) of Romania*

In the context of climate change and other global environmental problems, environmental management systems and approaches will become more important for companies in the near future. The book gives a complete overview of common standards and provides a valuable contribution to the topic of how sustainable development can succeed in business.

*Monika Brom, Deputy Head of Unit Sustainable
Development – Environment Agency Austria
Chair of EU EMAS Competent Bodies – Austria*

The book exhaustively covers all main environment issues related to third party audits and recognitions, such as endorsements and certifications, including an effective recall on audit techniques adopted by the certification bodies. A valuable reference for all the 'insiders'.

*Zeno Beltrami, Business Development Manager at DNV GL
Business Assurance, Region South Europe*

Environmental Certification for Organisations and Products

Management approaches and operational tools

Tiberio Daddi, Fabio Iraldo and
Francesco Testa

Routledge
Taylor & Francis Group

LONDON AND NEW YORK

First published 2015 by Routledge

2 Park Square, Milton Park, Abingdon, Oxon OX14 4RN
711 Third Avenue, New York, NY 10017, USA

Routledge is an imprint of the Taylor & Francis Group, an informa business

First issued in paperback 2016

British Library Cataloguing-in-Publication Data
A catalogue record for this book is available from the British Library

Library of Congress Cataloging-in-Publication Data
A catalog record for this title has been requested

ISBN: 978-1-138-78473-4 (hbk)
ISBN: 978-1-138-28360-2 (pbk)

Typeset in Goudy
by diacriTech

Table of contents

List of Tables and Figures

Tables

Figures

1 Perspectives on environmental management

Historical overview of environmental management and further needs

The relationship between human beings and the environment has always been interspersed with moments of conflict and harmony depending on the individual's ability to live with respect to the carrying capacity of the ecosystems.

Various studies indicate that acts of environmental pollution have accompanied human civilisations since ancient times (Nriagu, 1983). For instance, soot found on the ceilings of prehistoric caves provides ample proof of the high levels of pollution associated with the inadequate ventilation of naked flames (Brimblecomb, 1995). The forging of metals, which began in the Chalcolithic period, seems to be a turning point in the creation of significant levels of external atmospheric pollution and core borings of glaciers in Greenland indicate an increase in pollution associated with the production of metal by the ancient Greeks, Romans and Chinese (Hong et al., 1994).

Other examples may include the behaviour of the colonies on the North American prairies, which, in the space of a few decades, almost annihilated the buffalo population with which the Natives had found a balance for coexistence lasting thousands of years.

Other authors see the Industrial Revolution, which began in England in 1700 and a little later in North America, as the start of a conflicting relationship between man and nature. This is the onset of the industrialisation process, which lasted almost two centuries and gave birth to the capitalist economy (Hobsbawm, 1975). The first companies with increasingly mechanised equipment and factories were created; profit and wealth became the values influencing individuals' actions. A multitude of innovations radically changed peoples' way of life and with it their relationship with the environment. An increase in production and consumption often concentrated in enclosed locations like big cities such as London and New York caused a rise in the pollution of the atmosphere and waters and the first interventions for the management of organic waste.

This situation continued until somewhere between the end of the eighteenth century and the beginning of the nineteenth century when the first environmentalist movements such as the conservation movement (Buchholz, 1993) were born in the United States. This movement arose from the need to increase awareness in society about a more careful management of resources both by individuals and by businesses and it can be considered the forerunner of the environmental movement, which began in the mid-1960s.

It is, in fact, from the second half of the 1960s onwards that we can see the first change in the attitude of industrial organisations to the way they interacted with the environment. We can pinpoint the birth of the first green practices by companies to this period.

In the early 1970s, the economic and social effects of environmental degradation, caused by the unsustainable use of natural resources and as a consequence of industrial activity, began to exert a pressure on industry to improve its performance. The combined influence of public and community opinion, environmental pressure groups, 'green' political parties and the media (at local, national and global level) targeted policy makers and brought forth a regulatory regime that demanded high levels of compliance of the large industrial organisations. It is the period of the first global conference on the human environment (Stockholm, 1972), where scientific and political debates considered systems of consumption and production as a potential threat to human survival. Climate change, loss of natural resources, extinction of species and environmental damage caused by emissions and waste can result from unsustainable patterns of consumption and production.

The major catastrophes which occurred during the 1970s and 1980s (including Seveso, Three Mile Island, Bhopal, Chernobyl) served to strengthen the public belief that most environmental problems were connected with the activities of large organisations, mainly multinationals operating in specific industrial sectors such as chemicals, petrochemicals and nuclear power.

In consequence, public policy making bodies in charge of environmental control paid more attention to larger companies than to smaller ones. Industries and companies targeted had to spend their energies and resources in seeking solutions to environmental problems and demonstrating socially acceptable behaviour. During the 1990s, the public concern about small and medium enterprises' (SMEs) contribution to the deterioration of the environment has also rapidly increased. In order to effect a global improvement in industry's environmental performance, policymakers have become aware that environmental policy measures, supports and incentives should also target SMEs. During this period, it became increasingly urgent for many companies to play their part in finding reliable ways of managing environmental problems through innovative means, which place emphasis on effectiveness and integrated solutions, rather than conventional management and bolt-on 'end-of-pipe' means.

From the year 2000 onwards, the possibility of combining competitive advantages and eco-efficiency became more evident in businesses. The environmental variable became an integral part of corporate strategy and a factor to take into consideration in all corporate functions. Integration occurred both on a strategic and operative level and the environment became an almost moral obligation for business owners and was demanded by external stakeholders as well.

This process led Pane Haden et al. (2009) to an interesting definition of environmental management by attempting to combine and summarise the various aspects which characterise it, namely, 'Green management is the organisation-wide process of applying innovation to achieve sustainability, waste reduction, social responsibility, and a competitive advantage via continuous learning and development and by embracing environmental goals and strategies that are fully integrated with the goals and strategies of the organisation'.

This evolution in companies' attitude, combined with an even more efficient approach by regulatory bodies, has led to greater improvements even though some critical elements still remain.

For instance, the emissions from European Economic Area (EEA) countries have been reduced 17 per cent since 1990 and appear to be steadily decreasing, although they are still five times higher than the 2050 target for a sustainable level of greenhouse gas (GHG) emissions from Europe. At absolute level, production-related direct greenhouse gas emissions of the European Union (EU-25) remained nearly constant over the same period but showed a slight increase since 1999 (Watson et al., 2011).

On the contrary, direct emissions of acidifying gases and ground-level precursors related to European production saw an absolute decoupling from economic growth during the period 1995–2006 (they decreased by 27 per cent and 13 per cent, respectively despite an increase in economic output of 40 per cent) (Watson et al., 2011).

Moreover, long term improvements in material productivity and energy productivity have been less rapid than improvements in labour productivity: during the period 1970–2007, productivity per unit of labour in the EU 15 increased by 144 per cent, while productivity per unit of material and of energy increased by 94 per cent and 69 per cent respectively (Watson et al., 2011).

Looking at products, many of these are gradually becoming more energy-efficient during their use phase. Most energy using products for which data is available across Europe have shown improvements in energy efficiency since 1990. Petrol and diesel cars have reduced their fuel consumption per kilometer by roughly 10 per cent over this period, while washing machines and dishwashers reduced electricity use per cycle by 25 per cent and 37 per cent respectively (Watson et al., 2011).

Moreover, consumer spending is changing toward a higher share of overall spending on services. This development may contribute to relative decoupling of environmental pressures from economic growth, since service sectors generally have lower environmental intensities than average. However, further improvement should be addressed, mainly on product categories showing higher environmental intensities (i.e. transport, food and drink and housing goods). In particular, in each product categories demand should be oriented towards more environmental friendly products.

In summary, the need for further initiatives has been demonstrated from various perspectives.

1   Current trends in resources used for production and consumption show that this might trespass the biocapacity of the planet Earth. Concepts like Ecological Footprint or Human Appropriation of Net Primary Production (HANPP) show that the limits of our current economic system are rapidly reaching the biophysical limits of our environment.
2   Energy, resources and waste are all costs to the economy. By not utilising our resources more efficiently, competitiveness of companies may be at risk. A recent study showed that EU companies acknowledged the importance of resource efficiency as a viable strategy for cost reduction, product quality improvement and increased productivity, hence, a viable strategy for maintaining competitiveness in their global markets (Rademaekers et al., 2011).
3   The inclusion of sustainable production and consumption into decision-making processes may form an excellent case for the growing number of green jobs. Jobs in renewable energy have increased by 25 per cent in 2009 and 2010 (Eurobserver, 2011).

Overall, the challenge is to create a virtuous circle: improving the environmental performance of products throughout their life-cycle, promoting and stimulating the demand of better products and production technologies and helping consumers to make better informed choices. This calls for actions at the *microeconomic level* – i.e. for actions that directly affect individual economic actors and both institutional and private consumers – as well as for actions aimed at *integrating the resource efficiency issue* along three areas:

1   **Products**, in order to improve their environmental performance;
2   **Consumption**, in order to stimulate demand for 'green' products and to assist consumers to reduce their environmental impacts;
3   **Production**, in order to improve companies' resource efficiency and competitiveness while reducing their environmental impacts.

Theoretical perspectives on environmental management: from institutional theory to resource-based view theory

Environmental emergencies derived from unsustainable consumption and production patterns have led to the need to change the behaviour of firms and to adopt new solutions to combine economic success with the preservation of natural resources (Pane Haden et al., 2009).

In the literature, the determinants of environmental practices' adoption can be broadly divided into 'external factors', mostly linked to stakeholders' pressure; and 'internal factors', i.e. a specific business-led strategic process. These differ according to the source of the 'stimulus' that drives the development of an environmental strategy, and that encourages their diffusion through all a firm's functions or departments.

The adoption of environmental practices at the firm level has been mainly investigated within the framework of institutional and neo institutional theory (Henriques and Sadorsky, 1999; Delmas, 2002; Brammer et al., 2012; Gusmerotti et al., 2012). The institutional environment where a firm operates is made up of several institutions such as regulators, customers, trade associations and competitors who exert permanent pressure on a firm's decisions, leading to isomorphic behaviour (Meyer and Rowan 1977; Townley, 2002).

Di Maggio and Powell (1983) identified three institutional mechanisms – normative, coercive and mimetic – to explain the isomorphism or homogeneity in the adoption of environmental initiatives. According to this view, obtaining an official recognition for the implementation of an environmental management system (EMS) compliant with international standards such as ISO 14001 or ecomanagement and audit scheme (EMAS), does not stem from internal benefits such as greater resource efficiency (Christmann and Taylor, 2006) but is essentially driven by increasing or maintaining social legitimacy (Boiral, 2007). For instance, normative isomorphism can derive from customer requirements, which, according to many studies, are one of the first motivations behind the adoption of environmental management practices (Biondi et al., 2000; Boiral, 2003). Mimetic pressures result when the development of environmental practices in specific sectors or competitive arenas becomes so significant that it induces the adoption of them by followers (Testa et al., 2010).

Although the adoption of environmental initiatives may be genuinely motivated by the idea of gaining a competitive edge (Henriques and Sadorsky, 1996; Porter and Van der Linde, 1995; Ambec and Lanoie, 2008; Darnall et al., 2010), institutional pressures, and especially those associated with the adoption of EMSs, tend to encourage 'ceremonial behaviours' and a superficial and apparent conformity to the standard requirements (Boiral, 2007).

The literature on the effectiveness of certified EMSs shows that the 'organizational myth' is still a risk (Boiral, 2007). In fact, using different methodologies and data, and by focusing both on ISO 14001 and EMAS, many empirical studies have found contrasting results (Melnyk et al., 2003; Potoski and Prakash, 2005; King et al., 2005; Christmann and Taylor, 2006; Barla, 2007; Boiral and Henri, 2012).

Limiting the analysis only to 'institutional pressures' does not allow for a complete understanding of why organisations operating within the same context pursue different strategies, despite experiencing similar institutional pressures. There can be strategic motivations that encourage managers to adopt actions that aim at designing, rationalising, implementing environmental practices and that are not just spurred by external stimuli.

Environmental management is, therefore, developed by organisations not just as an *ad hoc* operational response to external pressures, but as a key-element of a business strategic vision, aimed at pursuing better environmental and commercial results.

Pursuing a better 'competitive performance' can have different meanings and be achieved in many ways. The three most diffused strategic approaches able to favour the adoption of environmental practices by firms are the following:

1   'reputation-led': the improvement of environmental performance of the whole product life-cycle can significantly contribute to positive corporate image (Darnall et al., 2008).
2   'efficiency-led': an environmental-oriented business strategy can reduce the use of raw materials per unit of product or reduce the weight and the thickness of the packaging thanks to innovative solutions. This leads to cost savings and enables the company to supply a cost-competitive product to the market (Delmas, 2002).
3   'innovation-led': An environmental-oriented approach can also be seen as the result of an innovation leader's strategy. Those companies that are front-runners in developing product and process innovations can find in pioneeristic environment-related practices an opportunity to strengthen their leadership and create a gap with respect to their competitors (Vachon and Klassen, 2007).

One of the predominant theories addressing the role that the natural environment can play in an organisation's competitiveness and success is the natural-resource-based view of the firm (Hart, 1995). The conceptual framework for this theory is comprised of the interconnected strategies of pollution prevention, product stewardship and sustainable development. Empirical evidence also lends support to this theory, finding that organisational capabilities that lead to a competitive advantage can be obtained via proactive responsiveness to ecological issues.

According to this approach, competitiveness and success of companies and products depend on the quality and quantity of the resources available and by the ability of companies/industries to optimise their use (Russo and Fouts, 1997). The resource-based view identifies five kinds of resources (Grant, 1991):

1   financial and economic resources;
2   physical resources;
3   human resources (and their competence);
4   technical (considering innovation capabilities);
5   intangibles (e.g. reputational, managerial, organisational).

This approach emphasises that also in the short run, the quality and quantity of internal resources can benefit from the adoption of an environmental-oriented strategy, especially if we consider it in dynamic terms.

Environmental management and business competitiveness: does it pay to be green?

In the last two decades, the debate on the strategic potential of corporate social responsibility (CSR) and the existence of a possible relationship between CSR and competitive edge has become increasingly relevant (Porter and Kramer, 2006;

Vilanova et al., 2009; Magrizos, 2012), and at the same time studies on the business case for CSR have become increasingly focused (Hart, 1997; Orlitzky et al., 2003; Kotler and Lee, 2005).

The realisation of commercial benefits as 'side-effects' of environmental improvement represent the most important motivating driver for companies to initiate more sustainable production patterns. It has been argued that success in addressing environmental issues may provide new opportunities for competition and innovative ways to add value to core-business activities (Fitjar, 2011).

The variety of perspectives and levels of analysis at which the concept of competitiveness may be considered requires a brief analysis of the several definitions of competitiveness, both at a theoretical and political level.

In order to formulate a better understanding of the concept of competitiveness, it needs to provide answers to three relevant questions linked to its definition:

1 *Who is the entity that competes with others?*
2 *What is the 'context' in which this entity competes with its competitors?*
3 *What are the drivers and factors that enable this entity to perform better than its competitors?*

The first question refers to the 'entities' that are the relevant actors in the competition 'arena'. Literature distinguishes three basic typologies of actors: (1) *a single firm* or *plant*, (2) *a cluster of firms*, i.e. an industry, a sector, a branch or a local productive system (e.g. an industrial district), and (3) *a territorial context* (i.e. a country or a region).

At the firm level, competitiveness implies that companies are able to produce goods and services more efficiently and/or effectively than their competitors. A strong competitive performance is achieved by relying on some 'competitive factors', often with a particular focus on process productivity and the efficient use and/or access to strategic inputs (Jenkins, 1998). Additionally a recent paper from the International Energy Agency defines competitiveness at the firm level as '*The ability to maintain and/or to expand [a] market position based on its cost structure*' (Reinaud, 2005).

At the sectoral level, competitiveness implies that competitive factors are activated and used by different 'clusters' of companies (e.g. all the companies operating in similar industrial sectors in different countries) to obtain better performance in the relevant market (local and/or international markets). This level is related to the previous one, but is not totally overlapping: in fact, a competitive industry can be composed by a high number of competitive firms, but also by some low-performing firms.

At the territorial level (country or region), the concept of competitiveness is not limited to a market perspective, but also to the 'standard of living' within a certain geographical area.

The second question refers to the 'dimension' of competitiveness. We can distinguish at least three dimensions: international, national and local, each strongly linked to one another.

Focusing on the international level, competitiveness refers to the success with which an entity (i.e. a country/region, sector/industry, firm/plant) competes against overseas counterparts (OECD, 2003).

Moreover, the fundamentals of international or national competitiveness rest on the efficiency with which resources are allocated and used at the national or micro level (i.e. at sectoral and/or firm level) (Esty and Porter, 2002).

The third question refers to the analysis of the *key variables* affecting competitiveness as well as the *ways to measure them*. Two major approaches can be distinguished:

1   the first tries to investigate the *drivers of the competitiveness* (e.g. the resource productivity at firm level, the degree of internationalisation at sector level);
2   the second approach focuses on the performances *of the competitive success* (e.g. the market performance measured by market share; the turnover growth rate; the financial performance measured by ROI or EBTIDA at firm level; the welfare of a nation measured by GDP *per capita*).

According to our framework of analysis, competitiveness can be measured at the *macro level* (territorial: international/national), the *Meso level* (cluster: sectoral/ industry/district) and the *micro level* (plant/firm).

- At the macro level, measurements of competitiveness aim at describing how successfully a country or a region (made up of different sectors and many firms) competes with counterparts in other countries. The most common indicators to compare competitiveness between countries are *Gross Domestic Product* (GDP) and *Gross National Product* (GNP), *GDP per capita* (Esty and Porter, 2002) and *international trade flows* (Mulatu et al., 2004).
- Measurements of competitiveness at the industry level refer to the ability of specific industries to compete for market shares with businesses operating in the same sector, but located in other countries or regions. Most studies use *trade* (e.g. net exports), *investment flows* and *productivity growth* as proxies or indicators of sectoral competitiveness (Constantini and Crespi, 2008; Lee, 2008). Other studies seek to consider the drivers of trade competitiveness at the sectoral level, such as the *Total Factor Productivity* (TFP) and/or proxy measures of *innovative capacity* (mainly R&D expenditure and patent applications) (Jaffe and Palmer, 1997). Finally, financial measurements such as *operating profit* and *Earnings Before Interest, Tax, Depreciation and Amortisation* (EBITDA), are also used even if rarely, in the literature, as a measure of sectoral competitiveness (Carbon Trust, 2004).
- At the *level of firms/plants*, competitiveness indicators relate to various aspects, such as the ability to sustain market shares, to sustain independent existence in the market or to sustain 'normal' levels of profitability and returns. At the firm level, *productivity* is the key variable, simply defined as the '*measure of output per unit of input*'. Productivity aims at measuring the efficiency with which production is carried out; in other words, the

ratio between the outputs and inputs that make production possible (raw materials, labour, capital, etc.). Many studies identify, as an optimal measure of productivity, the *Total Factor Productivity*, that is, a synthetic measure of how firms are organised, structured, use technology and are managed (see, for instance: Dofour et al., 1998; Berman and Bui, 2001; Lanoie et al., 2008). In contrast, other studies focus on business performance (Darnall et al., 2008; Testa and Iraldo, 2010), environmental innovation (Iraldo et al., 2009; Rennings et al., 2006) or on intangible assets such as corporate reputation (Iraldo et al., 2009).

Many studies have emphasised that under such circumstances the adoption of environmental practices has a positive relation on the different measurement of competitiveness.

For instance, there is evidence to suggest that good environmental performance can help enterprises get better economic result. Hart and Ahuja (1996) report that efforts to prevent pollution and reduce emissions drop to the 'bottom line' (Return on Sales [ROS], Return on Assets [ROA] and Return on Equity [ROE]) within one to two years of initiation: operating performance (e.g. resource productivity or savings leading to efficiency) is benefited in the following year, while at least two years are needed before financial performance is affected. Klassen and McLaughlin (1996) used the 'financial event methodology' to prove the positive link between environmental and financial performance. Also Al-Tuwaijiri et al. (2004) demonstrate, by a simultaneous equation model, that good environmental performance is significantly associated with good economic performance.

Environmental practices tend to pay off (even if not in a short time span), thanks to cost savings due to a better and more rational use of natural resources, innovation from emission reduction, lower litigation expenditures and lower insurance costs (Porter and Van der Linde, 1995).

In a customer perspective, positive effects of environmental practices have been demonstrated by D'Souza et al. (2007), especially in terms of customer satisfaction improvement, due to the 'greening' of the offered products. Manaktola and Jauhari (2007) emphasised the relevance of the increasing awareness among final consumers on corporate engagement in environmental activities. Boehe and Barin-Cruz (2010), showed how the attention paid to environmental impacts can enhance product differentiation and thus can particularly support the performance in export markets where green consumers are more active.

Other valuable examples were provided by the literature on supply chain-oriented management. Dodgson (2000) and Dyer and Singh (1998) argue that inter-firm relations provide formal and informal mechanisms that promote trust, reduce risk and in turn increase innovation and profitability. Some of the key elements of green supply chain management, such as involvement, analysis and control systems along the supply chain, based on environmental criteria, can reduce the risks of delivering interruptions or delays resulting from a critical supplier's compliance problem (Lipman, 1999).

Besides reducing risks and costs, environmental practices can also provide strategic and competitive benefits: the improvement of the brand's image, better relations with institutional stakeholders and increase of personnel motivation are possible effects of environmental management adoption described by the relevant literature.

For instance, Welford (1995) found environmental protection activities increasingly embedded in business operations and, thus, bring some benefits for firms such as an improvement in reputation and strengthened business relationships. In addition, Molina-Azorın (1999) indicated that pro-active environmental management has a positive effect on an organisation's market performance. Zhu and Sarkis (2004), which analyses green supply chain management practices in Chinese manufacturing enterprises, proved that enterprises that develop these kinds of practices have better competitive performance. Still, the analysis carried out by Rao and Holt (2005) found that 'greening' the different phases of the supply chain leads to a more integrated and co-operative supply chain, which ultimately results in greater competitiveness.

Research on human resource management has also provided evidence that programmes focused on environment reduce absenteeism (again increasing labour productivity), reduce costs connected with injuries (and related insurance tariffs) and yield other direct financial benefits (Aldana, 2001; Douphrate and Rosecrance, 2004). Moreover, several authors have, for instance, emphasised how human resource management positively influences the success of environmental initiatives (for an extensive overview, see Renwick et al., 2013). The active involvement of all employees in a management system can increase opportunities for environmental improvement and help identify better solutions in order to optimise the use of natural resources and reduce pollution (Brio et al., 2007). Reward mechanisms and employee incentives that contribute to achieving environmental objectives could be another important factor for the success of an environmental strategy (Fernandez et al., 2003; Cordeiro and Sarkis, 2008). Boiral and Paillè (2012) identified three main 'organisational citizenship' behaviours that are all relevant in terms of environmental success. They distinguished three employee behaviour models. The first, called 'eco-initiatives', identifies a proactive approach to reducing pollution. The second, 'eco-civic engagement', stresses the active participation in events and initiatives organised by the organisation. The third one emphasises a mutualistic behaviour focused on helping colleagues cope with environmental issues.

Finally, environmental initiatives can contribute to innovation abilities and performance in two different ways: innovation resulting from engagement with stakeholders (Buyssey and Verbeke, 2003; Wagner, 2010), and innovation stimulated by the implementation of environmental management tools (Rennings et al., 2006; Rehfeld et al., 2006; Iraldo et al., 2009). Other studies demonstrated a positive effect of environment-related CSR practices on networking with local stakeholders (Biondi et al., 2002) and improvement of companies' reputation and risk management (Orlitzy et al., 2011).

Environmental corporate behaviour: from a strategic approach to operational tools

Safeguarding the ecosystem and minimising the impact of the environment have in recent years taken on increasing importance in the eyes of business management and have become, over time, crucial components in evaluating management results: this has greatly influenced the development of new corporate strategies (Hart, 1997; Russo and Fouts, 1997).

Even though the degree of attention given by companies to ecological matters has been (and still is) extremely diversified, it now appears certain that the awareness of the importance of ecological factors has caused companies to internalise environmental protection within their own strategy (Henriques and Sadorsky, 1996.). It has become increasingly common for the heads of companies to take observations concerning the effects on the environment by their industrial and commercial operations into account when calculating the factors determining the strategic orientation of the business (Buyssey and Verbeke, 2003).

Before describing the development of corporate behaviour along green lines, the question should be asked as to what caused the transformation that decreed the final and irreversible acceptance of the 'environment' element among the decisional variables of corporations.

In order to identify the main underlying factors, we must first recall the changes which occurred in the four systems into which the 'external macro-environment' can be divided (Gilardoni et al., 1993), namely all the human and natural events which occur outside the company.

1) *The natural ecological system*

As shown in the first paragraph, the cause of the first 'green revolution' amongst companies, as well as the main reason behind the changes occurring in the other three systems, can undoubtedly be found in the substantial, and very worrying, deterioration of environmental conditions that has marked the last few years.

There is a universally shared statement that claims that the evolution of the relationship between companies and the environment through an increasing interest in ecological problems is a process that is, above all, determined by the progressive deterioration of the environmental situation. It is quite evident that without concrete proof of the problem, companies would definitely not have taken any interest in the questions raised exclusively by minority groups with a heightened awareness of the situation.

2) *The socio-cultural system*

Environmental degradation (even if quite evident, as in the case of ecological disasters) is, however, not enough to account for the explosion of the 'green revolution'.

It is quite legitimate to state that in the past some very serious episodes occurred whose widespread coverage did not, however, have any significant effect on the ecological conscience of the industrial world.

The deterioration of the planet's recorded environmental conditions in recent years has been influential in raising the awareness of those responsible for corporate strategies through an increased sensitivity towards ecology by society as a whole; despite the presence of additional evident degradation, the significance of environmental problems appears to be closely connected to a growing public awareness which gave a decisive push in putting environmental protection at the top of the list of priorities for civilised existence.

The birth and the evolution of a true environmental conscience represent the most significant change in the sociocultural system and in this context, can be seen as the main driving force of the transformation (Boiral and Paillè, 2012).

A second change in the same system, however, must be taken into consideration, which is more specifically related to the sphere of business culture.

3) The competitive economic system

The biggest incentive to internalising the environmental variable within corporate strategies most certainly comes from the possibility of obtaining an economic advantage (Hart and Ahuja, 1996).

The competitiveness of a 'green' product has effectively increased due to the expansion in ecological consumption practices marked by the propensity of customers to show their environmental awareness through their choice of purchases (Testa et al., 2013).

The establishment of this behaviour in a market sector generates an advantage for companies in the forefront of the field of eco-friendly production and for those companies, therefore, who have fully committed to the environmental challenge.

4) The political-institutional system

Some of the changes considered so far have prompted public institutions to provide an appropriate response through the competent authorities to the challenges emerging. This response, which takes the form of new regulations and innovative tools, has in turn, amplified the effect of incentives already caused by the changes of a social and natural character, thus accelerating the 'green revolution' (Porter and Van der Linde, 1995).

The first response of a political and institutional type occurred in the area of direct regulations.

The sociocultural changes have allowed the admission of the essential role of environmental matters (and even the sharing of some ecological petitions) from the business world, as well: this has meant that the acceptance of legislation to protect the environment has met less resistance and has become, as a result, less restrictive.

It is well known that the translation of the concept of sustainable development on a real-life basis can trace one of its key determining factors to the progressive crackdown on environmental legislation (Iraldo et al., 2011).

This crackdown has indeed convinced the management of many companies once and for all of the opportunity to assess the environmental variable correctly when determining their strategies, and of the need to consider eco-efficiency as an essential component of their objectives.

A second kind of response is the introduction of innovative measures to protect the environment.

As previously indicated, the exclusive use of command and control measures appears to be inadequate in developing an economic institutional context which rewards self-motivated ability and the innovative contribution of companies (Iraldo et al., 2011); for this reason, conventional economic measures have also been put in place: taxes, negotiable permits.

Changes in consumption trends have thus pointed the way to the use of voluntary measures (which has made it easier to recognise the potential competitive advantage and so, boosted the transformation of strategic models).

The slow process of transformation, which culminates in the 'green revolution' of businesses and is gradually affected from the onset to various extents by systemic changes now described, can be represented by the change in the meaning that the environmental question takes on for the industrial system.

The original starting point of this evolution is characterised, of course, by a notable indifference to the impact on the environment by industrial and commercial activities. Indeed, in the initial phase, businesses generally transfer private environmental costs with no restrictions onto the community by privatising and consuming external resources through methods that cause environmental impoverishment and imbalance.

The 'socialisation' of the costs has generated significant external diseconomies and has contributed in an indirect, but nevertheless primary way to the deterioration of environmental conditions. This brings us, then, to the second phase of the transition in which the environmental variable takes on the significance and form of an obligation for industrial organisations.

As mentioned above, in the major industrial countries, this phase corresponds to the period from the beginning of the 1970s to the latter half of the 1980s during which the problems linked to respecting environmental regulations meant companies only had to take any real notice when such regulations changed and usually became more restrictive.

As previously indicated, after structural changes in the external macro environment gradually take effect, companies then change their own attitude to the environmental question, which starts to be seen in terms of the potential economic advantages connected to it, and consequently, begins to take on the new meaning of competitive opportunity.

An initial indication of the gradual transition from obligation to opportunity can be found in the willingness of many companies to anticipate new legislative obligations by making changes in advance or by adopting the technologies which they believe will be requested, thus gaining a privileged position pending the implementation of the measures.

In the quest for better solutions to meet the requirements of the above-mentioned regulations, companies have been able to develop clean techniques and technologies which are more effective and economic, and have found that the pursuit (whether compulsory or voluntary) of environmental excellence often means greater efficiency of production processes, for example, in terms of saving resources and energy.

The final stage of the evolution towards the concept of eco-friendliness as a market opportunity is marked by the new frontier of ecological consumption, which also draws directly on competitive mechanisms because it rewards the products of those companies that are environmentally more advanced.

The transition of the environmental question from irrelevant strategic element to obligation and finally, to opportunity occurred or occurs in different ways (and timeframes) depending on the context in which the businesses operate.

The context is determined by the extent to which the transformation factors have been implemented and can be identified in the changes in the external macro environment: the more visible they are, the more the context is perceived to be environmentally evolved.

There are four main types of environmental context, which roughly include the cases that can be proved by trial and error.

The *stable context* is typical of less advanced industrialised countries, in particular developing countries and eastern European countries. Environmental regulations are basically non-existent in this context even though the problems linked to managing the natural environment are very serious: it is worth mentioning the indiscriminate exploitation of resources in developing countries and the catastrophic water pollution in former socialist countries. The lack of interest by institutions can be explained by the total absence of changes in the sociocultural system (and, even more so, in the economic-competitive system): public opinion in the countries concerned shows little interest in environmental problems (developing countries) or has insufficient power to influence political decisions (Eastern Europe) to succeed in putting ecology matters on the legislators' agendas.

The *reactive context* characterised most of the industrial sectors in Western countries in the decades preceding the 'green revolution'. In this context, active mobilisation for a solution to environmental problems was limited to small groups of people (environmental groups, residents of areas with high ecological risks, employees of dangerous factories, etc.), whilst the rest of public opinion was totally removed from any visible involvement on the environmental front. In addition to this, consumers showed very little interest in products that were environmentally friendly and so, there was no incentive to convert to ecology, even from a competitive point of view. In the absence of any real incentive, environmental legislation evolves very slowly and it is not uncommon for regulations to be agreed upon by governments and the biggest national corporations concerned, giving them time and the opportunity to adapt to the regulations without incurring any excessive costs.

In the *anticipative context*, public opinion, however, is very interested in environmental problems and quite often intervenes to ensure that stricter regulations are brought in. The most important consequence of this kind of pressure by the community and therefore, sufficiently effective, is to block agreements between governments and corporations and thus, reduce their influence on the change in regulations. Companies, therefore, are no longer guaranteed enough time to develop completely new technologies before the new legislation is enforced and are forced to anticipate changes (Porter and van der Linde, 1995). It is apparent how this context is characterised by the presence of the first element that marked the transition of the environmental question from obligation to opportunity: anticipation of regulations. Lack of ecological involvement by consumers, however, persists which basically means that the economic-competitive system remains static. A particularly significant example of the anticipative context is provided by the European Common Market where decisions concerning environmental regulations are taken at community level, thus avoiding any interference by single national companies.

The evolutionary path of the economic-competitive system is completed within it and records the consolidation of green consumption practices outlined in the previous contexts. The transformation of the significance of the environmental question, thus, comes to an end and becomes a source of opportunity for competitiveness. The *proactive context* can only be found in specific sectors of the market, although some are gaining in significance. Naturally, what has been described here is simply a rather generic reference framework since the approach to the environmental question is realistically not at all homogenous either for all the sectors making up any one type of context or for any business in a particular sector.

It is, however, opportune to mention that up until now the basic determinant of a company's behaviour towards environmental matters remains the context in which it can be found. After all, it makes no sense for a company to anticipate legislation when it has plenty of time to adapt to it and even influence its contents (as happens in a reactive context). It also makes no sense to adopt an ecological policy and a marketing policy wholly based on the environmental quality of products in a context that is not proactive. Consequently, all attempts to classify strategic behaviour by companies with regard to the environmental variable retain a certain explanatory value only if they remain in the social, economic and institutional context in which the company operates.

A sufficiently general overview of the classifications carried out must include at least the following three (as well as the original definitions, alongside each type of business, it must be indicated the type of contexts in which it might possibly be found):

1   an initial classification identifies three business models:

    a   the *adaptive business* (stable and reactive context): actions carried out for environmental protection are forcibly induced by a command and control policy by the public operator;

b   the *responsive business* (anticipative approach): even though called upon by regulations (both through standards and environmental taxes), it is characterised by the innovative way it pursues its goals; at the same time, its actions are not voluntary or systematic like those of the strategies of an active business;

c   the *active business* (proactive context): considers the environment to be a competitive challenge, which can allow it to identify new areas of profit and social consensus.

2   the second classification makes a distinction between the managerial models of environmental business management:

a   the passive model (stable, responsive and even anticipative context) which characterises businesses that resist change because they view environmental problems as a cost and not as an opportunity and they limit themselves to containing the impact on the environment to the extent to which it is imposed from the outside;

b   the adaptive model (anticipative and proactive context) relating to businesses which comply with regulations and at the same time, react to stimuli from society by putting innovative behaviour into place in both areas, where necessary;

c   the proactive model (proactive context) which concerns businesses that have understood the opportunity afforded by the environmental question in terms of ecoefficiency or efficiency across the board and the market.

3   the final classification concerns the environmental strategies of a business and presumably follows the first two:

a   the follower strategy (stable and reactive context) involves strict observance of all legislative standards or even the failure to observe them should this behaviour be less costly;

b   the market-oriented strategy (anticipative and proactive context) is clearly dominated by market considerations and foresees the improvement of the environmental quality of the business only if this increases profits (sales) or reduces costs;

c   the strategy that sees the environment as a key factor (proactive context) foresees the integration of the Environment and Total Quality and the inclusion of the ecological variable in corporate strategy at all levels.

References

Al-Tuwaijri S., Christensen T., Hughes K., 2004. 'The relations among environmental disclosure, environmental performance, and economic performance: a simultaneous equations approach'. *Accounting, Organizations and Society* 29, 447–471.
Aldana SG. 2001. 'Financial impact of health promotion programs: a comprehensive review of the literature'. *American Journal of Health Promotion* 15, 296–320.

Ambec S., Lanoie P., 2008. 'Does it pay to be green? A systematic overview'. *Academy of Management Perspectives* 22, 45–62.

Barla P., 2007. 'ISO 14001 certification and environmental performance in Quebec's pulp and paper industry'. *Journal of Environmental Economics and Management* 53, 291–306.

Berman E., Bui L.T.M., 2001. 'Environmental regulation and productivity: evidence from oil refineries'. *The Review of Economics and Statistics* 83, 498–510.

Biondi V., Frey M., Iraldo F., 2000. 'Environmental Management Systems and SMEs'. *Greener Management International* 29, 55–79.

Boehe D.M., Barin-Cruz L., 2010. 'Corporate Social Responsibility, product differentiation strategy and export performance'. *Journal of Business Ethics* 91, 325–346.

Boiral, O. 2003. 'ISO 9000: outside the iron cage'. *Organization Science* 14, 720–737.

Boiral O., 2007. 'Corporate greening through ISO 14001: a rational myth?' *Organization Science* 18, 127–146.

Boiral O., Henri J.F., 2012. 'Modelling the impact of ISO 14001 on environmental performance: A comparative approach'. *Journal of Environmental Management* 99, 84–97.

Boiral O., Paille P. 2012. 'Organizational Citizenship Behaviour for the environment: measurement and validation'. *Journal of Business Ethics* 109, 431–445.

Brammer S., Jackson G., Matten D., 2012. 'Corporate Social Responsibility and institutional theory: new perspectives on private governance'. *Socio-Economic Review* 10, 3–28.

Brimblecombe P., 1995: History of air pollution. In: Singh, H.B. (ed.), Composition, Chemistry and Climate of the Atmosphere. Van Nostrand Reinhold, New York, 1–18.

Brio J.A.D., Fernandez E., Junquera B., 2007. 'Management and employee involvement in achieving an environmental action-based competitive advantage: an empirical study'. *International Journal of Human Resource Management* 18, 491–522.

Buchholz R.A., 1993. *Principles of Environmental Management: The Greening of Business*, Prentice-Hall, Englewood Cliffs, NJ.

Buyssey K., Verbeke A., 2003. 'Proactive environmental strategies: a stakeholder management perspective'. *Strategic Management Journal* 24, 453–470.

Carbon Trust, 2004. The European Emissions Trading Scheme: Implications for Industrial Competitiveness. Available from: http://www.thecarbontrust.co.uk/carbontrust/.

Christmann P., Taylor G., 2006. 'Firm self-regulation through international certifiable standards: determinants of symbolic versus substantive implementation'. *Journal of International Business Studies* 37, 863–883.

Constantini V., Crespi F., 2008. 'Environmental regulation and the export dynamics of energy technologies'. *Ecological Economics* 66, 447–460.

Cordeiro J., Sarkis J., 2008. 'Does explicit contracting effectively link CEO compensation to environmental performance?' *Business Strategy and the Environment* 17, 304–317.

D'Souza C., Taghian M., Khosla R., 2007. 'Examination of environmental beliefs and its impact on the influence of price, quality and demographic characteristics with respect to green purchase intention'. *Journal of Targeting, Measurement and Analysis for Marketing* 15, 69–78.

Darnall N., Henriques I., Sadorsky P., 2008. 'Do Environmental Management Systems Improve Business Performance in an International Setting?' *Journal of International Management* 14, 364–376.

Darnall N., Henriques I., Sadorsky P., 2010. 'Adopting proactive environmental strategy: the influence of stakeholders and firm size'. *The Journal of Management Studies* 47, 1072–94.

Delmas M., 2002. 'The diffusion of environmental management standards in Europe and the United States: an institutional perspective'. *Policy Sciences* 35, 91–119.

Di Maggio P.J., Powell W.W., 1983. 'The iron cage revisited: institutional isomorphism and collective rationality in organizational fields'. *American Sociological Review* 48, 147–160.

Dodgson M., 2000. *Management of Technology*, Routledge, London.

Douphrate D.I., Rosecrance J., 2004. 'The economics and cost justification of ergonomics'. Colorado State University, National Occupational Research Agenda (NORA), 29–40. Available from http://www.mech.utah.edu/ergo/pages/NORA/2004/29-40_DouphrateDavid.pdf.

Dufour C., Lanoie P., Patry M., 1998. 'Regulation and Productivity'. *Journal of Productivity Analysis* 9, 233–247.

Dyer J.H., Singh H. 1998. 'The relations view: co-operative strategy and sources of inter-organizational competitive advantage'. *Academy of Management Review* 23, 660–79.

Esty D.C., Porter M.E., 'Ranking National Environmental Regulation and Performance: A Leading Indicator of Future Competitiveness?' in M.E. Porter, J.D. Sachs, P.K. Cornelius, J.W. McAuthur, and K. Schwab, (eds.) The Global Competitiveness Report 2001–2002 (2002). Oxford: Oxford University Press.

Eurobserver, 2011. The State of Renewable Energy in Europe. 11th EurObserv'Er report. Available at http://www.energies-renouvelables.org/observ-er/stat_baro/barobilan/barobilan11.pdf.

Fernández-Muñiz B., Montes-Peón J.M., Vázquez-Ordás C.J., 2007. 'Safety culture: Analysis of the causal relationships between its key dimensions'. *Journal of Safety Research* 38, 627–641.

Fitjar R.D., 2011. 'Little big firms? Corporate social responsibility in small businesses that do not compete against big ones'. *Business Ethics: A European Review* 20, 30–44.

Grant R. M., 1991. 'The Resource-Based Theory of Competitive Advantage: Implications for Strategy Formulation'. *California Management Review* 33, 114–135.

Gusmerotti N.M., Testa F., Amirante D., Frey M., 2012. 'The role of negotiating tools in the environmental policy mix instruments: determinants and effects of Environmental Agreements'. *Journal of Cleaner Production* 35, 39–49.

Hart S.L., 1997. 'Beyond greening: strategies for a sustainable world'. *Harvard Business Review* 75, 66–76.

Hart S.L., Ahuja, G., 1996. 'Does it pay to be green? An empirical examination of the relationship between emission reduction and firm performance'. *Business Strategy & the Environment* 5, 30–37.

Henriques I., Sadorsky, P., 1996. 'The determinants of an environmentally responsive firm: an empirical approach'. *Journal of Environmental Economics and Management* 30, 381–395.

Henriques I., Sadorsky, P., 1999. 'The relationship between environmental commitment and managerial perceptions of stakeholder importance'. *Academy of Management Journal* 42, 87–99.

Hobsbawm E.J., 1975. *The Age of Capital: 1848-1875*, Charles Scribner's Sons, New York, NY.

Hong S., Candelone J.P., Patterson C.C., Boutron C.F., 1994: 'Greenland ice evidence of hemispheric lead pollution two millennia ago by Greek and Roman civilizations'. *Science* 265, 1841–1843.

Iraldo F., Testa F., Frey M., 2009. 'Is an environmental management system able to influence environmental and competitive performance? The case of an eco-management and audit scheme (EMAS) in the European Union'. *Journal of Cleaner Production* 17, 1444–1452.

Iraldo F., Testa F., Melis M., Frey M., 2011. 'A literature review on the links between environmental regulation and competitiveness'. *Environmental Policy & Governance* 21, 210–222.

Jaffe A.B., Palmer K., 1997. 'Environmental regulation and innovation: a panel data study'. *The Review of Economics and Statistics* 79, 610–619.

Jenkins R., 1998. Environmental Regulation and International Competitiveness: A Review of Literature and Some European Evidence. United Nations University Institute for New Technologies.

King A.A., Lenox M.J., Terlaak A., 2005. 'The strategic use of decentralized institutions: exploring certification with the ISO 14001 management standard'. *Academy of Management Journal* 48, 1091–1106.

Klassen R.D., McLaughlin C.P., 1996. 'The impact of environmental management on firm performance'. *Management Science* 42, 1199–1214.

Kotler P., Lee N., 2005. *Corporate Social Responsibility: Doing the Most Good for Your Company and Your Cause.* Hoboken, NJ: Wiley.

Lanoie P., Laurent-Lucchetti J., Johnstone N., Ambec S., 2011. 'Environmental Policy, Innovation and Performance: New Insights on the Porter Hypothesis'. *Journal of Economics & Management Strategy* 20, 803–842.

Lee M., 2008. 'Environmental regulations and market power: The case of the Korean manufacturing industries'. *Ecological Economics* 68, 205–209.

Lipman S., 1999. *Supply Chain Environmental Management: Elements for Success, Environmental Management* 6, 175–182.

Magrizos S., 2012. 'SME corporate social responsibility and competitiveness: a literature review'. *International Journal of Technology Management* 58, 10–31.

Manaktola K., Jauhari V., 2007. 'Exploring consumer attitude and behaviour towards green practices in the lodging industry in India'. *International Journal of Contemporary Hospitality Management* 19, 364–377.

Melnyk, S.A., Sroufe, R.P., Calantone, R., 2003. 'Assessing the impact of environmental management systems on corporate and environmental performance'. *Journal of Operations Management* 21, 329–351.

Meyer J.W., Rowan B., 1977. 'Institutionalized Organizations: Formal Structure as Myth and Ceremony'. *American Journal of Sociology* 83, 340–363.

Molina-Azorin J.F., Claver-Cortes E., Pereira-Moliner J., Tarı J.J., 2009. 'Environmental practices and firm performance: an empirical analysis in the Spanish hotel industry'. *Journal of Cleaner Production* 17, 516–524.

Mulatu A., Florax R., Withagen C. 2001. Environmental Regulation and Competitiveness Tinbergen Institute Discussion Paper, T1 039 / 3.

Nriagu, J.O., 1983. 'Occupational exposure to lead in ancient times'. *Science of the Total Environment* 31, 105–116.

OECD, 2003. *Environmental Taxes and Competitiveness: An Overview of the Issues, Policy Options and Research Needs.* OECD Publishing, Paris.

Orlitzky M., Schmidt F.L., Rynes S.L., 2003. 'Corporate social and financial performance: a meta-analysis'. *Organization Studies* 24, 403–411.

Pane Haden S.S., Oyler J. D., Humphreys J. H., 2009. 'Historical, practical, and theoretical perspectives on green management: An exploratory analysis'. *Management Decision* 47, 1041–1055.

Porter M., Kramer M., 2006. 'The link between competitive advantage and corporate social responsibility'. *Harvard Business Review* 84, 78–92.

Porter M.E., van der Linde C., 1995. 'Toward a new conception of the environment competitiveness relationship'. *Journal of Economic Perspectives* 9, 97–118.

Potoski, M., Prakash, A., 2005. 'Covenants with weak swords: ISO 14001 and facilities' environmental performance'. *Journal of Policy Analysis and Management* 24, 745–769.

Prakash A., Potoski M., 2006. 'Racing to the Bottom? Trade, Environmental Governance, and ISO 14001'. *American Journal of Political Science* 50, 350–364.

Rademaekers K., Asaad S.S.Z., Berg J., 2011. Study on the Competitiveness of the European Companies and Resource Efficiency: Final Report. Available at ec.europa .eu/DocsRoom/documents/5189/attachments/1/.../en/.../native.

Rao P., Holt D., 2005. 'Do green supply chains lead to competitiveness and economic performance?' *International Journal of Operations & Production Management* 25, 898–916.

Rehfeld K.M., Rennings K., Ziegler A. 2006. 'Integrated Product Policy and Environmental Product Innovations: An Empirical Analysis'. *Ecological Economics* 61, 91–100.

Reinaud J., 2005. Industrial Competitiveness under the European Union Emission Trading Scheme, International Energy Agency, Information Paper.

Renwick D. W.S., Redman T., Maguire S., 2013. 'Green Human Resource Management: A Review and Research Agenda'. *International Journal of Management Reviews* 15, 1–14.

Rennings K., Ziegler A., Ankele K., Hoffmann E., 2006. 'The influence of different characteristics of the EU environmental management and auditing scheme on technical environmental innovations and economic performance'. *Ecological Economics* 57, 45–59.

Russo M.V., Fouts P.A., 1997. 'A Resource-Based Perspective on Corporate Environmental Performance and Profitability'. *The Academy of Management Journal* 40, 534–559.

Testa F., Iraldo, F., 2010. 'Shadows and lights of GSCM (Green Supply Chain Management): determinants and effects of these practices based on a multi-national study'. *Journal of Cleaner Production* 18, 953–962.

Testa F., Iraldo F., Vaccari A., Ferrari E., 2013. 'Why Eco-labels can be effective marketing tools: evidence from a study on Italian consumers'. Business Strategy and Environment DOI: 10.1002/bse.1821.

Townley B., 2002. 'The role of competing rationalities in institutional change'. *Academy of Management Journal* 45, 163–179.

Vachon S., Klassen R.D., 2007. 'Supply chain management and environmental technologies: the role of integration'. *International Journal of Production Research* 45, 401–423.

Vilanova M., Lozano J.M., Arenas D., 2009. 'Exploring the Nature of the Relationship Between CSR and Competitiveness'. *Journal of Business Ethics* 87, 57–69.

Wagner M., 2010. 'Corporate social performance and innovation with high social benefits: a quantitative analysis'. *Journal of Business Ethics* 94, 581–594.

Watson D., McKinnon D., Bjørn A., Hansen M. S., Wittmer D., von Geibler J., Saurat M., Schütz H., Tobias S., Zoboli R., Marin G., Mazzanti M., Volpi M., Beretta I., Dal Negro L., 2011. Progress in Sustainable Consumption and Production in Europe: Indicator-based Report. ETC/SCP Working Paper 1/2011. Available at http://scp.eionet.europa.eu/publications/SCP%20Indicators%20report%202010/wp/WP2011_1.

Welford, R., 1995. *Environmental Strategy and Sustainable Development: The Corporate Challenge for the 21st Century.* Routledge, London, UK.

Zhu Q., Sarkis J., 2004. 'Relationships between operational practices and performance among early adopters of green supply chain management practices in Chinese manufacturing enterprises'. *Journal of Operations Management* 22, 265–289.

2 Overview of environmental certifications

Introduction to the environmental certifications of product and process

The subject of certifications of organisations focuses on the correct management of the activities that come under their managerial control or over which they have significant influence. Examples of process certification that are dealt with in this volume are as follows:

- the European Regulation no. 1221/2009 on eco-management and audit scheme (EMAS);
- the UNI EN ISO 14001 standard, environmental management systems;
- the UNI EN ISO 50001 standard, energy management systems;
- the UNI EN ISO 14064, greenhouse gas emissions – Specifications and guidelines, on an organisational level, to quantify and report on greenhouse gas emissions and their removal (three parts).

The fact that the EMAS Regulation has more than three thousand registered organisations covering over ten thousand sites and that the ISO 14001 standard exceeds 285,000 certified sites worldwide is more than enough to comprehend the kind of interest that these certification schemes have aroused[1]. The other two standards, on the other hand, have not yet reached significant numbers since they are fairly new and are still in an embryonic, but nevertheless interesting, phase of dissemination.

All these standards have elements of strong commonality and synergy based on two fundamental aspects:

1   the 'organisation' is the field of common application;
2   the basic methodology is always based on the so-called *'Plan-Do-Check-Act (PDCA)'* approach or the Deming cycle

Field of application

The term 'organisation' is the subject of a specific, fundamental definition mentioned in both the EMAS Regulation and the ISO 14001 standard (which we can consider as the historical standards and which, in the way of definitions, have inspired and even fuelled the standardisation processes in this field): 'group, firm, company, business, body or institution or, part or combination thereof whether incorporated or not, public or private which has its own functional and administrative structure'.

This is a very broad definition and includes not only industrial organisations, but also, as will be shown in more detail, service companies, public bodies, institutions and even individuals all of which cover specific functions (not just EMAS). Everything that falls under this definition is considered a 'certifiable entity' and so, the 'field of application' can be determined therein. The delimitation of the activities and processes of the organisation to which the 'requirements' envisaged will be applied is intended when talking about the 'field of application' of a standard or a European regulation.

A crucial aspect in defining these boundaries concerns the so-called risk of 'cherry picking', which can compromise the importance and credibility of the certification. This practice, which is explicitly prohibited by the guidelines from the main parties involved in standardisation and endorsement in the different schemes (for example ISO and various national training institutions), basically means that the boundaries which are defined only encompass the 'good' part of the organisation, so that it can meet the requirements of the scheme in question and therefore, exclude any 'problematic' activities and processes from the field of application.

One element of the definition of 'organisation' which in some way limits its broad application, is the call for a 'functional and administrative structure', which should be interpreted as the organisation being in possession of the responsibility, authority, decisional power, independent management, human and financial resources and ability to control activities within the field of application, so that it fulfils all the requirements of the standard or regulation.

Aside from the intuitive interpretation of perimeters at the 'gates' of the company, it is clear, therefore, that the definition of boundaries (including the field of application) becomes much more complex in the case of companies with 'multiple sites' or the decision to divide up the certification of organisations into 'parts' (take the sectors of a public body, for example). For this reason, we have dealt with the topic of industrial areas and districts separately, as we have with public administration, so that the reader understands how to interpret the most complex cases.

The Deming cycle

Plan, Do, Check, Act: these are the four basic steps in the cycle that are taken into account by every environmental certification concerning the activities and processes of an organisation. The different steps of the cycle can be easily defined:

- Plan means establishing objectives and planning the business processes to deliver the results in accordance with the policy laid down by the organisation.

- Do means activating resources (human, technical and financial), actively pursuing the objectives through operations designed to improve the business structure, creating a management system and implementing the relevant work procedures to put the processes that have been established in place.
- Check means overseeing and monitoring the way the business processes are carried out, by reporting the performances and results and measuring them against the policy and objectives which the organisation set itself, as well as against any legal or non-legal requirements.
- Act means being able to implement any actions required to constantly correct and improve the performance of the management system.

The term 'processes' is intended to indicate a set of interrelated or interacting activities that transform incoming elements into outgoing elements by adding value and guaranteeing that results are achieved. Every organisation can, therefore, divide its management into various business processes on which to opt to carry out a Plan-Do-Check-Act type of operation at regular intervals.

The standards for management systems adopt this approach in full. The diagram in Figure 2.1 shows the PDCA logic previously described and again proposes the steps representing the 'classic' requirements in an environmental management system (EMS); by way of example: the definition of a policy for an organisation and the planning of the objectives and the system, its implementation, the verification and revision of the environmental management. Within this logic, continual improvement is seen as the recurrent process of building the management system, which leads to the achievement of improvements in the overall environmental performance in line with the environmental policy of the organisation.

Figure 2.1 Deming cycle (source: www.resultsresults.co.uk).

Product environmental certifications

Product certification focuses on the environmental aspects and impacts of the life cycle of a manufactured product or service. The product certifications discussed in this book are as follows:

- the European Regulation for the European Union (EU) eco-label (No. 66/2010, EU Ecolabel);
- the product environmental footprint (PEF) and the product carbon footprint;
- the validation systems for Environmental Product Declarations, with particular reference to the EPD Environmental Product Declarations scheme, IEC – International EPD Council;
- the so-called 'Energy labels' issued as a result of various EU directives.

Italy is the leading country in the EU for Ecolabel certified products (approx. 9000 as of January 2012), as well as for environmental product declarations (EPD). These two figures quite clearly show that numbers for certified products are still low, especially if compared with numbers for certified organisations, but show a particular interest in the productive systems of our country on this subject.

The sole exception within this framework is the energy label which is very different to the other certifications presented in this book: it is not regulated by any voluntary schemes, and, in fact, started out as a compulsory labelling system for many electrical appliances (fridges, ovens, bulbs, to name some of the better known examples) introduced into the European market. It goes without saying, therefore, that, in this case, there is no point evaluating the statistics for its application, but it is better to simply highlight the logic with which the European Commission has decided to make the standard compulsory by means of a clear 'label', and has thus enabled consumers to choose the best energy saving products. The prospects inherent in the future use of the 'EC' label envisaged for products affected by the ErP Directive (*Energy-related Products*) mean it is paramount to deal with this type of certification within the scope of this book.

The analysis of the life cycle is the same for all the product certifications presented below, with the exception of the energy label, which is only concerned with direct consumption (but not, however, with its evolution which is governed by ErP and is in line with the other certifications). This approach, which can be categorised quite simply as the product's path from 'cradle to grave', finds its highest level of application design, and technical and legislative detail in the field of the ISO standards for the 14040 series (see chapter 3). The evolution and dissemination of the life cycle approach within the scope of the voluntary standardisation processes have marked a fundamental and truly innovative change in the way in which environmental certification schemes have been applied.

Firstly, this approach is characterised by a long-term logic which, although it does not explicitly contemplate future generations, introduces into the realm of environmental management the consideration of the impacts created by a product after its useful life (take the case of non-biodegradable toxic substances or radioactive waste which remains harmful for decades) and before this, in the phases prior to the production process, where the company's choices may affect phenomena which concern those generations (for example, renewable resources).

Secondly, the *life cycle* approach aims to promote circularity by encouraging the producer to consider (and thus, take care of) all the impacts generated even when the product or part of it (packaging, waste, etc.) passes into the direct responsibility of other parties. This means, for example, that a company does not just need to ensure that its products are correctly disposed of at the end of their life, but that it must try to make sure they are recovered and reused.

Thirdly, this approach, as we have seen, helps the company to widen the focus of environmental management from a company and local dimension to 'system-product', that is to a wider field of operation of the different parties involved in managing the product, who are the 'targets' of the environmental impacts generated by it, or, more simply, hold an interest in preventing or minimising these impacts (basically they are *stakeholders*).

To support these requirements which make up the methodological 'backbone', the life cycle approach means that data and information which are not held in the organisation seeking certification must be collected and analysed (e.g. the need to influence environmental choices when extracting raw materials or treating end of life waste products) hence, the difficulties in implementing the tool are significantly increased. The life cycle approach interacts with the certification scheme in different ways. In some cases, the company is asked to carry out a life cycle assessment (LCA) to rigorously compile a set of environmental guidelines to use in communications to the market – take an environmental product declaration (EPD), for example. Sometimes, the life cycle assessment is not given to the company seeking the label, but is carried out on a one-time basis by a person who classifies the impacts by product category and who defines a series of thresholds with regard to the environmental parameters. The company must then gather data and guidelines on this basis and demonstrate full compliance with the assessment in order to obtain certification (take the European Ecolabel, for example).

The overall picture of potential certifications for products is much more varied than that for organisations and presents a series of possibilities, which, although they start from the same common base, take on substantial differences when actually applied.

As we will see in further detail, there are three different types of so-called environmental 'claims' that could be certified and also identified by the ISO standard (the 14020 series is the reference). In particular these types of 'claims' can be classified as follows:

- TYPE I: voluntary ecological labels based on a multi-criteria system which analyses the entire product life cycle, subject to external certification by an independent body (the European mark for ecological quality, ECOLABEL, falls under this category, for example) (ISO 14024);
- TYPE II: environmental self-declarations by manufacturers, importers or product distributors without the intervention of an independent certification board (self-declarations also include 'Recyclable', 'Compostable', etc.) (ISO 14021);
- TYPE III: eco labels (or *Eco-profiles*) which include declarations based on pre-established parameters and which contain a quantification of the environmental impacts associated with the product life cycle through an

LCA system. They are subject to an independent check and presented in a clear and comparable format. The 'Environmental Product Declarations' (EPD) are amongst these, for example, (ISO 14025).

Some types of product certifications can be used directly on the product or even on the immediate packaging, others are accompanied by claims (including advertising) or declarations intended to attract the attention of potential buyers and influence their choice. Product certification cannot, however, be used to identify a specific manufacturing facility or advertise environmental excellence (for the reasons indicated earlier). To be more precise, it is commonly held that due to their characteristics, type I and II labels are mainly aimed at the end consumer (business to consumer or BtoC), whilst the type III labels are better used for relations with commercial partners in the production chain (business to business or BtoB), although there are some notable exceptions (for example, the Ecolabel for graphic paper or the EPD for a car or a washing machine).

The product certification schemes presented in this book concern type I and II labels since they offer better assurances of data transparency, credibility of the scheme and the possibility to develop regulations governing incentives. Attempts to start certification schemes for type II claims are, however, on the increase and judging by some of the single theme labels (e.g. 'carbon footprints' or 'water footprints') could already fall into this category.

Refer to Chapter 4 of this book for a further discussion on the subject of product certification.

The environmental certification of organisations and their processes

The Eco-Management and Audit Scheme (EMAS) is a European Union Regulation concerning 'the voluntary participation of organisations in a Community eco-management and audit system'.

The first version of the Regulation was published in 1993, aimed solely at industrial enterprises, but it was revised five years later with the main goal of extending participation in it to all organisations in any area of business. The last version was approved in 2009 (Regulation 1221/2009) and all three versions have kept the original objective alive; to build a new relationship between organisations (industrial or not, public and private), institutions and the public based on cooperation, reciprocal support, and transparency with the aim of preserving and improving the quality of the environment for the benefit of current and future generations.

One of the most significant features of the Regulation lies in the fact that the Community Legislator does not set quantitative limits or organisational constraints on how the organisation's business is carried out, but merely outlines the characteristics of an environmental management system which, if correctly introduced within the same organisation, can lead to an improvement in its environmental performances.

For an organisation, introducing an environmental management system and maintaining compliance with Regulation requirements means organising and carrying out its activities by means of gradual but long-lasting interventions that minimise the impacts they have or could have on the environment.

After an organisation has joined a scheme of this kind and obtained the required results, it will receive public recognition by being entered in a special European register and by being allowed to make this result known to its partners.

It is becoming increasingly common, however, for organisations not to start from scratch when structuring their own environmental management system: in addition to numerous companies which leverage the experience gained in quality schemes such as those provided by the ISO 9000 standards, there are also organisations which obtain EMAS registration by capitalising on their own environmental commitment which has already been recognised by way of certification as provided by the ISO 14001 standard. ISO 14001 is the standard for environmental management schemes published at the end of 1996 and updated in 2004 by ISO, the international standardisation organisation. Whilst the Community Regulation entails the entry of the organisation in the Community register and the acquisition of the right to use the EMAS logo in accordance with the provisions laid down by the Regulation itself, compliance with ISO allows the organisation to obtain a certificate of conformity which is valid internationally (see table 2.1 for further differences between ISO14001 and EMAS). In 2001, the EMAS Regulation stated the compatibility of its own requirements with those foreseen by international standards and fully incorporated section 4 of ISO 14001 relating to the management scheme. This resolved the problem of inconsistency between the two schemes, thus allowing a gradual, controlled changeover, which was relatively easy for EMAS, for those organisations with ISO certification that were interested in obtaining registration[2].

The interest in the transition may arise from the distinctive and defining features of EMAS with respect to ISO 14001: the benefits linked to the guarantee of legislative conformity, the emphasis on improving environmental performance, external communication and dialogue, the active participation of employees. In 2009, the two standards came even closer together, since EMAS extended its validity internationally with the so-called EMAS Global' (Testa et al., 2014).

As with ISO 14001, adherence to EC Regulation no. 1221/2009 is voluntary and means that greater benefit can be derived from the commitment of an

Table 2.1 Main differences between ISO 14001 and EMAS

Topic	ISO 14001	EMAS
Nature	Private standard	Public Regulation
Validity	Valid at international level since its first issuing	Valid in Europe until 2009 and at the international level since 2010
External communication	It is not mandatory	It foresees to make available for the public an Environmental Statement
Scope	Organisations of all sectors	Organisations of all sectors and experimentally applied in industrial clusters

organisation to environmentally correct management: the voluntary process is a condition for participating in an effort to improve management that is documented and transparent.

The institutional layout and the steps for obtaining process certification

In order for an organisation to be eligible to take part in the EMAS scheme, the country in which it carries out its business must have two organisations: a Competent Body and an Accreditation Body.

The Competent Body enters those organisations in the Community register that have successfully completed the registration procedure and then publishes the list. It also controls the maintenance of such organisations in the register and suspends or deletes the entries in the case of breach of the provisions in the Regulation.

The Accreditation Body defines the accreditation criteria of the environmental verifiers (for EMAS) and the environmental certifiers (for ISO 14001) and monitors their actions. The accredited environmental verifiers are the decision-makers who are authorised to verify that the characteristics of the environmental management scheme of an organisation correspond to the requirements for EMAS and ISO 14001. These third parties are independent of the organisation and perform their task with competence, knowledge and ability as ensured by the accreditation system. Independent verification is one of the key requirements of the Regulation because it guarantees that the organisation operates in compliance with the objectives and guidelines specified by the Community Legislator. This activity is based around the analysis of documentation, site visits and meetings with personnel with the aim of assessing the effectiveness of the organisation's environmental management in accordance with the Regulation.

In short, an organisation seeking to obtain EMAS registration or ISO 14001 certification must:

1   implement an internal environmental management scheme

    a   by carrying out *an initial analysis* that identifies and evaluates all the environmental aspects connected to the business in order to identify the most significant ones;

    b   by developing and adopting an environmental policy which unequivocally endorses the commitment and strategies of the organisation in favour of environmental protection;

    c   by defining and applying an environmental programme which contains the description of concrete plans of action through which the organisation intends to convert the general principles of its environmental policy into specific objectives for improvement defined on the basis of the results which have emerged after completion of the environmental analysis;

    d   by adopting a *dedicated management and organisational structure* – assimilated into the overall management scheme – capable of pursuing the environmental programme and staying true to the commitments it has undertaken;

e   by planning and implementing *a periodic verification process* to evaluate the efficiency and the effectiveness of the management scheme and the environmental performance.

2   develop an environmental declaration which illustrates the commitments undertaken, the programmes defined and the results achieved and takes into account the information requirements of the stakeholders (applicable only to EMAS and not to ISO 14001);

3   submit the management scheme for *verification by an accredited environmental verifier* who can ascertain compliance with the requirements of the Regulation or the ISO 14001 standard;

4   having obtained registration, make the environmental declaration available to the public and adhere to the rules laid down in the Regulation and the Registration Procedure to maintain registration in the EMAS Register (valid only for EMAS).

Both for ISO 14001 and EMAS, the organisations are required to provide proof that the Environmental Management Scheme is maintained over the years and that the objectives established for improvement are regularly achieved by constantly seeking to improve its performance.

Other types of environmental certifications

Certifications for carbon emission: The ISO 14064 standard

Accession to local, national and international initiatives to reduce the impact generated by climate changes makes the assumption that the organisation is capable of calculating, monitoring over time and reporting on climate-changing emissions (or greenhouse gas emissions) and/or the reduction of emissions or the removal of greenhouse gases from the atmosphere generated by the activities or specific projects which it carries out.

This capability will allow the organisation to properly manage its strategic positioning with regards to the issue of climate change, with a view to

• reducing the risks linked to failure to comply with the requirements for good environmental practice on the issue of 'climate change', which the market or the stakeholders consider to be increasingly important and, indeed, providing effective communication about the opportunities offered by a 'virtuous' position.

• being able to participate reasonably and effectively in voluntary initiatives and schemes that are coherent in reducing emissions and support the strategies and policies undertaken (whether corporate or public).

• acquiring the necessary tools to fulfil any mandatory obligations that the Community and national legislation has decided to apply to the organisation.

• introducing the organisation to the idea of the new tools (standardised or voluntary) based on the mechanisms of the market through which it is possible to capitalise directly in economic and financial terms on the results obtained from the operations or projects that have been carried out to reduce or remove emissions.

These innovations have, over the years, led to the development, at the head of companies, institutions, public administrations and other types of organisations, of the need to correctly and effectively quantify the production or removal of emissions linked to their activities or to specific projects which they have undertaken by allowing them to produce reports on these emissions or on their contribution to climate change mitigation.

The standardisation community has developed several standard rules on this matter in order to provide certainty about any methods needed to fulfil these requirements.

Currently, the reference standards are summarised in the ISO 14064 standard with regard to the requirements for quantifying, monitoring, reporting on emissions or the reduction of emissions achieved by an organisation in its business operations or with reference to specific projects which it has planned and developed. The ISO 14064 standard consists of three separate parts that are more or less independent. The first two (ISO 14064-1 and 14064-2), in particular, establish the requirements for reporting on emissions and the reduction of overall emissions linked to an organisation's activities (the ISO 14064-1 standard) or linked to the completion of a specific project aimed at reducing emissions or increasing removal of greenhouse gases (the ISO 14064-2 standard).

Two different subjects for reporting, therefore, (on the one hand, the activities carried out by the organisation and on the other, the focus on a specific single project) to satisfy the different requirements of standardisation, resulting from the opportunity or the necessity to guarantee requirements for accuracy, performance and credibility of the claims regarding greenhouse gas emissions. A third standard in the same group (ISO 14064-3) is dependent on the application of the previous two and identifies the principles and requirements for checking greenhouse gas inventories (14064-1) and validating or checking the projects for reducing greenhouse gas emission (14064-2). This third standard can be used by the same organisations for an internal audit (verification of the first or second parts) on the inventory or the project that has been carried out, and should be used as a reference by independent parties (typically verification and certification bodies) who are responsible for the audit. Indeed, the application of the ISO 14064 standard is justified, above all, if it is subjected to external audits, and therefore, validated by an independent and accredited party. The ISO 14064 standards are verifiable standards (not certifiable), namely, they can be verified by a third party, resulting in a report (namely, an audit) containing proof of compliance with the requirements laid down.

At the same time, the application of the standards means that the approaches and the rules laid down for reporting on emissions can be standardised, so that different experiences and the results associated with them can be compared both when they refer to the same voluntary or mandatory scheme and when they refer to different schemes or are developed independently with respect to potential schemes and initiatives. The objective pursued is to propose general requirements for application characterised by the necessary stringency. For example, the results obtained on an organisational or project level are not evaluated in absolute terms but in comparison with a baseline scenario (consisting, on an organisational level, of a framework of the production and/or removal of emissions in the absence of ad hoc policies that have been already structured, and on a project level, of a foreseeable future scenario in the absence of the project itself).

In particular, the ISO 14064-part 1 standard defines the requirements for quantifying and reporting on the greenhouse gas emissions generated by an organisation and the reduction or removal of the emissions produced. This refers to a specific tool, namely the inventory of greenhouse gases. The inventory gives a complete picture of the emissions produced by each of the sources of emissions (for example, phases of the production process, individual plants) linked to the organisation's activities, as well as the removal of greenhouse gases carried out by so-called 'absorber' elements. The standard, therefore, establishes the methods by which the inventory should be planned and developed, managed, used in communications to report the results attained and lastly, checked. The inventory, in accordance with the standard, can be included in a programme or an initiative to which the organisation has adhered to achieve the reduction of emissions (and not just for the purposes of verification, or more precisely, third party validation)[3], and in this case, can demonstrate that participation in the programme will be carried out properly.

The inventory takes all the different greenhouse gases into account[4] and considers the specific potential impact on global warming showing all the values as a single unit of measurement given in tons of CO_2.[5] The inventory must also respect a series of basic principles indicated by the standard to guarantee a 'proper and fair' accounting (including, by way of example, those of coherency, accuracy and transparency) and must be a coherent tool for the requirements of the so-called 'intended user', namely the party (internal or external to the company) identified as the person who will use the information contained therein to carry out assessments and make decisions. The ISO 14064-part 2 standard, however, defines the requirements to quantify, monitor and report on activities aimed at obtaining reductions in greenhouse gas emissions (or increases in removing them) organised as projects.

What is meant by 'project'? A project to reduce greenhouse gas emissions (or remove them) is intended to be a series of activities aimed at modifying a trend (namely a situation that would occur in the absence of activities to carry out) generating a reduction in greenhouse gas emissions (or an increase in them). The results obtained from this kind of project can be quantified, monitored and communicated for reporting purposes in order to be acknowledged and validated. Validation of the results obtained through the project can produce tools that are open to economic exploitation, such as emission credits (a tool used, for example, by the flexible mechanisms in the Kyoto Protocol based on projects like the Clean Development Mechanism).

Unlike part 1, part 2 of the ISO 14064 standard has, in fact, been expressly developed to provide methodological support in carrying out projects which are typically placed in schemes (or programmes) with voluntary or mandatory participation, of a local, national or international nature aimed at accounting for and recording the results obtained from single projects carried out by the party concerned who is given the possibility of capitalising on the reduction of emissions or the removal of greenhouse gases obtained through the recognition and validation of permits for certified emission reductions. These reduction permits can be used, where necessary, to fulfil the commitments undertaken by the applicant or forcibly allocated, or even traded in a market that gives them a financial exchange value.

The aim of the ISO 14064-part 2 standard, therefore, is to define requirements that allow the results obtained from an emissions reduction project to be effectively quantified, monitored and communicated and thus, guarantee the efficiency of the process leading to the completion of the project. These requirements could, thus, coincide with or be adopted by market-based programmes or tools which, on the basis of the reporting carried out, result in the allocation of emission credits or other securities which are eligible to be bought or sold in a market.

The execution of a project on greenhouse gases is typically divided into two main phases: the planning phase and the implementation phase. The ISO 14064 standard recognises these two phases and establishes the requirements that must be taken into consideration for their development.

The project and compliance with the provisions of ISO 14064-2 must be verified and validated by a third party. The verification process starts with a claim or a statement made by the applicant on the results achieved by the project.

This requirement also calls for an appropriate reporting tool for the project in the form of a 'Report on greenhouse gases' which serves as the organisation level report provided for by the ISO 14064-1 and must, therefore, serve the needs of the person (the 'intended user') who receives the information contained therein. The report will, therefore, include a summary of the project and its main points (location, duration, and timeframe), the baseline scenario and the reduction or removal of emissions achieved including any other features.

If the project under examination fits the framework of a greenhouse gas emissions programme aimed at capitalising on the results achieved, then it could put appropriate methods and procedures in place for: certification and recognition of the units of greenhouse gases reduced or removed (as shown by the periodic monitoring carried out); a final check on the reduction of emissions or the overall increase in the removal of emissions established by the project (for the final report on greenhouse gases); final certification of the results achieved.

The ISO 50001:2011 standard and the synergy with environmental management systems

The topic of energy consumption and in particular, of the efficiency with which this consumption occurs has been the subject of debate for many years among the institutions which are responsible for drafting policies on a national and European level. There are numerous reasons why there is a strong push within Europe to reinvigorate the programme to promote energy efficiency on all levels of society. Firstly, according to numerous studies, the EU could save at least 20 per cent of its current energy consumption for a sum of 60 billion Euros per year, the equivalent of Germany and Finland's combined energy consumption. Secondly, energy savings are without doubt the quickest, most effective and most efficient way in terms of costs of reducing greenhouse gas emissions to honour the commitments that the various states made to Kyoto. Lastly, it must be pointed out that, on the basis of current trends, by the end of 2030, Europe will be 90 per cent dependent on imports to fulfil its needs for oil and 80 per cent for gas. It is impossible to predict the price of oil and gas in 2020, particularly if the demand from developing countries continues to grow as rapidly as today.

Energy efficiency is, therefore, one of the key instruments for addressing this problem and an effective energy efficiency policy could make a major contribution to improving EU competitiveness and employment.

These and other considerations have led to the recent introduction of the ISO 50001 standard. The Energy Management System (EnMS) proposed by the standard allows organisations to develop and implement policies covering problems related to energy consumption.

The standard specifies the requirements for establishing, implementing, maintaining and improving an energy management system. It enables any organisation to follow a systematic approach in achieving continual improvement of energy performance through a more efficient use, irrespective of the energy source or process. In the field of Management Systems, the Standard seems to be a natural extension, as far as energy is concerned, of the 9001 standards on quality management systems, ISO 14001 standards on environmental management systems and OHSAS 18001 standards on occupational health and safety management. As in the case of the equivalent environmental standard (ISO 14001), ISO 50001 does not establish the requirements for energy performance, but supplies the elements, to the companies intending to adopt it, required to implement an organisational system for improving energy efficiency.

ISO 50001 can be applied to any organisation seeking to ensure compliance with its energy policy and demonstrate this compliance through third party certification of its energy management system.

ISO 50001 defines the Energy Management System as 'the set of interrelated or interacting elements of an organisation to establish an energy policy and energy objectives, and the methods of achieving these objectives' (Figure 2.2).

Within the EU, Energy Management Systems have also been the subject of voluntary standardisation quite similar to ISO 50001. In 2001, Denmark published its own standard titled 'DS 2403 Energy Management System Standard' based on ISO 14001, Sweden followed suit by publishing the 'SS 627750 Energy Management Systems standard', and then Ireland in 2005 with the standard titled 'I.S. 393 Standard on Energy Management System'. In 2007, two further standards were published for Energy Management Systems, the 'UNE-216301:2007 Energy Management System standard' by Spain and the

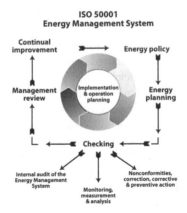

Figure 2.2 ISO 50001 Energy Management System (source: www.sistemiconsulenze.it).

standard titled 'VDI 4602/1 Technical rule on Energy Management' published by the German Association of Engineers. It appears quite clear, then, that compulsory or voluntary standards for Energy Management Systems cannot be considered a novelty linked to the ISO 50001, even though it has contributed to organising multiple existing approaches in various European states into one standard, as is often the case with such standards.

All the voluntary type standards preceding the publication of this standard had a common denominator: they were based on the ISO 14001. This feature was confirmed by the ISO 50001 standard, which was modelled on the previous and more widespread standard for Environmental Management Systems, but is also complementary to other types of management systems like those for quality in accordance with ISO 9001 or the Health and Safety Management System in accordance with the OHSAS 18001 standard.

The first feature of the ISO 50001 standard highlighting the integration and synergy with other Management Systems is the model on which it is based. In this case, too, as in numerous other types of standards for management systems, the European standard is based on the Plan-Do-Check-Act methodology. The 'Plan' step identifies the legislative requirements, the objectives and the energy targets, outlines a policy for energy saving, and defines the actions for continual improvement towards energy saving. The 'Do' step aims to allocate resources and responsibilities; promotes awareness of the organisation as well as internal and external communication and performs systemic, procedural, infrastructural and behavioural actions envisaged in the 'Plan' step. The 'Check' step, as mentioned in the previous paragraphs for the Environmental Management System, establishes a programme for energy monitoring and auditing to check conformity with legal obligations and systemic, procedural, infrastructural and behavioural requirements, and manages non-conformity.

The 'Act' step puts the revision of the energy management system in place by implementing the improvements made necessary by the feedback acquired during the check phase.

In the 'Plan' step, one of the fundamental steps for both standards on which the structure of the system is based is the identification and evaluation of the features. As we have seen, in the ISO 14001, the document that summarises this activity is titled Initial Environmental Analysis, whereas it could be called Energy Analysis for the ISO 50001. The Initial Environmental Analysis within the report identifies and evaluates all the direct environmental aspects of the organisation including energy. This permits a high level of integration between the two documents, even though a series of distinctions can be made. The biggest difference encountered on a first reading of the standard is that less importance is given to the indirect aspects of energy consumption in the ISO 50001 standard. The standard frequently touches on the criteria and selection methods for suppliers in the section relating to the energy management system, but does not mention the need to identify and evaluate the indirect aspects connected to energy consumption. This, on the one hand, simplifies the execution of the Energy Analysis of organisations, but on the other hand, poses questions about whether the standard is still applicable to all types of organisations including services and public entities. Take a local authority, for example, which may 'influence' energy-intensive activities in the area or an environmental consulting agency that only shows consumption of electric energy by computers and air conditioners. In these cases, the identification and assessment of the indirect aspects would be the predominant part of the phase for identifying and assessing them. From this point of view, even though the standard is applicable to any organisation, it seems to revert to the 1836/93 Regulation (EMAS I) when the environmental management system described by it was only applicable to manufacturing sectors and indirect environmental aspects were not taken into account. For this reason, we are waiting for the release of the first explanatory Guidelines by the training and/or accreditation bodies that could comment on this subject.

There are some other minor aspects that need to be taken into account if the Initial Environmental Analysis is going to be integrated with the requirements of the ISO 50001 standard. Firstly, the standard requires that during the Energy Analysis an estimate of future consumption be made as well as a reconstruction of past and present energy consumptions. Secondly, the standard asks for the people who work for the organisation and may influence the organisation's energy consumptions to be identified. Both these points seem to be supplementary to the requirements of the ISO 14001 standard.

Another element that needs to be considered is the level of detail that Energy Analysis should have with respect to conventional methods of addressing the direct aspect of 'Energy consumption' in the Initial Environmental Analysis. The standard states that the level of detail depends on the size of the organisation, even though the minimum requirement is that all sources of energy (gas, fuel oil, electricity, diesel, etc.) and all uses (drying, lighting, air conditioning, etc.) should be identified. It is often difficult to separate consumption by production departments or by type of use in small organisations, even though this information is very essential for planning improvements in the next step.

Table 2.2 shows an example of a summary table for methane consumption, which can be included in the Energy Analysis.

Table 2.2 Example of summary table for energy consumption to include in the Energy Analysis

Process	Nominal power	Load factor	Power absorbed	Work hours per day	Working days	Hours of work	Energy absorbed	Energy absorbed	%
	kW	%	kW	hours/ day	day/year	hours/ year	Sm3/ hour	Sm3/year	
Heating Area 1	2.000	60%	1.200	24	140	3.360	125.1	420.310	56%
Heating Area 2	300	50%	150	24	140	3.360	15.6	52.539	7%
Office boiler	150	30%	45	14	140	1.960	4.7	9.194	1.2%
Office + cafeteria boiler	250	30%	75	14	140	1.960	7.8	15.324	2%
Changing room boiler	35	35%	12.3	14	220	3.080	1.3	3.933	0.5%
Process 1	300	55%	165.7	24	300	7.200	17.3	124.350	16.6%
Process 2	300	55%	165.7	24	300	7.200	17.3	124.350	16.6%

The section on planning the system is completed by the paragraphs about the applicable legal requirements, the objectives and the goals. The paragraphs for formulating the criteria are identical to those for ISO 14001. Tools in the form of documents such as the fulfilment timetable or the register for legal requirements will definitely be much shorter than the ones relating to the Environmental Management System. By contrast, the energy improvement programme should show details of the processes and the areas targeting increases in energy efficiency if it wants to be consistent with the survey carried out in the Energy Analysis.

Moreover, since energy is also an important aspect not only of the economy, but also of an organisation's budget for reaching its goals, it should contain an estimate of the return of investment achieved by actions aimed at saving energy.

The 'Do' section of the Deming cycle contained in the ISO 50001 standard appears to be exactly the same as the one in the ISO 14001 standard, if you exclude the absence of requirements for managing emergencies as indicated in the previous paragraphs, and so, can be integrated quite easily. The need to define roles and responsibilities is virtually identical and the considerations made in the previous chapters can be repeated for this standard. The documentation and the document check are less detailed than in ISO 14001 and so, any procedure for an Environmental Management System concerning this aspect can be considered exhaustive. The same consideration can be made with regard to communication where the organisation is given the choice of communicating its most significant energy features to the outside world. There are a few minor differences concerning training. The first difference refers to the EMAS Regulation in particular rather than to ISO 14001. The standard does not make any reference to the active involvement of personnel in the Energy Management System, either in the training or communication sections. Moreover, the ISO 50001 standard specifies that the Management Representative for the EnMS must be qualified in energy management, whereas this requirement is not quite so distinct in the ISO 14001 standard and so, in this particular case, it would appear necessary to include something more accurate in the EnMS for the tasks or requirements of competence which are often indicated in the EnMS. The 'Check' part is in line with the EnMS. There are no substantial changes with respect to the ISO 14001 standard in the periodic assessment of compliance with the standard in terms of energy, management of non-conformities, corrective and preventive actions, checks on registrations and management of internal audits. The paragraph on Monitoring and Measuring introduces several new concepts in this section. Firstly, the topic of the ratio between energy consumption and the factors that influence them is touched upon. The organisation needs to periodically monitor this ratio by assessing actual consumption and estimated consumption. The need to predict and conserve records of 'unexpected' energy consumption including the causes and the solutions put forward to reduce this consumption is linked to this requirement. Lastly, when talking about performance indicators, on the one hand, key performance indicators should be developed per unit of product or square meter of surface area, whilst on the other hand, benchmarking operations need to be carried out comparing these indicators both internally and externally with other similar organisations. Compared to the first point, it should be noted that the suggested indicators are compatible with the 'key performance indicators' indicated in the annex IV of the 1221/2009 Regulation (EMAS III), even though, as described in the previous chapters, the Regulation goes further by specifying that the term 'unit of production' means one ton of the finished product and, if such information is unavailable for certain production categories, then it is possible to use revenue or added value.

Costs and benefits of environmental certification

One of the topics that primarily interests companies and organisations considering environmental certification concerns the estimate of the financial commitment required and the benefits and advantages that can be obtained by adopting this tool. Twenty years after the implementation of the first certified environmental management systems, there are now numerous methodological guidelines available to help identify the main items for cost and the types of benefits linked to acquiring and enhancing the different forms of environmental certification. What organisations (whether 'novices' or already certified) still require, however, is the comfort of empirical confirmation and practical evidence that demonstrate which costs and which benefits carry more weight in the certification process and, above all, the extent to which they can be quantified economically.

The area in which the most amount of feedback is available is, without a doubt, the one for environmental managements systems, given the 'seniority' of the EMAS schemes and ISO 14001 and their widespread use. This area can be referenced for some guidelines on the estimate of costs and the benefits of environmental certification.

The first feature to consider in identifying and estimating the management and economic effort required to sustain the implementation of an environmental management system concerns the commitment required to achieve and fine tune the different requirements envisaged by the standards (EMAS and ISO 14001).

An initial estimate can be made by quantifying in man-months the time required to implement the different steps needed to meet the requirements. This approach avoids distortions linked to the different costs of human resources (internal and external) that can be found in each specific area of a company or local market. The costs which must be sustained to obtain the initial ISO certification or EMAS registration can be measured based on the following figures: the management system requires 4–5 man-months, the initial analysis commitment can be estimated in 2–3 man-months whilst the other parts probably require less time (policies, objectives and programmes: 1 man-month; environmental declaration: 1–2 man-months). It must be pointed out that the above-mentioned estimated costs in terms of man-months refer to the implementation of the environmental management system[6] and only take internal costs into account.[7]

Furthermore, the costs of certification can vary quite significantly in relation to how long the existing environment management system has been in place in the company embarking on the process of obtaining ISO certification or EMAS registration. It is actually quite clear that the costs involved in attaining this result depend on the 'starting point' from which the company moves on various levels; the environmental performance of the production processes, the definition of environmental responsibility and the organisational set-up, the progress of the monitoring and verification activities on environmental aspects, etc.

The so-called fixed costs for the certification must be added to the variable costs, namely the expenses for certification or registration of the company including any fee for the accredited certifier/verifier and the amount due for the EMAS registration of the organisation.

Over the last few years, there have been several attempts to quantify the overall financial cost to the company of implementing the environmental management system and obtaining certification or registration thereof.

An indication of the financial cost required of the organisation can be given by quoting the EMAS toolkit created by the European Commission, which provides an estimate of the average cost according to the size of the organisation:

- € 10,000 for micro organisations (< 10 employees);
- € 20,000 for small organisations (< 50 employees);

- € 35,000 for medium organisations (< 250 employees);
- € 50,000 for large organisations (> 250 employees).

Further studies (e.g. Milieu Ltd, 2009) have shown that these estimates are often based on weak empirical grounds that are simply derived from approximate indications attained through questionnaires by the companies interviewed (which rarely have internal systems accounting for environmental costs). This explains the lack of uniformity in the reported estimates. Table 2.3 collates the main data gathered from the latest studies of EMS implementation costs in compliance with the EMAS Regulation in different countries.

In particular, the recent study commissioned by the European Commission on the costs and benefits of EMAS registration (Milieu Ltd, 2009) estimated the total average cost of EMAS for a 'typical' registered organisation (approximately 48,000 Euros the first year; approximately 26,000 from the second year onwards) showing that the lion's share of the costs are concentrated in the first year (the need to learn about EMAS, the implementation of administration and management systems, the need to resort to external expertise) which then gradually shrink through the economies of learning.

As far as the ratio between the different costs is concerned (internal, external and fixed), the study shows a big discrepancy based on the size of the organisation, from a micro organisation where the fixed costs exceed 50 per cent and the internal costs 30 per cent, to large organisations where the ratios are inverted. The external costs are stable at an average of about 10 to 15 per cent irrespective of the organisation's size.

It is important to underline, however, that the estimates given are merely indications and subject to significant variations not only in relation to the sometimes notable size differences within each category, but also because the specific characteristics covering sector, location, technology and management are not taken into account despite being, as we have seen, the real determinants of commitment by the company.

Table 2.3 Study of EMAS implementation costs

Country Size	Small < 100 employees	Medium < 500 employees	Large > 500 employees	Average
Austria	€ 109,000	€ 225,000	€ 153,000	
Denmark				€ 62,000
Germany	€ 37,000	€ 84,000	€ 85,000	€ 59,000
EU member States	€ 21,000 € 38,000	€ 17,000 € 40,000	€ 38,000 € 66,000	€ 26,000 € 48,000

The benefits of environmental certification

The attention paid by companies and observers to a fundamental question has grown in proportion to the dissemination of the different forms of environmental certification: can these tools create 'value' for the companies that adopt them?

Numerous studies and empirical research have looked into some areas linked to the main competitive strategies of a company in order to find out if environmental certification can guarantee an advantage over competitors. It is possible to give a general overview of the main environmental certifications.

Here again, as in the case of costs and commitment required, the area offering the most ideas and pointers lies in environmental management systems certification.

The results of the EVER study (IEFE et al., 2006), for example, are summarised in Figure 2.3, which puts the competitive benefits produced by participating in the scheme in order of relevance as revealed by the sample survey.

As can be seen, there are many obvious benefits indicated by organisations registered with EMAS, which can be traced back to different 'areas' of competitiveness, each of which highlights interesting features.

As far as the area of efficiency and productivity of company resources is concerned, the results are moderately positive: 56 per cent of organisations with EMAS registration made savings in production costs, mostly by optimising the use of resources and capitalising on their reuse or recovery (especially energy and materials).

The benefits deriving from the reduction of emissions in air and water were not quite as high.

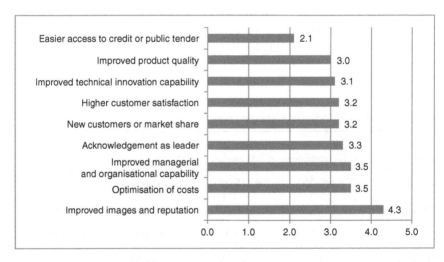

Figure 2.3 The competitive benefits of EMAS (source: Authors' own).

This is confirmed by numerous other surveys on the efficiency of environmental management systems figuring in a broad range of literature (Milieu Ltd, 2009).

Benefits deriving from improved management and organisation of business activities quite often figure alongside production efficiency. It is no coincidence that the development of human resources (motivation and training), organisational efficiency, the planning of business activities and document management are indicated in studies as the greatest benefits perceived by companies with environmental certification. The above-mentioned EVER study confirms these indications: following EMAS registration no less than 61 per cent of participating companies perceived an improvement in motivation and participation of personnel, whilst 63 per cent noticed a better definition of roles and responsibilities within the company's organisation.

A second, very important area of competitiveness for a company lies in its ability to develop both technological and managerial innovations making it possible to gain a margin of advantage over competitors. Studies in this area reveal a reasonable level of 'stimulus' towards innovation from EMAS and ISO 14001. One of the most prominent studies carried out on 1277 organisations registered with EMAS in Germany showed that participation in the European scheme made 'a substantial contribution to environmental innovation, particularly to management and organisational innovation' (Rennings et al., 2003).

Undoubtedly, the most prominent strategic area for corporate competitiveness is in market performance. The EVER study shows that, in this area, EMAS can actually generate competitive advantages in revenue and market share, even if to a lesser extent compared to other types of benefits. Suffice to say that a consistent number of organisations registered to EMAS have reported positive results in terms of increased market share and/or numbers of customers (45 per cent), as well as in terms of increased customer satisfaction (39 per cent). On the other hand, however, it is important to remember that the sample surveys indicate a lack of market response as the main reason why some companies have abandoned the scheme (particularly in countries like Germany and Austria).

The main studies that have been published, however, provide mixed indications. For example, a recent European study (Rennings et al., 2006) investigated the impact of different aspects of EMAS on economic performances and on the ability of organisations to produce technical innovations. The results identified a tenuous relationship between EMAS and other indicators of market success. A positive impact was registered, however, in an increase in revenue and exports, above all for those organisations reporting organisational improvement after implementing the EMS. Similar conclusions were reached in the study conducted by Iraldo et al. (2009) on a sample of 100 organisations operating in different EU countries. The authors carried out an analysis on whether adopting an EMS in compliance with the EMAS scheme had a positive effect on the organisation's environmental and competitive performance. The econometric analysis showed a positive impact of a *well-designed* environmental management system on environmental performances, and as a result, on the innovative capability of the organisations; less strong evidence emerged on the positive effect of EMAS on market performance.

Granly and Welo (2014) interviewed nine Norwegian manufacturing SMEs. The study demonstrated that customer pressures and improved environmental routines are the main drivers for ISO 14001 certification while increased aware-ness of environmental issues and reduced environmental impact are perceived like the most important benefits by the investigated sample. Heras and Arana (2010) report on the results of a survey that involved 262 companies of Basque Autonomous Region. The research aimed to investigate the drivers, barriers and benefits of Spanish SMEs in the adoption of the Spanish standard named Ekoscan and ISO 14001. The sample involved 169 ISO 14001 certified companies and 93 Ekoscan certified companies. The results show that the main driver that led SMEs to implement the Ekoscan standard is related to an improvement in the environmental situation of the company (51.9 per cent of the answers) while motivation behind companies implementing ISO 14001, the replies were rela-tively heterogeneous and the highest value is achieved by the aim to improve the environmental performance of the company of the company (25.8 per cent).

Lim and Prakash (2014) studied the country-level relationship between the number of ISO 14001 certificates issued and the registered patents. They examined the data of 79 countries for the period 1996–2009. They considered registered patents related to the following categories: Air pollution abatement, water pollution abatement, waste management (such as solid waste collection and recycling), soil remediation, and environmental monitoring. The authors found that country-level ISO 14001 participation is a significant predictor of a country's environmental patent applications. Martín-Peña et al. (2014) carried out a survey collecting 228 questionnaires from Spanish companies of the auto-motive industry (manufacturers and suppliers). More than 80 per cent of the sample was composed by ISO 14001 certified companies. According to the survey results, the benefits are improvements in the firm's market position, stakeholder relations, environmental performance and access to environmental technologies. De Oliveira et al. (2010) performed in 2008 a questionnaire survey on Brazilian ISO 14001 certified companies. The main benefits identified are related to the development of preventive environmental actions, reduction in the consump-tion of power, water, gas and fuel oil, and a positive influence on other internal management processes.

Turk (2008) looked at reasons for ISO 14001 certification (or not) and ben-efits in 68 large firms in the construction sector in Turkey. He found ISO 14001 certification contributes to construction firms not only in terms of environmental benefits but also with corporate management and marketing effects. The biggest negative factor was determined to be the operational cost.

A final interpretation by which the benefits connected to environmental certification can be better evaluated is linked to a specific competitive advantage: benefits in image and relationships. Although the benefit is 'intangible' and difficult to quantify, it is the competitive advantage that is most commonly perceived, for example, by organisations registered with EMAS: no less than 84 per cent (IEFE et al. 2006).

There is one type of benefit in particular that merits special attention which is placed mid-way between internal benefits and external relations. According to some companies and observers, the environmental management system has made it is easier to monitor, update and maintain compliance of corporate activities with the applicable environmental laws and rules. This is a benefit which is often underestimated by many companies which believe they are in a position of relative tranquillity until they have to restructure and rationalise the corporate activities dedicated to the management of environmental regulations in order to comply with the requirements of EMAS and ISO 14001 (identification of pertinent regulatory requirements and regulations, registration of the applicable regulations, update of procedures, external communication procedures, etc.). The guarantee of legislative conformity is an advantage not only for the continuity of a company's activities (internal), but also for institutional figures with whom the company interacts (external) in various capacities starting with supervisory authorities who are increasingly appreciative of a management system in a company that is subject to verification. According to the EVER study (IEFE et al., 2006), for example, EMAS is considered a very useful tool for registered organisations to increase awareness about the applicable regulatory requirements and to monitor their evolution (70 per cent), to guarantee compliance (69 per cent) and to plan adjustments well in advance (67 per cent).

The indication seems particularly important for small businesses which traditionally seem to endure limitations and shortcomings (above all in resources and skills) when compared to a constantly changing regulatory and legislative framework for the environment which is sometimes characterised by significant uncertainties (take the recent change in the Environmental Act in Italy, for example). Furthermore, this indication has already been acknowledged by the European Commission, which, in the Action Plan supporting SMEs (European Commission, 2007), identifies EMAS as a strategic operative priority to fill the gap in applying regulations that these companies currently occupy indiscriminately in the European Union.

Finally it must be stressed that the 'benefits' of Environmental Management Systems should not be restricted to the environmental performance of the organisation that adopts them. Along with tangible benefits, such as improved environmental performance, in evaluating the effectiveness of the instrument those intangible benefits that are difficult to assess should also be taken into account. For example, the entrepreneurs' increased environmental awareness, the employees' participation and involvement in effective environmental management practices, the greater cooperation with those agencies in charge of permits and inspections, the increased ability to handle environmental emergencies, the increased ability to manage compliance with environmental regulations, etc. (Steger 2000), all indirectly contribute to environmental improvement in a wider sense.

Competitive benefits of product certification

Another form of environmental certification that is often used to increase the perceived value of a company and its products/services is environmental product labels or better defined as *ISO type 1 environmental labels.*

Feedbacks should be measured above all in terms of market response in order to evaluate the benefits and the competitive effectiveness of these 'product certifications' since this is their primary goal.

From this point of view, some studies conducted by the European Ecolabel suggest that this type of label can rely on an increasing awareness and willingness to buy in specific countries. In Italy, for example, a study by Astra-Demoskopea in 2003 highlighted how the vast majority of consumers, once they were given precise information about Ecolabel and the guarantees it provides, were willing to consider certification as an important factor when choosing to buy (76 per cent) or to always opt for products with the European label (65 per cent), where possible.

A direct verification of the benefits perceived by companies with product certification can produce very positive indications. The EVER study, as previously mentioned, examined the feedback obtained from companies using the Ecolabel on some of their products in a competitive context and identified the main categories of benefits shown in Table 2.4.

The biggest advantage perceived comes from benefits which are intangible, but considered essential in guaranteeing a good competitive performance: namely an improved image, which helps position the company as market leader. In this respect, it is symbolic that 95 per cent of certified companies using Ecolabel in advertising campaigns or other marketing activities are satisfied with the result of these activities and consider the label effective. It should also be noted that the vast majority of companies interviewed see a definite improvement in communication and relations with intermediate customers (74 per cent) and final customers (66 per cent).

One of the most interesting competitive advantages concerns the impact of the Ecolabel on the market. This area registered an effective increase in competitiveness by certified companies: in 57 per cent of cases, increases in market share and/or the acquisition of new customers were seen after adopting the Ecolabel. The data is probably underestimated since many companies have only recently obtained certification and have not yet been able to appreciate the changes in sales and market share.

The study has also tried to measure the percentage of increase in revenue induced by the Ecolabel. Although many certified companies have not succeeded in isolating and quantifying the specific contribution of the label in revenue trend, the data recorded in the study is extremely encouraging: on average (based on companies that could give an answer) the Ecolabel generated a revenue increase of 3 to 5 per cent in a year, with peaks reaching 30 to 35 per cent.

It must also be emphasised that, in many cases, the Ecolabel makes companies adopting it for their products more competitive since they are able to guarantee a

Table 2.4 Competitive benefits of the European Ecolabel

Recognition as leader (and benchmark) by competitors or other economic actors (trade associations, rating agency, etc.)	3.6
Improved our environmental performance	3.6
To improve selection of raw materials	3.5
New customers (or contracts) or market shares acquired	3.4
Increased knowledge of products environmental impacts	3.4
Satisfy a specific request by (one or more of) our customers	3.3
Increased customer/consumer interest	3.3
Higher customer satisfaction	3.3
To improve waste management	3.3
Improved employee/management commitment to environmental performance	3.3
Keep up with our main competitors or with the other members of our trade association	3.2
Improved our international competitive capabilities	3.2
Improved our managerial capabilities in the environmental area	3.2
Improved product design and product development of all our products	3.2
To improve production methods and processes	3.2
Improved our national competitive capabilities	3.1

high level of environmental innovation and thus, keep abreast of the changes in the reference standards, which are becoming increasingly stringent. It is no accident that no less than 84 per cent of the companies interviewed declared that the Ecolabel could be exploited as a basis for compliance with the requirements for EC Directives known as 'New Approach' or with other national regulations. The 'Energy-related Products' Directive (better known as the 'EcoDesign' Directive), for example, has set up a framework to draft specifications for the environmentally friendly design of products that consume energy. In practice, the Directive requires manufacturers of 'energy-related' products to integrate environmental features into the design of the product to improve the environmental performance for the duration of its life cycle. The same Eco-Design Directive stipulates that if a product has obtained the European Ecolabel, then it can benefit from presumed conformity with regard to the implementing measures required thereby.

Whilst on the subject of product certification, it is worth remembering that certification schemes for type III labels have recently joined the ISO type I labels, for example, the EPD – Environmental Product Declaration. The main aim of this tool is to highlight the environmental performance of a product/service by increasing its public visibility and acceptability and by encouraging a comparison between products with the same functions.

This underlines the enormous potential for products which are offered to intermediate customers and consumers in sales outlets and exposition spaces where a direct comparison can be made of their characteristics and sometimes their performance (including their environmental performance) with competitors. As indicated in the introduction, this tool was designed as a support for environmental communication mainly aimed at the production chain (the so-called 'B2B') and therefore, useful in providing more detailed technical information to other companies which presumably have the skills to read it, understand it and compare it with declarations from other manufacturers of the same goods or services (even if the use of EPDs is sometimes encountered in the field of consumer goods).

The EPD can enable the customer to find out, for example, about the potential greenhouse effect caused by the product he is about to purchase and so choose the one that causes less CO_2 emissions. The European market, in particular, has been able to exploit the opportunities offered by this new environmental marketing tool, which combines an impressive communication ability with a solid scientific base and give credibility to the manufacturer.

The use of environmental product certification is beginning to be more widely used as a central tool for corporate communications to the market within the framework of strategies for so-called green marketing. A recent Italian survey on ecological advertising conducted by the Sant'Anna School of Advanced Studies (Frey et al., 2013) showed how 8 per cent of environmental advertising appearing in major newspapers and national weekly journals included in the sample survey used a form of environmental certification to guarantee the environmental quality of the product or the production process.

Public demand as a competitive opportunity for certified companies and products

An important market opportunity for all environmental certifications is thus linked to the possibility conceded to the Public Purchaser to include environmental criteria in purchasing procedures (the so-called *Green Public Procurement*). It is indeed quite evident that the *green public procurement*, or the insertion of environmental criteria in the purchasing choices of public administrations plays a fundamental role in reducing the environmental impact and the promotion of a better informed market. There have been numerous interventions by the legislator directed at the promotion of purchasing choices by public bodies that are able to consider certain environmental criteria; and there have been many important initiatives aimed at supporting and sustaining local authorities in adopting green procurement practices.

Today, the GPP represents something more than just a virtuous practice by a few public administrations: it is an essential element of the European and national environmental policy which should strengthen the link between environmental and competitive benefits on the basis of a concrete model for sustainable development. The latest changes to it are indeed aimed at obliging public administrations to comply with some minimum environmental requirements to be included in tenders. Furthermore, the European Legislator and, as a result, the legislators of Member States have adopted measures aimed at adding value to those products and organisations, within the GPP, that have received official recognition, such as Ecolabel certification or EMAS registration for the important steps they have taken towards protecting the environment. It is, in fact, an accepted practice to refer to environmental certification for products and schemes as proof that the criteria for respecting the environment have been included in public tenders.

In particular, the inclusion of environmental criteria may distinguish each phase of the public tender procedure, namely that it can occur:

- between technical specifications, that is, the required characteristics that can be objectively verified so that the products and services reflect the use for which they are intended (e.g. raw materials, recycled glass/wood for windows, or a particular production process); the inclusion of environmental performance or functional requirements may occur when reference is made to the specifications defined by so-called (multi)national European 'eco-labels' as long as they respect certain conditions, such as being based on scientific information or being adopted through a decision-making process involving all the *stakeholders*, etc. The reference to eco-labels such as type I (ISO 14024) and, in particular, the Ecolabel certification is clear;
- during the evaluation of the technical capability of the participants by asking the bidders for service tenders and, only in appropriate cases[8], to demonstrate their technical capability of applying environmental management measures through possession of EMAS registration or ISO 14001 certification;
- in the choice of the award criteria between minimum price or most economically advantageous tender for the contracting authority in which inter alia environmental type criteria can be used, as long as such criteria are linked to the subject matter of the contract, do not confer unrestricted freedom of choice on the contracting authority, are expressly referred to and respect the Community principles;
- in the execution of the contract for the supply or for the service (e.g. environmentally-friendly transport, packaging recovery, reuse of finished products, concentrated chemical products that are diluted only when actually used).

The effectiveness of certified environmental management systems in the improving of environmental performance

In recent years, the issue of 'continuous improvement', a founding principle of voluntary certification schemes (such as EMAS and ISO 14001), has been the subject of strong debate among scholars in the area of environmental management systems (EMSs). How much this principle is then translated into real improvements in performance of organisations that have adopted an environ-mental management system has to be empirically assessed in order to confirm the effectiveness and validity of the environmental voluntary instruments adopted by policy makers, who devote increasing financial support to these policies (Arimura et al., 2008).

EMAS-registered companies are suited to carry out research related to the analysis of environmental performance, as the regulation requires the annual publication of the Environmental Statement, a record which shows the main data and environmental indicators of the organisation, data verified and vali-dated by an independent third-party.

The difficulty of assessing the link between EMAS and environmental performance stems from a number of methodological challenges. Firstly, performance improvement can be operationalised in very different ways, for example as absolute reductions of emissions or improved eco-efficiency; as short-term or long-term improvement; an upwards performance trend or one which is better than that of similar organisations; and so on. In practice, organisa-tions will usually see improvement on some indicators and worsening on others. Secondly, the environmental performance of companies can be characterised by a strong inherent variability, e.g. due to short and medium term changes in capac-ity utilisation, raw material prices, product characteristics, etc. Shifts in perfor-mance may also be the outcome of larger business decisions (e.g. outsourcing or re-location of resource-intensive production steps, plant modernisation) or external pressures (e.g. environmental legislation, media reporting) (Al-Tuwaijri et al., 2004). Finally, most studies relied on perceptions by environmental manag-ers on the ability of EMAS or ISO 14001 to improve environmental performance (and not on primary data referred to environmental parameters, such as emis-sions or resource consumption). Moreover, although environmental statements provide reliable quantitative data on performance of EMAS organisations, there are a number of problems with the availability and comparability of those data: lack of harmonisation (indicators, measurement units), different reporting levels (process, site, firm, group), lack of time series data, insufficient information on products, processes and output, etc.

These difficulties, and the range of approaches to address them, explain why studies have come to different results.

ISO 14001 and environmental performance

The difficulty of assessing the link between EMAS and environmental perfor-mance stems from a number of methodological challenges. Firstly, performance improvement can be operationalised in very different ways, for example, as absolute reductions of emissions or improved eco-efficiency. Secondly, the envi-ronmental performance of companies can be characterised by a strong inherent variability, e.g. due to short and medium term changes in capacity utilisation, raw material prices, product characteristics, etc. Finally, most studies relied on perceptions by environmental managers on the ability of EMAS or ISO 14001 to improve environmental performance (and not on primary data referred to environmental parameters, such as emissions or resource consumption). Moreover, although environmental statements and reports provide reliable quantitative data on performance of organisations, there are a number of problems with the availability and comparability of those data: lack of harmonisation (indicators, measurement units), different reporting levels (process, site, firm, group), lack of time series data, insufficient information on products, processes and output, etc.

These difficulties, and the range of approaches to address them, explain why studies have come to different results. Although the literature does not provide a simple answer to the question of ISO 14001 and EMAS effectiveness, a number of recent studies have produced interesting insights.

While most studies tend to highlight the positive nature of these impacts and the fact that ISO 14001 certification improves environmental performance (Goh Eng et al., 2006; Melnyk et al., 2002; Potoski and Prakash, 2005; Pun and Hui, 2001) other studies question these benefits (Boiral, 2007; Christmann and Taylor, 2006; King et al., 2005; Welch et al., 2003; Boiral and Henri, 2012).

Some studies (Ammenberg et al., 2002; Brouwer and van Koppen, 2008) evidenced that ISO 14001 determines improvements in the initial implementation phase when the companies have to face the compliance with environmental laws or are developing the Environmental review. On the contrary, other studies didn't find clear positive effects once the certificate has been obtained (Ilomaki and Melanen, 2001; Moxen and Strachan, 2000).

Several studies observe a positive effect of ISO 14001 adoption on environmental performance. Molina-Azorin et al. (2009) according to a literature review carried out in their article affirm that most of the empirical studies analysed demonstrate a positive relationship between Environmental Management practices (included ISO 14001 adoption) and firm performance. The performances investigated were both input (resources consumption) and output (air and water emissions, waste) oriented.

In their empirical research, Nishitani et al. (2012) illustrate the result using panel of data of 500 Japanese manufacturing firms and referred to the period 2002–2008 collected by Japan's Pollution Release and Transfer Register (PRTR). In the mentioned sample around 60 per cent of firms have adopted ISO 14001 for more than four years. The statistic model performed reveals that firms that implement an EMS are more likely to reduce pollution emissions.

The article of Melnyk et al. (2002) shows significant improvement related to waste indicators using a sample of 1510 manufacturing firms of the United States. Another study regarding U.S. plants revealed that ISO 14001 could conduct to the improvement of performance. This study involved a sample of 7899 manufacturing facilities collecting the data from the Toxics Release Inventory (TRI) (King et al., 2005).

Russo (2009), using a large sample of electronics manufacturing facilities and data from 1996 through 2001, points out that the adoption ISO 14001 was associated with lower emissions and the longer a facility operated under ISO 14001, the lower were its emissions.

Iwata et al. (2010) examined 216 Japanese manufacturing facilities operating in 2002 and found that there was a positive relationship between ISO 14001 adoption and the reduction of toluene emissions.

The paper of Franchetti (2011) reveals positive quantitative effects of ISO 14001 certification on solid waste generation. He performed a survey on US firms belonging to several manufacturing sectors collecting 121 self-reported data questionnaires.

Nawrocka and Parker (2009) analyse 23 studies connecting environmental performance to environmental management systems. The results showed a not univocal relationship between the two issues due two main reasons: a different method used in the studies to measure the environmental performance, the modalities on how the EMS should improve the performance.

Nee and Wahid (2010) study the relationship between ISO 14001 certified Malaysian SMEs and the related performance. Based upon 61 responses questionnaire survey, the authors confirm that ISO 14001 implementation has a positive and significant relationship with SMEs's performance.

Barla (2007) highlights how the plants certified ISO 14001 improve their biological oxygen demand of water releases while not improving other parameters of the same environmental aspect, and Anton et al. (2004) also find that 'the adoption of a more comprehensive EMS has a significant impact in terms of reduction of the intensity of toxic releases' and point out that the importance of these measures tends to be especially visible in companies with initially poor environmental records.

Despite the aforementioned studies that pointed out positive effects of ISO 14001 on environmental performance, other studies reveal a not clear correlation.

Guoyou et al. (2012) illustrates a survey carried out in 246 certified organisations of the Chinese construction sector. The survey was performed through self-reported data included in a specific questionnaire in order to monitor the performance related to six environmental topics: solid waste, dust emissions, complaints, noise emission, raw material consumption and energy consumption. The study shows a not clear correlation between ISO 14001 and environmental performance even if the authors affirm that 'the internalizing practices underlying ISO standards can lead to corporate environmental improvements'.

Zobel (2013), using a sample of 66 certified and 50 not certified Swedish companies, performed a t-test investigating the relationship with environmental performance in the period 1994–2000 for the following environmental aspects: air emissions, water emissions, resource use, energy use, waste. The author didn't find any statistically significant differences between the environmental performance of certified and non-certified firms at 95 per cent confidence.

Gomez and Rodriguez (2011) focused their study on four Spanish regions: Asturias, Cantabria, Galicia and Castilla-León. They observed the Toxics Release

Index of 56 certified companies, comparing it with the Index of 70 not certified companies. Through a statistical analysis they concluded that ISO 14001 does not represent a leverage to improve companies' environmental polluting index.

Lam et al. 2011, observing the performance of firms of construction sector with implemented EMS, don't find a clear relationship with improvement performance.

Focusing on a survey of 40 Western Australian companies certified ISO 14001, the research of Annandale et al. (2004) using self-reported data shows that the EMS is perceived as a tool that can influence the environmental performance of companies even if with a not high magnitude.

Hertin et al. (2004) perform regressions and times series analysis on European industrial companies and production sites with different EMS policies. Their main finding was that the link between a company's EMS and environmental performance (measured with eco-efficiency indicators) is weak and ambiguous: companies with a formal EMS performed better on a number of indicators, but worse on several others and only a small number of correlations were statistically significant. Hertin et al. (2008), reporting the outputs of a research project named MEPI based on data of 274 companies and 400 production sites in six manufacturing sectors in six EU countries, confirm the weak link between EMS and environmental performances.

Agan et al. (2013) performed a survey collecting data from a sample of 500 Turkish SMEs ISO 14001 adopters and non-adopters. Among these 152 companies were certified ISO 14001. The study demonstrated that the Turkish SMEs having ISO 14001 certification are likely to perform better on environmental activities and they seem to be more vigilant in the management of environmental aspects.

EMAS and environmental performance

Despite the numerous studies focused on the relationship between EMS and environmental performance, only a few of them are specifically aimed to observe the effects of EMAS registration on performance.

Daddi et al. (2011) perform an analysis of the trends of the environmental performance of a sample of 64 Italian companies pertaining to six different industrial sectors that have achieved EMAS registration for at least three years. The performances were analysed, collecting and verifying the companies' Environmental Statements validated by the third party verifiers. The study pointed out a positive influence of EMAS on performance on some environmental aspects like water consumptions and waste while observing a weak influence on energy consumptions.

A survey of German EMAS companies find that the adoption of the management system has had a positive impact in a range of areas (especially waste generation, resource use and water consumption), but was unable to quantify the magnitude of improvement (UNI/ASU 1997); and using the same list of environmental aspects in a survey of French EMAS sites, Schucht (2000) obtain similar results (reduction of liquid effluents and water pollution is reported as another important effect in the French case).

Rennings et al. (2003) found in a survey of 1277 EMAS certified German facilities and 12 in-depth case studies that environmental managers consider the implementation of EMAS as a substantial contribution to the introduction of environmental innovations, especially organisational ones.

Morrow and Rondinelli (2002) studied the relationship between EMAS and performance improvement of five German domestic energy and gas companies using qualitative self-reported data.

Iraldo et al. (2009) performed an econometric analysis based on data collected through questionnaires in the framework of EVER Study, pointing out positive effects of EMAS registered organisations on environmental performance.

The article points out only minor environmental improvements achieved thank to EMAS according to the opinion of the interviewed managers.

Other scholars have studied the effects observing a sample composed by both ISO 14001 and EMAS companies as well.

Analysing a sample of 306 German manufacturing firms, Wagner (2002) found no significant differences in energy efficiency between firms with and without EMS (EMAS and ISO 14001), either for the year 2001 or for the period 1991 to 2001.

Rennings et al. (2004) show a weak but significant positive influence of ISO 14001 and EMAS on environmental product innovations.

Johnstone et al. (2004) observe that EMSs (including both ISO 14001 and EMAS) played 'a distinct role in encouraging firms to undertake measures to improve their environmental performance in a number of areas'. The impact of EMS was particularly important in the generation of wastewater and air emissions and in the reduction of environmental impacts from accidents.

Testa et al. (2014) investigate the impacts of EMAS and ISO 14001 on the reduction of carbonic anhydride emissions on 229 energy intensive plants in Italy. By applying a rigorous statistical method, the results suggest that the implementation of an environmental management system in energy intensive industries has a clear influence on environmental performance, both in the short and in the long term, but a different effect of ISO 14001 and EMAS on environmental performance occurs.

Notes

1 2014 Data.
2 The ISO certification and the EMAS verification are often carried out at the same time to allow the organisation to avoid unnecessary duplications in terms of time and costs.
3 As previously indicated, the standards in the ISO 14064 group are considered 'verifiable', but not 'certifiable' standards; so it is preferable to use the more intuitive term 'validation' rather than the stricter one, 'certification'.
4 The greenhouse gas emissions (indicated in the standard itself) are carbon dioxide (CO_2), methane (CH_4), nitrous oxide (N_2O), sulphur hexafloride (SF_6), hydrofluorocarbon gases (HFC) and perfluorocarbon gases (PFC).

5 Every greenhouse gas is characterised by its potential impact on global warming (denominated GWP = Global Warming Potential), an index used to set parameters for the potential climate-changing impact of the gas with respect to a standard measurement indicated by the potential impact of CO_2. For example, methane has a GWP of 21: which means that a given mass of methane released into the atmosphere will generate a climate-changing impact equal to a similar mass of carbon monoxide multiplied by 21. The application of GWP to quantified emissions of different greenhouse gases means that the whole inventory can be expressed with a single unit of measurement expressed as 'CO_2 equivalent'. The standard unit of measurement is a ton of CO_2 equivalent (tCO_2 eq.).

6 The maintenance of the environmental management system entails different kinds of annual costs: organisational costs, training costs, time dedicated by the system manager and resources used to carry out audits.

7 For a complete overview of the quantifiable financial commitment, the costs of employing internal resources have to be combined with the cost of acquiring external resources and services which are necessary and useful in obtaining certification or registration of the system (e.g. the use of outside consultants to carry out specific in-depth surveys or technical analyses, legal consultants, etc. investments for modernising factories or adopting new technology to improve checks on or prevention of significant environmental impacts in view of certification).

8 The term 'appropriate cases' means tenders that may cause damage to the environment when being completed and as such, measures to protect it are called for.

References

Agan, Y., Acar, M.F., Borodin, A., 2013. 'Drivers of environmental processes and their impact on performance: a study of Turkish SMEs'. *Journal of Cleaner Production*, 51, 23–33.

Al–Tuwaijri, S., Christensen, T., Hughes, K., 2004. 'The relations among environmental disclosure, environmental performance, and economic performance: a simultaneous equations approach'. Account. *Organizations and Society*, 29, 447–471.

Ammenberg, J., Hjelm, O., Quotes, P., 2002. 'The connection between environmental management systems and continual environmental performance improvements'. *Corporate Environmental Strategy*, 9, 183–192.

Annandale D, Morrison-Saunders A, Bouma G., 2004. 'The impact of voluntary environmental protection instruments on company environmental performance'. *Business Strategy and the Environment*, 13, 1–12.

Anton, W.R.Q., Deltas, G., and Khanna, M., 2004. 'Incentives for environmental self-regulation and implications for environmental performance'. *Journal of Environmental Economics and Management*, 48, 632–654.

Arimura, T., Hibiki, A., Katayama, H., 2008. 'Is a voluntary approach an effective environmental policy instrument? A case for environmental management systems'. *Journal of Environmental Economics and Management* 55, 281–95.

Barla, P., 2007. 'ISO 14001 certification and environmental performance in Quebec's pulp and paper industry'. *Journal of Environmental Economics and Management*, 53, 291–306.

Biondi, V., Frey, M., Iraldo, F., 2000. 'Environmental management systems and SMEs: barriers, opportunities and constraints'. *Greener Management International* 29.

Boiral, O., 2007. 'Corporate greening through ISO 14001: a rational myth?' *Organization Science* 18, 127–146.

Boiral, O., Henri, J.F., 2012. 'Modelling the impact of ISO 14001 on environmental performance: A comparative approach'. *Journal of Environmental Management*, 99, 84–97.

Brouwer, M.A.C., van Koppen, C.S.A., 2008. 'The soul of the machine: continual improvement in ISO 14001'. *Journal of Cleaner Production* 16, 450–457.

Christmann, P., Taylor, G., 2006. 'Firm self-regulation through international certifiable standards: determinants of symbolic versus substantive implementation'. *Journal of International Business Studies* 37, 863–878.

Daddi, T. Magistrelli M., Frey, M. Iraldo, F., 2011. 'Do Environmental Management Systems improve environmental performance? Empirical evidence from Italian companies'. *Environment, Development and Sustainability*, 13, 845–862.

De Oliveira, O.J., Serra, J.R., Salgado, M.H. 'Does ISO 14001 work in Brazil?' *Journal of Cleaner Production*, 18, 1797–1806.

European Commission, 2007. Small clean and competitive – a programme to help small and medium sized enterprises comply with environmental legislation [online]. Communication from the Commission to the Council, the European Parliament, the European Economic and Social Committee and the Committee of Regions, COM (2007)379 final. Available from: http://ec.europa.eu/environment/sme/programme/programme_en.htm.

Franchetti, M., 2011. 'ISO 14001 and solid waste generation rates in US manufacturing organizations: an analysis of relationship'. *Journal of Cleaner Production*, 19, 1104–1109.

Frey, M., Testa, M., Iraldo, F. 2013. 'The determinants of eco innovation in green supply chains: evidence from an Italian sectoral study'. *R & D Management*, 43, 352–364.

Goh Eng, A., Suhaiza, Z., Nabsiah, A.W., 2006. 'A study on the impact of environmental management system certification towards firms' performance in Malaysia'. *Management of Environmental Quality* 17, 73–93.

Gomez, A. and Rodriguez, M.A. 2011: 'The effect of ISO 14001 certification on toxic emissions: an analysis of industrial facilities in the north of Spain'. *Journal of Cleaner Production* 19, 1091–1095.

Granly, B.M., Welo, T., 2014. 'EMS and sustainability: experiences with ISO 14001 and Eco-Lighthouse in Norwegian metal processing SMEs'. *Journal of Cleaner Production*, 64, 194–204.

Guoyou Q., Saixing, Z., Xiaodong, L., Chiming, T., 2012. 'Role of internalization process in defining the relationship between ISO 14001 certification and corporate environmental performance'. *Corporate Social Responsibility and Environmental Management*, 19, 129–140.

Heras, I., Arana, G., 2010. 'Alternative models for environmental management in SMEs: the case of Ekoscan vs. ISO 14001'. *Journal of Cleaner Production*, 18, 726–735.

Hertin, J., Berkhout, F., Wagner, M., Tyteca, D., 2004. Are 'soft' policy instruments effective? The link between environmental management systems and the environmental performance of companies. SPRU Electronic Working Papers Series. Available from: http://www.sussex.ac.uk/spru/research/sewps (accessed Feb 2012).

Hertin, J., Berkhout, F., Wagner, M., Tyteca, D., 2008. 'Are EMS environmentally effective? The link between environmental management systems and environmental performance in European companies'. *Journal of Environmental Planning and Management* 51, 259–283.

IEFE, Adelphi Consult, IOEW, SPRU, Valor & Tinge, 2006: EVER: Evaluation of eco-label and EMAS for their Revision – Research findings, Final report to the European Commission – Part I–II, DG Environment European Community; Brussels. Available from www.europa.eu.int/comm/environment/emas.

Ilomaki, M., Melanen, M., 2001. 'Waste minimisation in small and medium-sized enterprises-do environmental management systems help?' *Journal of Cleaner Production* 9, 209–217.

Iraldo F., Testa F., Frey, M., 2009. 'Is an environmental management system able to influence environmental and competitive performance? The case of the eco-management and audit scheme (EMAS) in the European union'. *Journal of Cleaner Production* 17, 1444–1452.

Iraldo, F.; Testa, F. and Frey, M. 2009. 'Is an environmental management system able to influence environmental and competitive? The case of the eco-management and audit scheme EMAS: in the European Union'. *Journal of Cleaner Production*, 17, 1444–1452.

Iwata, K.; Arimura, T., Hibiki, S. 2010. 'An empirical analysis of determinants of ISO 14001 adoption and its influence on toluene emission reduction'. *JCER Economic Journal*. 62, 16–38.

Jaeger, T., 1998. 'Umweltschutz, umweltmanagement und umweltberatung – ergebnisse einer befragung in kleinen und mittleren unternehmen'. *ISO Bericht 55*. Koln: ISO Institut.

Johnstone, N., Scapecchi, P., Ytterhus, B., Wolff, R., 2004. 'The firm, environmental management and environmental measures: lessons from a survey of European manufacturing firms'. *Journal of Environmental Planning and Management*, 47, 685–707.

Khalid, A, Babakri, K.A., Bennett, R.A., Rao, S., Franchetti, M., 2004. 'Recycling performance of firms before and after adoption of the ISO 14001 standard'. *Journal of Cleaner Production* 12, 633–637.

King, A.A., Lenox, M.J., Terlaak, A., 2005. 'The strategic use of decentralized institutions: exploring certification with the ISO 14001 management standard'. *Academy of Management Journal* 48, 1091–1106.

Lam Patrick T.I., Edwin H.W. Chan, C.K. Chau, C.S. Poon, K.P. Chuna, 2011. 'Environmental management system vs green specifications: How do they complement each other in the construction industry?' *Journal of Environmental Management* 92 788–795.

Lim, S., Prakash, A., 2014. 'Voluntary Regulations and Innovation: The Case of ISO 14001'. *Public Administration Review*, 74, 233–244.

Martín-Peña. M.L., Díaz-Garrido, E., Sánchez-López, J.M., 2014. 'Analysis of benefits and difficulties associated with firms' environmental management systems: the case of the Spanish automotive industry'. *Journal of Cleaner Production*, 70, 220–230.

Melnyk, S.A., Sroufe, R.P., Calantone, R.L., Montabon, F.L., 2002. 'Assessing the effectiveness of US voluntary environmental programmes: an empirical study'. *International Journal of Production Research* 40, 1853–1878.

Melnyk, S.A.; Sroufe, R.P. and Calantone, R. 2003: 'Assessing the impact of environmental management systems on corporate and environmental performance'. *Journal of Operations Management*, 21, 329–351.

Milieu Ltd. 2009: Study on the Costs and Benefits of EMAS to Registered Organisations. Final Report for DG Environment of the European Commission under Study Contract No. 07.0307/2008/517800/ETU/G.2.

Molina-Azorín, J.F.; Tarí, J.J.; Claver-Cortés, E. and López-Gamero, M.D. 2009: 'Quality management, environmental management and firm performance: A review of empirical studies and issues of integration'. *International Journal of Management Reviews*, 11, 197–222.

Morrow D, Rondinelli D., 2002 'Adopting corporate environmental management systems: motivations and results of ISO 14001 and EMAS certification'. *European Management Journal* 20, 159–171.

Moxen, J., Strachan, P.A., 2000. 'ISO 14001: a case of cultural myopia'. *Eco-Management and Auditing* 7, 82–90.

Nawrocka, D. and Parker, T., 2009. 'Finding the connection: environmental management systems and environmental performance'. *Journal of Cleaner Production*, 17, 601–607.

Nishitani, K., Kaneko, S., Fujii, H., Komatsu, S., 2012: 'Are firms' voluntary environmental management activities beneficial for the environment and business? An empirical study focusing on Japanese manufacturing firms'. *Journal of Environmental Management* 105, 121–130.

Potoski, M., Prakash, A., 2005. 'Green clubs and voluntary governance: ISO 14001 and firms' regulatory compliance'. *American Journal of Political Science* 49, 235–248.

Pun, K.F., Hui, I.K., 2001. 'An analytical hierarchy process assessment of the ISO 14001 environmental management system'. *Integrated Manufacturing Systems* 12, 333–345.

Rennings, K., Ziegler, A., Ankele, K., Hoffman, S., Nill, J., 2003. The influence of the EU Environmental Management and Audit Scheme on Environmental Innovations and Competitiveness in Germany: An Analysis on the Basis of Case Studies and a Large-Scale Survey. ZEW Discussion Paper n. 03–14. Available from: http://ideas.repec.org/s/zbw/zewdip.html. (accessed July 2013).

Rennings, K., Ziegler, A., Ankele, K., Hoffmann, E., 2006. 'The influence of different characteristics of the EU environmental management and auditing scheme on technical environmental innovations and economic performance'. *Ecological Economics* 57, 45–59.

Rennings, K., Ziegler, A., Rehfeld, K., (2004). Integrated Product Policy and Environmental Product Innovations: An Empirical Analysis'. ZEW Discussion Paper n. 04–71. Available from: http://ideas.repec.org/s/zbw/zewdip.html. (accessed Feb 2010).

Russo, M.V., 2009. 'Explaining the impact of ISO 14001 on emission performance: a dynamic capabilities perspective on process and learning'. *Business Strategy and the Environment.* 18, 307–319.

Steger, U., 2000. 'Environmental management systems: empirical evidence and further perspectives'. *European Management Journal*, 18, 23–37.

Steger, U., 2000. 'Umweltmanagementsysteme – erfahrungen und perspektiven'. *Zeitschrift für umweltpolitik und umweltrecht* 4, 467–506.

Testa, F., Rizzi, F., Daddi, T., Gusmerotti, N.M., Iraldo, F., Frey, M., 2014. 'EMAS and ISO 14001: the differences in effectively improving environmental performance'. *Journal of Cleaner Production* 68, 165–173.

Turk, A. M., 'The benefits associated with ISO 14001 certification for construction firms: Turkish case', *Journal of Cleaner Production*, Vol. 17, 2009, pp. 559–569.

UNI/ASU, (1997). Öko-Audit in der mittelständischen Praxis – Evaluierung und Ansätze für eine Effizienzsteigerung von Umweltmanagementsystemen in der Praxis. Unternehmerinstitut e.V., Arbeitsgemeinschaft selbständiger Unternehmer, Bonn.

Wagner, M., 2002. The relationship between environmental and economic performance of firms and the influence of ISO 14001 and EMAS: an empirical analysis and implications for government policy. In: Paper Presented at the 5th Environmental Management Accounting Network Europe (EMAN-Europe) Annual Conference, University of Gloucestershire, Cheltenham, UK, pp. 11–12.

Welch, E.W., Rana, S., Mori, Y., 2003. 'The promises and pitfalls of ISO 14001 for competitiveness and sustainability: a comparison of Japan and the United States'. *Greener Management International* 44, 59–73.

Yen, N.G., Abdul, W. N., 2010. 'The Effect of ISO 14001 Environmental Management System Implementation on SMEs Performance: An Empirical Study in Malaysia'. *Journal of Sustainable Development*, 3, DOI: 10.5539/jsd.v3n2p215.

Zobel, Thomas, 2013. 'ISO 14001 certification in manufacturing firms: a tool for those in need or an indication of greenness?' *Journal of Cleaner Production* 43, 37–44.

3 The environmental certification of organisations: the standard ISO 14001 and the EMAS Regulation

The drivers of EMAS and ISO 14001 adoption

There are many studies that deal with drivers of European Eco-management and Audit Scheme (EMAS) Regulation and other forms of environmental management system (EMS). There are a huge number of factors driving companies towards EMS. Drivers can be either economic/strategic or 'environment-led' external factors, such as the desire to gain a competitive advantage from fiscal/normative incentives and facilitations.

The internal motivations

The need to improve internal environmental management is surely one of the most important drivers for organisations that decide to adopt EMS. This can be motivated by the need to improve the management of environmental compliance, an aim to improve environmental performance and resource efficiency and the aim to improve organisational and managerial capabilities.

Milieu Ltd. and RPA Ltd (2009) interviewed more than 400 European EMAS-registered companies and competent bodies about the costs, benefits, drivers, barriers and added value of EMAS. The main internal drivers they found were improvement of resources and production efficiency and the desire to improve legislative compliance. Similar results were observed in EVER, the previous EMAS evaluation study (IEFE et al., 2006). It found that drivers of EMAS adoption (and also for EMSs) are heterogeneous and are subject to change according to the sector, size and location of the organisation. Moreover, the study found that the interviews conducted all report environmental and internal drivers to be in no way marginal. Key internal drivers such as better management of legal compliance, the need to improve environmental performance and the capacity of EMAS to prevent environmental risks and liabilities were cited as the main drivers of EMAS adopters.

In addition to the previous two studies mentioned, other studies have investigated drivers of the implementation of other standards such as ISO 14001 in European countries.

Grolleau et al. (2007) used empirical methods to work out which factors determine voluntary adoption of Environmental Management System (EMS) certification (ISO 14001 or EMAS) in agricultural industries. A discrete choice model of EMS certification is applied to a sample of 1,000 French agricultural firms. The findings suggest that internal management-related factors drive certification more strongly than economic incentives. French farmers also expressed their willingness to increase the value of their organisation by cleaning up/structuring their paperwork, meeting legal requirements and being attractive to the market.

Another key internal driver is the aim to improve environmental performance. Heras and Arana (2010) report on the results of a survey that involved 262 companies in the Basque Autonomous Region. The research aimed to investigate the drivers, barriers and benefits to Spanish small and medium-sized enterprises (SMEs) in the adoption of the Spanish standard Ekoscan and ISO 14001. The sample involved 169 ISO 14001 certified companies and 93 Ekoscan-certified companies. Results showed that the main driver leading SMEs to implement the Ekoscan standard is improvement in the environmental performance of the company (51.9 per cent of the answers), while responses regarding the motivations behind companies implementing ISO 14001 were relatively heterogeneous, the highest value achieved in this case (25.8 per cent) being the aim to improve the environmental performance of the company. Marazza et al. (2010) confirm improvements in environmental performance to be drivers in the public sector. The authors observe that one of the drivers spurring public administrations to implement EMS is environmental and management performance improvement. ISO (2005) conducted an international survey of SMEs to determine why they are less likely to be ISO 14001-certified than larger firms and what related costs, benefits, drivers and barriers they experience. In that study, similarly to the EVER study conducted in the same period, the capacity of EMAS to improve environmental legal compliance was considered to be both a driver and a benefit.

The ISO report on ISO 14001 survey (ISO, 2014) found that the main driver to implement the standard is the commitment to environmental protection and conservation, followed by the reduction of risk related to adverse environmental impact. The survey involved 5000 organisations.

Broadening the perspective of this research brings us to Fryxell et al. (2004) on Chinese organisations. They examined the motivations of Chinese facilities in seeking ISO 14001 certification and the links between these motivations and organisations' own reports on the effectiveness of major environmental management system components. The study was conducted in 2002 in three major urban cities – Beijing, Shanghai and Guangzhou – with a sample size of 128 facilities. The main drivers for certification were reported to be ensuring regulatory compliance, enhancing the firm's reputation and improving environmental performance. The study pointed out how internal motivations have an influence on most EMS components.

The wish to improve corporate image and reputation in the minds of external stakeholders

The opportunity to obtain third party certification is seen by both policy makers and organisations as a chance to show environmental commitment to external stakeholders. Public institutions, local communities, trade associations and

NGOs belong in this category. The studies analysed show that the organisations can decide autonomously to obtain certification, or they can adopt this decision to respond to specific external pressures exerted by external stakeholders.

SSSUP carried out a survey in 2012 as part of its BRAVE study (SSSUP, 2013), interviewing 224 EMAS registered companies in several European countries. Part of the study focused on stakeholders that stimulate actions geared towards environmental improvements. The study shows that pressure from public authorities (included inspection agencies) plays a key role. In particular, the role of public entities is shown to be very important for 44 per cent of respondents in Italy and for 67 per cent in Portugal, whilst it is less significant in countries such as Austria and Germany. The relevance of external stakeholders was also observed by the German Federal Environment Agency (2013). Their research shows the results of a survey on 573 German organisations registered for EMAS. The main drivers identified by the research are transparency of relevant consumption toward external stakeholders and improvement in operational environmental protection and energy/resource efficiency.

Another example is the aforementioned report by Milieu Ltd. and RPA Ltd. (2009). It pointed out that general improvement to an organisation's reputation was identified as a key driver by 16 per cent of the EMAS organisations interviewed, whilst about 12 per cent were driven by the need to increase transparency with local stakeholders.

Other studies have investigated drivers linked with external stakeholders in organisations certified ISO 14001.

Granly and Welo (2014) looked at nine Norwegian manufacturing SMEs. The study demonstrates that customer pressures and improved environmental routines are the main external and internal drivers for ISO 14001 certification.

Neugebauer (2012) is based on 21 interviews with industrial and institutional representatives from the German automotive and engineering industry. This study found that different external pressures affect the adoption of the two standards: the choice to adopt ISO 14001 is mainly induced by external stakeholders whilst the implementation of EMAS is mainly influenced by internal drivers. These findings have been confirmed by Salomone (2008). The author surveyed 103 Italian companies with integrated management systems certified ISO 14001, ISO 9001 and OHSAS 18001. The aim of the study was to identify the main drivers and barriers to adopting EMS in the presence of an integrated system. The motivations prompting companies to adopt EMS were linked mainly to enhanced image (80 per cent) and continual improvement (74 per cent). Similar results were observed by Kassolis (2007). In his paper, he questions the extent to which the adoption of ISO 14001 in Greece is motivated by environmental sustainability or processes of economic globalisation. The study also addresses whether the new system of harmonised regulation, driven by economic globalisation and sustainability discourses, inherently benefits environmental policy through differentiated national contexts. The findings indicate that to pursue sustainability through environmental management, proper institutional arrangements and a legal framework must be established and implemented by government and in civil society. The pressures driving companies towards ISO 14001 come not only from specific institutional actors and elements in society at large, but also from economic actors.

Darnall et al. (2008) examined OECD survey data to determine if the motivations behind EMS adoption had any influence on the benefits the companies received from EMS. Their conclusions were that facilities are driven to adopt more comprehensive EMSs in response both to institutional pressure for greater external legitimacy and desire to build upon existing complementary resources and capabilities.

By focusing on studies that used a sample of non-EU countries, Lannelongue and Gonzalez-Benito (2011) set out to explain the impact that stakeholder pressure has on the implementation (or non-implementation) of EMS, its certification by a firm and its subsequent relationship with environmental proactivity. The study analysed a sample of 3748 plants from seven Organisation for Economic Co-operation and Development (OECD) countries (United States, Canada, France, Norway, Hungary, Germany and Japan), to check if certification is also a mechanism that firms use to discriminate between stakeholders, allowing firms to only react to the pressure of certain stakeholder. Findings reveal that the implementation of EMS responds to pressure from stakeholders, but only once this system has been certified. In respect to drivers to adopt EMS, organisations basically respond to pressure from internal primary stakeholders, ignoring pressure from external primary and secondary stakeholders and regulators.

Studies on Chinese and Brazilian samples drew different conclusions. Qi et al. (2011) analysed the effects of community, regulatory and organisational stakeholders on the diffusion of ISO 14001 certification at Chinese provincial levels. Panel data on ISO 14001-certification from each province for the period of 2004–2008 provides evidence of such relations. Findings reveal that signals to foreign customers and community stakeholders play the main roles in encouraging diffusion of ISO 14001 certification. Foreign investors are not considered to be relevant drivers in the diffusion of ISO 14001 in China. Gavronski et al. (2008) explored the determinants of 63 Brazilian companies from the chemical, mechanical and electronic industries to adopt ISO 14001. An exploratory factor analysis identified four sources of motivation: reaction to pressures from external stakeholders, proactivity in expectation of future business concerns, legal concerns and internal influences.

Boiral (2007) carried out nine case studies of Canadian companies implementing ISO 14001. He found that many organisations implement ISO to improve their reputation but do not always follow through on effective implementation.

Market-based drivers

The literature on market-based drivers presents contradictory results. Some studies show this category to be less important than drivers mentioned in previous paragraphs whilst other studies indicate that these drivers assume a significant role in the decision to adopt EMAS or other forms of EMS.

For example, Johnstone and Labonne (2009) performed a survey aimed at exploring the motivation for the introduction of environmental management systems, and their certification. They distinguished between their role in bringing about: (1) better compliance or improved performance, and (2) as external indicators of good environmental practices to both other market participants and regulatory authorities. Drawing upon a database of approximately 4000 facilities in seven OECD countries, the authors found empirical evidence for the role that both factors play in encouraging the adoption and certification of EMS, even if the relative importance of different factors varies according to facility size. Their results support the view that facilities implement and certify EMS to signal to other players in the market, particularly when there is significant potential asymmetry of information between the facility in question and those that they are trying to signal. In addition, they found strong evidence that certification serves as a signal to regulatory authorities, although the intended recipients of the signal appear to differ by facility size.

Bracke et al. (2008) found that decisions to participate in EMAS are positively influenced by the solvency ratio, the share of non-current liabilities, the average labour cost and absolute company size as well as the relative size of a company compared to its sector average. The profit margin exerts a negative influence. They also found that companies whose headquarters are located in a country that actively encourages EMAS are more likely to participate. Finally, this paper suggests that rather than attracting other kinds of companies, a favourable institutional context succeeds in convincing similar companies to participate.

Price (2007) compared EMS systems in the UK, with a particular focus on the impact of changes made to the ISO 14001 standard during the revision of 2004. He found that organisations adopted ISO because of market-based drivers (increase of turnover). Other less important drivers included the need to respond to pressure from external stakeholders and changes in organisational policy and personnel. Similar economic drivers were observed by Prakash and Potoski (2006) even if they looked more to exports than turnover. They observe the effect of international trade on countries' ISO 14001 adoption rates, examining both countries' structural dependence on exports and how often their main trading partners have high rates of ISO certification. They found that international trade influences ISO 14001 adoption through bilateral trade but not through structural trade. Countries whose export destinations have higher levels of ISO 14001 certifications have higher certification levels themselves.

The ISO report 'ISO 14001 Continual Improvement Survey 2013' (ISO, 2014) includes survey results on 5000 participants in 110 countries worldwide. One of the aspects investigated showed that the main driver influenced organisations to adopt ISO 14001 was the customer requirement.

The authors also observed market base drivers in non-European countries. Nishitani (2010) analyses the environmental preferences and pressures of customers in environmentally conscious markets influencing the number of adoptions of ISO 14001 in a country. The research was carried on over eight years using a sample of 155 countries. Its aim was to confirm whether environmental preferences and pressure from customers in environmentally conscious markets are greater. The findings show that environmental preferences and pressure from customers in environmentally conscious markets (including Finland, Japan, Germany and Denmark) are more likely to encourage domestic along with foreign suppliers from adopting ISO 14001. Some conclusions on market-based drivers have been drawn by authors that studied a sample of ISO 14001 companies in two BRICS countries: India and China. Singh et al. (2014) aimed to empirically determine the primary factors influencing adoption of environmental management practices in Indian firms. The paper focused on 104 observations. Survey respondents included firms from the agricultural, chemical, manufacturing and servicing sectors, 43 per cent being comprised of SMEs and 57 per cent large enterprises. The survey was conducted in 2011–12. A wide range of samples – in terms of different firm size and sector – have been collected. The study found that internal and market pressures are significant drivers governing the adoption of proactive environmental management practices. In any case, external pressures from regulatory and social stakeholders were not found to be important in India. Moreover, the analysis showed that firm's feature (e.g. firm size and age, kind of sector) also play a role in defining the positive behaviour of firms, as large firms are more proactively engaged in environmental management initiatives. Zhang et al. (2008) looked at motivations for ISO 14001 registered firms in China and factors affecting implementation. The result indicates that the major motivation for the system was to seek entrance to the international market.

The environmental review

The initial environmental review represents one of the crucial phases in the implementation process of EMAS and ISO 14001 because it not only requires the organisation to carry out a detailed study and complex self-evaluation not currently covered by legislation (or at least not for environmental aspects), but also because the results stem from the commitments and objectives for improvement that the organisation intends to pursue and determine a large part of the choices on the structure and characteristics of the management system. The review is, therefore, the first fundamental step that the organisation must carry out when it begins the process of complying with Regulation requirements.

The term initial environmental review means an 'exhaustive initial review of the problems, impact and environmental performances connected to the activity of an organisation'.

The main objectives of an initial environmental review are

- to identify, assess and document the most important environmental aspects connected with the activities carried out;
- to study the interaction between these aspects and the technical and management organisation of the activities carried out by the organisation within its operations;
- to verify compliance with the legislative and regulatory requirements;
- to draft an initial appraisal of the environmental performances in view of the environmental policy (if the organisation has already formulated one);

- to provide the necessary information and indications to establish priorities, objectives and the environmental programme on the basis of the previous points;
- to create a traceable reference to make the reason behind the choices for the programme and the environment management system with regard to the requirements of the Regulation[1] clear to the environmental verifier during the initial stage of verification and validation.

The initial review takes into account all the environmental aspects that are connected to the activity and to the products and services provided by an organisation in order to highlight the most important ones to use as a foundation on which to 'build' the different components required by the Regulation (the environmental policy, programme, management system, audit and statement of activities).

The basic activities making up the initial review must, above all, be able to

1   identify the legal or regulatory requirements needed to fulfil and assess compliance with them;
2   identify and analyse all the environmental aspects connected to the activity carried out and to the products and services provided;
3   assess these aspects and select the most significant ones;
4   keep a record of the environmental aspects;
5   analyse the processes and procedures for existing environmental management and assess the lessons learnt from the review of any environmental accidents that have occurred.

In order to set up this activity correctly, the organisation should conduct an initial detailed review of

- the production processes and/or the services it carries out,
- the raw and semi-finished materials, and the services it uses,
- the products and services it provides,

with the aim of identifying their effects (actual or potential) on the environment.

In order to get an overall picture as a reference point to use in the subsequent phase of assessing environmental aspects, the organisation should gather data and information about the following:

- the current organisational layout of the company (including relations, where present, with the parent company) and its development;
- the layout of the production facilities and the infrastructure in which it operates (e.g. production plants for industry, network structure for energy distributors, transport for couriers and haulers, etc.);
- the environment by showing, where possible, the relevant territorial, urban, housing, landscape, economic, social and environmental (geology, hydrography, etc.)[2] context.

In short, the initial review is the tool that enables the organisation to establish its current position with regard to environmental problems concerning the activities it carries out. The review can, therefore, be equated to a 'snapshot' that depicts the environmental conditions of the organisation at the time it was taken, forming the 'starting point' from which the organisation will be able to assess the progress of its environmental performance over time.

At this point, the elements allowing the snapshot to be 'developed' need to be looked at in more detail.

The key elements for conducting an initial environmental review; identifying legal or regulatory requirements for compliance

The Regulation and the ISO 14001 standard view compliance with legislation to be among the most important elements for obtaining registration.

Firstly, the initial review must verify that the organisation knows all the pertinent regulations and complies with them.

The basic requirements with which the organisation must comply can be quite different and stem from different regulations. Environmental laws (EC, national, regional or local), for example, may concern the organisation's specific type of production and its effect on the environment (air, water, waste, soil, noise, transport, etc.), the products and services it provides and the specific sector in which it operates.

In addition to examining any relevant legislation, the review may also take a look at existing internal regulations, corporate directives concerning the environment and its commitments arising from voluntary agreements or participation in initiatives promoted by external parties (environmental groups, local associations, etc.).

The Regulation, however, does not require the organisation to simply assess its status with regard to legal conformity by intervening in a timely manner to correct any shortcomings, but also to verify and ensure that legal conformity is continually maintained.

This requirement can be fulfilled not only by pursuing efficiency in technology, plant design and production (which aims to ensure that limits are respected by working on the environmental performances), but also by defining the managerial and organisational methods required to continually monitor the legislative provisions and requirements concerning the organisation's activities.

The execution of the environmental review is, therefore, a very important phase in pinpointing, completing and updating the applicable regulation and in defining the appropriate ways to 'handle' it correctly.

The box shown below indicates several possible ways of carrying out a check on legal conformity by an organisation that can be applied to its different environmental aspects. The last question in the list could represent a starting point from which the organisation could initiate an additional process to check and examine in detail the way legislative provisions are managed and compliance is approved.

Box 3.1 Guidelines for checking legislative conformity with all environmental aspects

- Is the organisation aware of all the laws and regulations connected to the production activities concerning the aspect under examination?
- Has the organisation identified the relevant legislative provisions, fulfilled all the administrative and authorisation requirements?
- Has the organisation initiated and completed the authorisation procedures correctly?
- Has the organisation obtained the relevant authorisations and received certifications?
- Has the organisation respected all the methods and timeframes to renew the authorisations?
- Is the organisation in compliance with the provisions and any regulatory limitations? Are there any disputes or on-going cases affecting relations with the competent authorities?
- Has the organisation initiated ways and means of collecting, updating, recording and archiving references to legislation and relevant regulations?

The ability of the organisation to guarantee continuity in conforming to laws and regulations and the extent to which it fulfils its commitments in the various areas of environmental protection and prevention is an initial indication of the significance and difficulties connected to a particular environmental aspect. The organisation may decide to initiate corrective actions or improvements with different levels of priority depending on how critical the different situations concerning legislative compliance are (based on the results of the review) and its ability to maintain conformity (Table 3.1).

The ISO 14001 standard and EMAS Regulation stipulate that the organisation shall '*establish and maintain a procedure which allows legal or other provisions regarding the environmental aspects of its activities, products and services to be identified and accessed*'.

The organisation may set up a *registration system* of legal and regulatory provisions to fulfil this requirement, which is regulated by a *procedure* defining the responsibilities and the methods to manage, update and archive the registrations in question.

The organisation is allowed to choose the structure of the system based on its requirements and features, provided that it fulfils the following objectives:

- to ensure that all the applicable regulations and relevant provisions are known (in short: the organisation must know what to do to comply with current legislation);
- to guarantee control of all the activities dealing with administrative and authorisation conformities (what it has to do).

The organisation can make use of resources that facilitate the identification of the relevant regulations (the Official Journal of the European Union or its own country, as well as the Competent Body, local environmental protection agencies, trade associations or magazines, or specialised internet sites, databases, consultancy firms, conventions, etc.) to maintain and revise legal requirements.

Table 3.1 Situations and priority of actions

Situation	Example	Priority of action
Substantial non-conformity	No authorisations or failure to respect regulatory limits	Immediate action with absolute priority
Formal – procedural non-conformity	Substantial compliance, but lack of authorisation documents required by competent authorities	Immediate action (e.g. direct contact with competent authority or written notification)
Full conformity but with insufficient control mechanisms	Deficiencies in the collection, update and recording of the relevant legislations	Actions to be planned
Full, adequate conformity – in other words, correct and effective – control mechanisms to maintain conformity		No specific action

The identification phase and analysis of environmental aspects

The Regulation stipulates that 'an organisation must consider all aspects of its activities, products and services and decide which aspects have a greater impact on the environment on the basis of the criteria it has set itself'.

Furthermore, the organisation must initially look at all the environmental aspects connected with its activity and, after careful evaluation, concentrate on the ones it considers to be most significant.

The Regulation makes a distinction between direct and indirect environmental aspects to enable organisations in any sector to better articulate and complete the picture of environmental impacts that may result from their activities.

The Regulation uses the concept of *management control* as a means of distinguishing between direct and indirect environmental aspects. Direct environmental aspects are defined as those aspects 'under (full) management control of the organisation' and indirect environmental aspects as those over which the organisation 'may only have partial management control'.

A more detailed analysis of the definitions provided by the Regulation concludes that the indirect aspects (that is, those aspects over which, according to the definition, the organisation has only partial control) occur also because of the contribution (whether conscious or not) of at least one other party external to the organisation – hereinafter referred to as the intermediate party – with which the organisation shares management control.

Box 3.2 Aspects and environmental impact

The definition of

- environmental aspect is an 'element of an organisation's activities, products and services that has or can have an impact on the environment';
- environmental impact is any 'change to the environment, whether adverse or beneficial, wholly or partially resulting from an organisation's activities, product and services' (art. 2 EMAS Regulation).

Some examples may help clarify the meaning of these concepts.

Take, for example, a fine chemical production process being carried out at a given industrial site that generates secondary wastewater with a medium-high organic waste content. These substances may produce an increase in biochemical oxygen demand (BOD) in the receiving water body (the water course they discharge into), which may cause a lack of oxygen and result in the death of fish.

The nature and the entity of the environmental change caused by the organic substances discharged into the receiving water body depend on a series of factors (the concentration of these substances in the waste water, the state of the water course into which the waste was discharged, the simultaneous presence of other sources of pollution which have an impact on the same receiving water body, the type and nature of the organisms living in it, etc.).

Given the difficulties identifying the relationship of cause and effect, on the one hand, and the measurement of the final consequences on the environment, on the other hand, there is no point in distinguishing between primary impact (the first consequences: in the example, the level of BOD in the discharged waste water provoking a change in the quality of the receiving water course) and the secondary impact (the final consequences: the reduction in the number and variety of fish in the receiving water course) caused by the environmental aspect considered (the presence of organic substances in the discharged wastewater). The organisation is required to identify the environmental aspects connected to its activities and evaluate its own primary environmental impact by taking into account, where possible, the relationship between the known cause and effect and the gravity of the possible secondary environmental impact.

The gradual refinement of the knowledge of the relationship between cause and effect and the measurability of the changes in the environment will increasingly enable the focus and evaluation of the performance of the activities to be shifted onto the secondary impact in order to plan and improve ways of intervening with regard to the final consequences of environmental activities.

During this learning curve, having access to reference documents may prove useful for the organisation (studies on specific aspects, environmental review of the area or other documents such as the most common Reports on the State of the Environment), which on different levels of territorial review – local, provincial and regional – provide a picture of the state of the environment, the pressures put on it by human activity and environmental policies (responses) put in place in the area in question to limit their consequences.

(Continued)

Box 3.2 Aspects and environmental impact (*Continued*)

> The development – by National and International Organisations or research bodies (Ocse, Eurostat, etc.) – of global warming indicators for reference may provide further useful insight as in the case of the Global Warming Potential (GWP), for example, which translates the impact of non-carbon dioxide greenhouse gases into CO_2 equivalents. The emission of these gases caused by human activity, even though they do not have a local impact, generate environmental consequences on a global level affecting the composition of the atmosphere and greenhouse gas emissions. Having access to this data can help evaluate, for example, the significance of the impact caused by carbon dioxide emissions produced by combustion in a thermoelectric power plant (the environmental aspect) which – according to the review submitted – creates a primary impact (the change in the quality of the air after emission of a certain quantity of CO_2) and a secondary impact (a rise in the Earth's temperature).

Some examples help to clarify this concept. The Regulation provides two (not exhaustive) lists of direct and indirect environmental aspects. The list has been recently updated by the USERS Guidelines (Commission Decision of 4 March 2013).

As far as the direct aspects are concerned, the Regulation requires the organisation to at least take into account the following aspects:

- Air emissions
- Water emissions
- Waste
- Use of natural resources and raw materials
- Local issues (noise, vibration, odours)
- Land use
- Air emissions related to transport
- Risks of environmental accidents and emergency situations

The list, which is not exhaustive, of the indirect aspects includes the following aspects:

- Product life cycle related issues
- Capital investment
- Insurance services
- Administrative and planning decisions
- Environmental performance of contractors, subcontractors and suppliers
- Choice and composition of services, e.g. transport, catering, etc.

Whilst the impacts caused by a direct aspect are exclusively generated by the activities and decisional processes of the organisation (which, however, can obtain full management control over them through an appropriate and effective management system), those caused by an indirect aspect also depend on the activities and decisional powers of other parties that figure as active parties in the interaction between the organisation and the environment.

An example of this could be shown as follows: if, on the one hand, the quantity of outbound waste from the production process of an electrical appliances factory (point c in the list of direct aspects) results from the factory's capacity to manufacture with minimum waste, on the other hand, the correct disposal of any of its electrical appliances at the end of the life cycle (point a of the list of indirect aspects) is dependent on the behaviour of the customer who acquires the product (intermediate party).

It must be pointed out that it is not a matter of simply classifying the aspects as direct or indirect, but of ensuring that 'all the aspects have been identified in order for them to be managed by the system'.

For this reason, the Regulation suggests that the identification and assessment process should be instigated by a review of the organisation's ability to influence the aspect under analysis.

In other words, it is necessary to assess the level of control or influence the organisation may exert (or effectively exert) on the individual aspect; this assessment, in conjunction with the one for relevant environmental impacts, may make it possible to establish the significance of the indirect aspect.

This type of approach may envisage different levels of control that can be exercised by the organisation in order to apply the different environmental aspects uniformly, irrespective of the sector in which it operates. The identification of the direct and indirect aspects requires a significant effort in terms of analysis, assessment and building of relationships to be able to go beyond the organisation's boundaries. The rule of thumb that can be adopted by organisations committed to continuous improvement of their environmental performance connected to indirect impacts is one of graduality: efforts should be concentrated initially on involving intermediate parties with whom the organisation has stable, consolidated relationships and gradually extended to parties which take part in indirect aspects that are less 'controlled' or 'influenced'.

The Box below shows an example of an initial environmental review carried out by an industrial organisation, the Example company, which, in examining its activities and organisational set-up, identifies the packaging of the Indirect product as an indirect environmental aspect since it 'shares' the management of the environmental impacts connected to it with other parties over which it can only exercise partial influence and control.

During the identification and assessment process of the environmental aspects, the analysis must be carried out in consideration of the

- routine operating conditions (with regard to normal business operations including, for example, ordinary and extraordinary maintenance planned for the production plant);
- non-routine operating conditions (including, for example, start-up conditions and shutdown of operations or production plants);
- accidents, unforeseen situations or foreseeable emergencies (in this case the initial review should assess the possible consequences and measures adopted to prevent them in conjunction with the probability that the event will take place);
- past, present and planned activities.

Box 3.3 Example Ltd – Initial review

The EXAMPLE Ltd. company produces Indirect, a product used in numerous industrial sectors as an intermediary product. The company, registered to EMAS and certified to ISO 14001 since 2005, had looked, in its management system, at the packaging of the products it sold in the form of different sizes and types of polythene bags dictated by the customer requirements, from the environmental aspect connected to its activities only in relation to raw material consumption since 'the environmental impact' on phases after the production process was considered outside the company's jurisdiction. The EMAS Regulation and, above all, the indications contained in Annexes regarding the identification of all the environmental aspects, whether direct or indirect, connected to an organisation's activities and products has persuaded the company to review its position regarding the product packaging.

When revising the Initial Environmental Review (IER), the review of the organisation's activities and set-up confirmed that the packaging was an environmental aspect over which the company only had partial control. The information collected and the interviews carried out in the IER revision did, in fact, highlight how some corporate activities interacted with other parties (outside the company) in the management of the packaging. The Marketing Department is responsible for the analysis of market requirements regarding the features of the packaging; the Procurement Department for the management of packaging suppliers; the R&D department for the composition and performance characteristics of the packaging based on customer requirements. In this sense, the company realised that the packaging of its products represents an 'indirect' environmental aspect since it only has partial control over it which it shares with other intermediate parties (suppliers, customers).

One of the first requirements was, therefore, to identify and propose a measurement of the environmental aspect that enabled the scale to be evaluated. Since the aspect was indirect, the company decided it should concentrate on quantifying its contribution to the environmental impact caused by intermediate parties (such as the creation of waste at the end of life) and, for this reason, difficult to measure. In this context, the data supported by the initial review is

- kg of packaging procured over one year
- kg of packaging used per product unit
- per cent of packaging recovered

The indications emerging from the International Energy Agency (IEA) review also meant that the phases of the packaging life cycle in which management control was more closely 'shared' with intermediate parties could be identified and therefore, that there were ample margins for collaboration aimed at improving the environmental impact: namely the design, use and end of life phases.

In order to assess the significance of this indirect environmental aspect, the company collected and reviewed a series of additional information concerning the life cycle phases of the packaging identified as possible 'common ground' for action:

- Design: the product specification sheets (i.e. for the packaging) provided by the packaging suppliers were reviewed in order to study the environmental and performance characteristics; a screening of customer procurement orders was carried out to identify the production and business requirements (storage and usage methods of Indirect at its sites, storage requirements, movement on site, etc.); sector-related data (on the packaging used) was analysed with regard to the environmental performance of the product and lastly, the requirements for advertising and distribution by Marketing were compared with potential actions for environmental improvement which were deemed technically feasible.

- Use and end-of-life: given the overlap of these two phases in the packaging life cycle (its usage is reflected in its correct recycling and disposal), the company reviewed the sector-related data (on the packaging used) regarding the destinations of the product at end-of-life and its environmental impact and compared it with the data requested from its customers through a questionnaire about their 'habitual' use (that is, disposal) of the packaging.

Analysis of the data gathered from customers highlighted, in particular, the possibility/opportunity of producing the product in polyethylene bags with a uniform composition and format, so that they could be recovered by the customers, treated appropriately (washed and relabelled) and re-used in production. In other words, Indirect could be packaged in a 'universal' polyethylene bag (in terms of format, composition, content capacity and resistance), which could be used by all customers for other unrelated production purposes.

This solution, however, will transform the packaging for indirect into a direct environmental aspect which will then have to manage the recovery and treatment of the packaging.

The information and data gathered will enable the company to correctly identify the indirect aspect 'packaging' and assess the degree of influence it can exercise over its customers in optimising the environmental performance of the packaging of Indirect during the design and use/end-of-life phases. Preventive analysis of the repercussions of the proposed solution, that is, the recovery of the packaging from the customers, will also enable assessment of the feasibility of other possible ways of tackling the problem of re-use (e.g. agreements with the packaging suppliers).

Assessment of environmental aspects and identification of the significant ones

Having identified and analysed all the environmental aspects related to the activity carried out, the organisation must assess them in order to select the ones which are considered significant and merit special attention in structuring the environment management system. The first step is the study of interactions between environmental aspects and connected impacts. Table 3.2 shows some examples of those interactions.

Then the Regulation invites the organisation to

- assess the level of significance of the environmental aspects based on the criteria established by the organisation itself;
- identify the areas in which improvements can be made;
- organise the most suitable methods to achieve the improvements.

The definition of the criteria for attributing significance to the environmental aspects is, therefore, left to the organisation and represents an essential phase

Table 3.2 Environmental aspects and impacts

Environmental aspects	Type of impacts	Method of interaction between aspect and impact
Use of paper for office machines	Paper consumption	Increase computer use to reduce consumption
Delivery of packaged goods	Creation of waste packaging	Select packaging to allow partial recovery
Distribution of finished products	Impact linked to transport	Identify transport companies able to guarantee use of vehicles which create less pollution
Transport route planning	Impact linked to transport	Modify routes in areas with heavy traffic
Loans	Direct impact of organisations requesting loans	Fix the loan to minimum requirements in terms of environmental impact on project earmarked for loans
Maintenance	Impact on damage caused to other networks	Coordinate execution of maintenance work with administrators on other networks
Loading and unloading of goods	Impact linked to goods handling	Establish rules for loading and unloading and supervise activity to limit environmental impact
Production of disassembled products	Impact linked to the creation of waste at life cycle end	Allow qualified disposal companies to easily separate components of homogeneous material from products
Management of authorisation processes	Improve environmental performance of certified or registered companies	Encourage the use of ISO and EMAS by simplifying the procedures for participating organisations
Concession of loans	Eligible actions which affect the environmental performance of the applicant organisation	Propose subsidised credit loans, particularly for small and medium companies
Customer awareness	Direct impact linked to guests' behaviour	Initiate awareness campaigns directed at hotel guests (for example, changing and washing of towels; electricity consumption for lighting)
Information and customer awareness	Impact linked to the life cycle of products offered	Take on a key role to develop environmentally-friendly consumption through, for example, recycling platforms, sales promotions and advertising

in the initial review. The Regulation, however, makes it clear that these criteria must be 'comprehensive, capable of independent checking, reproducible and made publicly available'.

It also requires the organisation to take into consideration the elements shown in the first column of Table 3.3 during the phase for defining the criteria, as well as some operational indications given in the right-hand column.

By way of example, an environmental aspect can be judged significant if one or more of the following circumstances occurs:

- the surveys conducted indicate that the measurement of a parameter of an environmental aspect is frequently (or constantly) close to the limits provided by law;
- the initial review identifies a particularly critical environmental aspect with regard to the size, frequency or reversibility of its impact;

Table 3.3 Indications for defining criteria of significance

Information about the condition of the environmental to identify the organisation's activities, products and services	Data gathered by area, local and national action plans, results of monitoring campaigns, reports on the state of the environment, scientific studies, etc.
Organisation's existing data on material and energy inputs, wastes, and emissions data in terms of risks	Review of data and information collected by the analysis activities involving personnel; comparison with other organisations in the same sector; contact with associations in the same sector, contacts with trade associations
Views of interested parties	Gathering of opinions amongst employees, local communities, environmental and consumer associations, local institutions, study centres through interviews, surveys, circulation of information; assessment of media reaction to the organisation's initiatives and results, etc.
Environmental activities that are regulated by the organisation	Analysis of laws and regulations; voluntary agreements; internal standards, etc.
Procurement activities	Gathering of information through direct contact with suppliers, in situ audits
Design, development, manufacturing, distribution, servicing, use, re-use, recycling, and disposal of the organisation's products	Life Cycle Analysis, criteria for attributing eco-labels, information and contacts with designers, suppliers, intermediate customers and end users of products and services, etc.
Organisation's activities with most significant environmental costs and benefits	Environmental accounting, Life Cycle Costing, feasibility analysis, etc.

- the environmental review highlighted the fragility of a local, regional or global situation linked to a specific environmental aspect;
- some of the organisation's characteristics compel it to pay particular attention to its environmental impact (sites within residential areas using specific production processes or dangerous substances, etc.);[3]
- the organisation received frequent notifications from its stakeholders (local community, employees, public administration) about the persistence of specific unpleasant impacts that can be traced back to its activities (e.g. odours, 'suspicious' air emissions, death of fish, etc.);
- the organisation foresees that in the near future certain environmental aspects will be regulated more stringently and decides to concentrate its efforts on these aspects and anticipate changes to legislation.

In cases like these, or in any other case for that matter, where specific environmental aspects are judged to be significant, the environmental management system will take particular notice of their existence and the organisation's need to manage them with great care. In other words, the system will be 'tailored' to the characteristics of the organisation, so that it can guarantee effectiveness in controlling the environmental aspects considered to be significant.

Furthermore, it is essential that the management system is structured in a way that will ensure that the review of environmental aspects due to a change in circumstances and conditions (the introduction of new plants, products, procedural changes, changes in the organisation or lay-out, new parameters monitored by law, etc.) guarantees the continuing appropriateness of all the environmental aspects considered to be significant for production, organisational and management characteristics of the organisation's activity and the related environmental impacts.

The Regulation leaves the choice of method to identify the environmental aspects and the assessment of the most significant ones to the discretion of the organisation, which can be based on quantitative index mechanisms or be linked to quality type assessments. The part which interests the management system (and the verifier called to express an opinion on the method for the process of identification and assessment of the environmental aspects) is that the analytical and assessment process is *traceable* and thus, guarantees the accuracy of the conclusions on the significance of the environmental aspects (used as a basis by the organisation in planning its improvement actions).

Choice of indicators and layout of the register of environmental aspects

The Regulation indicates that after the review and assessment of the environmental aspects connected to the organisation's activities have been completed, a register of the aspects considered most 'important' should then be compiled. The results of the environmental review are, therefore, the starting point for the systematic compilation of the register and subsequent assessment of any changes occurring over time.

Box 3.4 Identification and assessment of direct environmental aspects: example

---

The following diagram can be applied to all the activities under full management control of the organisation and is aimed at identifying and assessing direct environmental aspects.

a) Construction of the Matrix for Direct Interactions and Identification of Environmental Aspects

According to the definition given in the regulation, identifying the environmental aspects connected to the activity, products and services (hereinafter, 'activity') of an organisation means identifying the elements of that activity that interact with an environmental subsystem.

An environmental interaction, therefore, describes the relationship between an activity carried out by the organisation and an environmental subsystem.

The 'Matrix for Direct Interaction' is a useful graphical representation and logical guide in the process of identifying the different interactions (matrix cells) resulting from the intersection between activities (shown horizontally) and the environmental subsystem (in columns).

In order to construct this matrix, therefore, the organisation

- identifies and lists the subsystem elements in a column (water quality, air quality, consumption of resources, soil quality, wastes, noise…) with reference to the indications in the Regulation, to other relevant scientific information (e.g. sector-related studies) and the specifics of the process, the products and the services;
- identifies and lists in a line the activities (past, present and planned) which can determine environmental interaction (current, previous, potential) with the environment.[4] Each activity is analysed in normal conditions, not routine or emergency conditions.

The matrix, constructed in this way, is then compiled by 'picking' the cell in correspondence with which the organisation verifies the existence of the interaction; for each interaction identified, data and information are collected about the element or the way in which it occurs.

The matrix for environmental interactions enables an initial selection of the environmental aspects based on the relevant criteria by excluding the activities/ subsystems with no interactions (empty cell).[5]

b) Assessment of the significance of the relevant environmental aspects and identification of the priority of actions

The assessment process is aimed at selecting the significant environmental aspects[6].

(Continued)

Box 3.4 Identification and assessment of direct environmental aspects: example (*Continued*)

Each environmental aspect identified on the basis of the criteria in point a) is analysed according to three distinct assessment axes, each of which is alternately articulated in two parameters of significance:

Assessment axis x   INTERNAL IMPORTANCE (II)

- criticality in terms of effective and potential environmental consequences;
- criticality in management and control methods;[7]

Assessment axis z   EXTERNAL IMPORTANCE (EI)

- criticality with regard to legal compliance;[8]
- sensitivity of environmental context;

Assessment axis y   FREQUENCY (F)

- frequency of event;
- duration of event.

Each assessment axis is assigned a value by applying the same scale or frequency/importance:[9]

- High with a value of 3;
- Medium with a value of 2;
- Low with a value of 1.

For internal and external importance, the predominant opinion is the one for environmental consequences and criticality of legal compliance respectively.

A significance value S (with $1 \leq S \leq 27$) is attributed to each environmental aspect equal to the sum of the values of frequency, internal and external importance ($S = F \times II \times EI$).

Any environmental aspects with $S \geq 8$ are considered significant. This means that the organisation deems that these aspects have a significant impact on the environment based on the quantitative and qualitative considerations resulting from the analytical process.

The next step is to identify the priorities within the significant environmental aspects which will help the organisation to tackle the successive phase of defining the improvement goals and planning the actions: the basis for identifying priorities is to attribute increasing priority to increasing values of significance.

The register of environmental aspects is based and built on the data traced back to the organisation's environmental conditions at the time of the initial review. The relevant primary environmental impacts are identified and systematically monitored for each environmental aspect deemed to be significant by monitoring the parameters deemed important for understanding the interaction with the environment.

It is important to take a great deal of care over the layout of the register since it represents one of the key tools for assessing continual improvement of the effectiveness of the management system by allowing the evolution of primary impacts of significant environmental aspects to be followed over time. It must also consider all the changes in the environment surrounding the organisation that

Box 3.5 Identification and assessment of indirect environmental aspects: example

The following diagram can be applied to all activities under partial management control of the organisation and is aimed at identifying and assessing indirect environmental aspects.

1. Construction of the matrix for indirect interactions and identification of indirect environmental aspects

An environmental aspect is indirect when the organisation has partial control and shares it with a third party. A possible way of identifying environmental aspects may, therefore, be to start by identifying the activities through which the organisation may, indirectly, (or via the contribution of an intermediate party) interact with the environment.

A possible logical sequence for identifying the indirect environmental aspects is the following:

*   identification of the activities which may interact indirectly with the environment (the creation of a checklist of possible activities could prove useful for this step, itemised for each phase/operation or product/service life cycle);
*   identification of the intermediate party involved in the interactions;
*   analysis of the ways in which the indirect interaction occurs in the environment and identification of the level of control;
*   construction of a Table of indirect interactions. The Table serves to organise the environmental aspects identified according to the level of control/ influence exercised.

The indirect aspects identified and analysed in this way are divided in the Table into

*   first level indirect aspects: the aspects linked to the activities of parties external to the organisation operating independently; the organisation is able to design, coordinate and monitor these activities using its own personnel;
*   second level indirect aspects: the aspects linked to the activities of the organisation which go beyond its boundaries and are directly controlled by third parties; the behaviour of these parties can only be influenced by the organisation.

2. Assessment of the significance of indirect environmental aspects and identification of the priority of actions

Once the indirect aspects have been classified according to the proposed subdivision, then the assessment of the significance is carried out by applying different assessment parameters according to category (first and second level environmental aspects).

When defining the assessment criteria, the organisation's partial control, as well as the limitations of collecting comprehensive data or carrying out direct analyses or surveys at independent third party sites must be taken into account.

The suggestion is, therefore, to back up the assessment of the 'intrinsic' significance of the environmental impacts produced with an assessment of the management control that was actually detected at the time of the initial review.

Box 3.6 Assessment of management control in the event of first or second level indirect environmental aspects

a)   In the event of first level indirect environmental aspects, the assessment criteria and relative indices could be the following:

a.1 – Checks on the aspect

- Contracts with external parties (directly responsible for the aspect) include requirements for the aspect in question: score 1
- Contracts with external parties (directly responsible for the aspect) include requirements for environmental aspects in general, but not for the aspect in question: score 2
- Contracts with external parties (directly responsible for the aspect) do not envisage requirements for any environmental aspects: score 3

a.2 – Monitoring of external parties (Mo)

- Systematic checks are regularly carried out on external parties on management of the aspect under examination: score 1
- Partial checks are carried out (sporadic, documented or spot-checks): score 2
- No checks are carried out on external parties: score 3

b)   As far as the second level indirect environmental aspects are concerned, since no power of direct control was indicated at the first assessment level, it would be necessary to substitute the assessment parameters (a.1) and monitoring (a.2) in the previous point with the following, indicating the effective degree of influence on the indirect aspect.

b.1 – Empowerment of external parties (Ee)

- Explicit requests or incentives are sent to external parties to encourage correct control of indirect aspects: score 1
- Comprehensive information is sent to external parties to encourage correct control of indirect aspects: score 2
- No initiatives are taken for external parties: score 3

b.2 – Involvement of external parties (Io)

- External parties are regularly involved in coordinating activities causing an indirect aspect: score 1
- Managers of external parties are asked for feedback on management of indirect aspects (e.g. data requests): score 2
- There is no interaction with external parties in charge of indirect aspects: score 3

In both cases (first and second level indirect aspects), the assessment of the level of effective management control can simply be extrapolated from the multiplication of the relevant parameters (CxMo for the first level indirect aspects and EexC for the second level indirect aspects) by a value between 1 and 9.

Assessment of the 'intrinsic' significance of the environmental aspect

In order to perform a correct assessment of the indirect aspect, the 'intrinsic' significance of the environmental aspect must also be taken into account regardless of which party has management control over it and the level of control exercised.

If the data and information required to assess the significance using the same approach applied to the direct aspects is not available, then a scale (from 1 to 18) will be applied based on the qualitative criteria listed below according to which an indirect environmental aspect is judged to be more or less significant in relation to

- The results deriving from studies or literature;
- Indications provided by an external party (e.g. with an environmental management system);
- The need for additional data and information in the event of suspicion of significance;
- Sensitivity proved by contacts and stakeholders.

If the available data is applicable, the method for direct aspects can be applied.

A greater incidence in the assessment process of indirect aspects is attributed to significance based on direct data; the value obtained in this assessment (from 1 and 27) is, in fact, multiplied by 2/3. Once this value has been extrapolated (S), it can be summed to the previous value (G) to achieve a maximum level of 27 again.

Review conclusion

The proposed method allows significance values (from 1 to 27) of the indirect aspects identified to be reached which are attributed on the basis, on the one hand, of the environmental impacts of the aspect (intrinsic significance) and on the other hand, of the possibility and opportunity of existing controls. Indirect aspects with higher values will, therefore, be given more attention by the organisation which will assess the possibility of initiating actions to gradually reduce their significance.

---

may possibly change the environmental impacts of its activities (e.g. if a nursery school is built in proximity to an industrial area which was previously deserted, the environmental impacts of the site will change significantly).

The gathering of data in response to the need to assess and monitor environmental performance, and the management of the information required to understand its progress are both very important steps in the cognitive path initiated by the organisation through the environmental review. These activities mean that the existing surveillance and monitoring systems can be analysed and assessed and any weak areas and margins for improvement can be identified.

Data registration should be carried out by adopting the following precautions to facilitate consultation and review:

- measure the measurable and estimate the rest;
- always specify the methods employed to carry out the measurements and the criteria on which the estimates are based;

- use consolidated indicators by referring to standards stipulated by current regulations, but also to specific recognised techniques, and to indicators provided by existing databases or studies performed by industry associations (e.g. the *Responsible Care* programme for the chemical industry).

The definition of appropriate indicators means that the organisation can monitor the significant environmental parameters and assess the progress of its performance over time with respect to legal compliance and/or to industry averages.

Analysis of existing environmental management procedures and assessment of lessons learnt from previous analyses of occurrences of environmental accidents

As already seen, environmental review is the identification and assessment of environmental aspects through the examination of interactions – either direct or mediated by intermediate parties – of an organisation's activities, products and services with the environment. The way in which these interactions are manifested can be better understood if the organisation carries out a detailed, accurate analysis of existing internal procedures and practices (even if only to ensure compliance with current legislation) of the individual aspects of environmental management.

By taking into consideration the completeness and the appropriateness of the work already carried out by the organisation, the initial environmental review can then provide a comprehensive description of the organisation's situation concerning environmental management and organise the management system in such a way that it does not duplicate, overlap or contradict the work already carried out by the organisation.

The box below shows an example of a reference scheme for interpreting how suitable the operational and management work methods used are (whether they are practices or embedded in management or operational procedures).

Furthermore, the use of this model serves to identify any weak points in the existing management, control and monitoring methods and any margins for improvement in them and is essential for creating a management system that is 'clad' in the characteristics and the experiences of the organisation.

The Regulation requires that particular attention be paid to emergency procedures and analysis and assessment of previous accidents when carrying out this activity.

By way of example, in Box 3.8, the above-mentioned model is applied to this specific aspect.

Box 3.7 Checklist for work method analysis

- Is the environmental aspect known to the organisation? (yes – no)
- Does a specific work method need to be defined for correct management?

  If required:

  - does the work method exist? (yes – no)

If it exists:

- has it been defined correctly? (yes – no)
- do the employees concerned know about it? (yes – no)
- has it been correctly made known to these employees? (yes – no)
- has it been made into a procedure? (no, into a practice – yes, into a procedure or an operational instruction)

If it has been made into a procedure:

- is an updated version available in the relevant departments? (yes – no)
- do the employees concerned know about it? (yes – no)
- has it been correctly made known to these employees? (yes – no)
- is it subjected to periodic controls and relevant updates? (yes – no)
- has it been adequately documented (see $) (yes – no)
- ...

Box 3.8 Checklist for the analysis and assessment of emergency procedures and accidents that have occurred

- The organisation identifies and assesses the potential risks and emergency situations distinguishing between those occurring internally and those externally.
- Are there resources, systems, vehicles and equipment to respond to an emergency situation? Are periodic trials with simulations of potential emergency situations carried out and regularly documented?
- Is there a procedure that describes the ways in which risks and emergency situations are identified and assessed?
- Is there a procedure that describes the criteria and methods of setting up, instructing and training emergency teams?
- Has the procedure been introduced correctly?
- Are accidents and emergencies documented?
- Are accidents and emergencies reviewed and the analysis results circulated among all personnel to share the findings?
- Are the emergency plans communicated to the competent authorities?
- Are the emergency plans communicated to other companies in the vicinity and the local inhabitants?
- Has the procedure taken the domino effect into account?
- ...

Environmental policy and programme

Once the initial review has been completed, the organisation will have a comprehensive, detailed picture of all the information at its disposal concerning:

- the nature and scale of the significant environmental problems connected to its business practices;

- the strengths and weaknesses encountered in the organisational, management, technological, technical and operational methods which it adopts to manage these problems;
- the potential margins for improvement and priority for actions.

This picture provides the organisation with all the elements necessary to define an environmental policy and action plan (which will be discussed in the next paragraph) suited to its characteristics and unique setup.

The environmental policy

The environmental policy defines the commitment that the management of the organisation intends to adopt to protect the environment and states 'the general objectives and principles for action', which will guide all its actions in managing environmental problems connected to its business practices.

Given its strategic importance in the general operation of the organisation, the environmental policy must be viewed as an asset at the highest management level, be coherent and integrated into the set of general principles and objectives which represent the organisation's values and identity and inspire its decisional and management processes, must translate into specific objectives and concrete actions aimed at improving the management of environmental aspects and related performances. In the case of complex organisations (e.g. multinational and/or multisite organisations), the environmental policy must be integrated with the parent organisation.

The policy must also be clearly stated in writing, signed by the highest echelons of corporate management, implemented, maintained and updated over time: the total and unequivocal buy-in at management level is essential for the start-up process and maintenance of the management system to guarantee that environmental aspects are included in the key components of the organisation's strategic planning.

The reference standards also require that the environmental policy is communicated to all personnel and made available to the public: it should not, therefore, be considered a purely formal act, but on the contrary, interpreted as an unequivocal statement of the organisation's commitment to its employees – who are asked to share it and participate in its application – and external stakeholders.

As far as the content of the environmental policy is concerned, the EMAS Regulation and the ISO 14001 standard clearly point out some of the content to include in the document:

- compliance with the law and standards of the organisation; the commitment to scrupulously observe environmental legislation is an essential prerequisite for an organisation's participation in EMAS. The Regulation identifies in this condition the first, basic guarantee of a broader, tangible and active commitment to the protection of the environment. Top management must, therefore, base its environmental policy, first and foremost, on the principle of respect for all the provisions concerning the environment in relation to any activities that it carries out;
- commitment to continual improvement: incorporating this principle into the organisation's environmental management is one of the main

objectives in applying environmental certification. Improvement in environmental performance is defined as a 'process of improvement, year by year, of the measurable results of the environmental management system relating to an organisation's management of its significant environmental aspects based on the policy and its objectives and goals; the improvement of these results does not necessarily have to occur at the same time in all operating sectors'. The Regulation, therefore, specifies that continual improvement must refer to the overall results of the organisation and may be highlighted by just some of the indicators measuring the environmental performance and not necessarily by all of them. There may also be areas in which the organisation has already improved its performance in the past where the margins of improvement will, therefore, be understandably inferior: in these cases, it is in the organisation's interest to endeavour to maintain a constant level of performance and emphasise the efforts made in the past;

- participation and involvement of personnel; EMAS, in particular, places great emphasis on participation of all personnel by highlighting the opportunity to create a sense of responsibility towards the environment among employees at all levels and encourage the appropriate use of methods for ensuring participation and involvement;

- commitment to dialogue with external parties: there are numerous references to external communication and information within the EMAS Regulation. Among these, the most evident is the one expressed by the complexity and the obligation of the requirements of the environmental statement and by the primary role given to it. The more necessary and pressing the need to communicate with external parties appears, the less the organisation's environmental communication seems to be developed and up-to-date with the increasing pressure for information by the public. This seems to be the case of many PMIs, which are often poorly prepared, when they compare themselves to the growing interest of many external parties in the impact of their activities on the environment. The intention alone of subscribing to EMAS by a PMI is an indication of a notable and commendable commitment towards environmental communication (given the implications arising from the legal requirements of the environmental statement).

In addition to the above-mentioned principles, which are shown to be fundamental by the Regulation, the environmental policy may contain commitments aimed at guaranteeing the following:

- the prevention and management of emergencies;
- the involvement of customers and suppliers;
- the safety and environmental compatibility of the product;
- the use of clean technology;
- the commitment to pursue sustainable development;
- the participation in agreements or other voluntary type initiatives;
- the health and safety of employees.

Reference to these principles which could be applied to all realms of the organisation should not give the impression of an 'impersonal', standardised policy document. The first action required of the organisation is to translate its actual position in relation to the environment into the policy and define general objectives tailored to its own characteristics and unique features.

The environmental programme

Once the significant environmental aspects have been identified and the commitment in conjunction with the environmental policy have been established to prevent, manage and monitor these aspects, the organisation must then define specific objectives for improvement and plan appropriate actions accordingly.

It is essential that there is coherence between the organisation's environmental policy, the significant environmental aspects and the objectives for improvement. The transition from the general objectives to specific objectives allows the commitments undertaken by management to be translated in performance objectives tailored to the organisation's actual operational, organisational, technological and financial situation regarding the significance of environmental aspects. The requirement for coherence should not be interpreted rigidly when looking for a specific objective for *each* commitment undertaken against a corresponding environmental aspect identified as significant: what is important is that the environmental programme as a whole reflects the organisation's characteristics, responds to the priority of actions identified by the analysis and actually contributes to the pursuit of the environmental policy.

The Regulation also requires that the objectives be quantified where possible and translated into goals, or detailed objectives and/or intermediate steps aimed at achieving the objectives themselves: quantification and creation of goals provides, on the one hand, measurable indicators of the results achieved and, on the other hand, to have references to verify the progress of the environmental programme.

On the basis of the critical events which emerged from the initial review, specific objectives can be pursued through technical type actions directed at preventing or reducing the environmental impact or actions which aimed at rationalising, from a management and organisational point of view, the organisation's activities which interact with the environment. When identifying the actions required to achieve a specific objective (e.g. the reduction of a particular pollutant from wastewater), the organisation should assess the opportunity of adopting preventive type solutions first (which act on the causes, e.g. the substitution of material used in the process causing the presence of the pollutant in the waste) against protective type solutions (which act on the effects, e.g. the improvement of the purification system). It is also important for the organisation to assess the way effects may overlap due to a particular action: quite often, in fact, the performance improvements of an environmental aspect can have an adverse effect on those for other aspects connected to it (for example, the introduction of a new abatement plant for a specific pollutant may cause an increase in the amount of mud being expelled during the purification process).

Table 3.4 Contents of the environmental improvement programme

Environmental Aspect	Objective	Goals	Actions	Timeframe	Resources	Responsibilities

Having defined the improvement objectives and identified the actions required to pursue them, the organisation then develops the environmental programme based on the model and summarised contents shown in Table 3.4.

An essential and unavoidable component of any environmental programme is the involvement of the organisation's top management in the quest to achieve the objectives and initiate the operational plans defined. It is true to say that the initiation of the entire environmental management scheme cannot be achieved without the buy-in of whoever runs the organisation. Commitment by top management becomes tangible, visible, effective and systematic by implementing the environmental programme, initiating the management system and maintaining its effectiveness. For this reason, it is essential that top management provides and guarantees adequate means, defines coherent procedures and assigns clearly defined responsibilities and powers.

Another fundamental aspect is the involvement of personnel in the environmental improvement programme. This can be interpreted as the minimal commitment of informing employees about the objectives in which they will be directly involved and subsequently establishing the roles, responsibilities and tasks to be pursued. However, the phase for analysing and defining the objectives may also be a fundamental step towards encouraging active participation by employees: through suitable methods to involve them (e.g. creating work groups aimed at specific objectives), the organisation could take advantage of employee expertise, by assessing and encouraging their contribution through a gradual process, whereby the objectives and means to successfully achieve them are shared.

The case of programmes and improvement objectives in Abbott Italia

Abbott Laboratories, founded in 1888, is today one of the most important companies in the healthcare sector and a global leader in the research, development, production and marketing of pharmaceutical products, medical devices and nutritional formulas.

The company headquarters are in Chicago, Illinois; the company has 83,000 employees and operates all over the world, marketing its products in over 130 countries. Currently, Abbott has 10 specialised research centres and over 100 production plants located in 66 countries worldwide.

Abbott's mission is to operate responsibly towards society by contributing every day to the creation of responsible production processes and organisational methodologies shared within the company and to initiating serious, innovative and sustainable corporate policies.

In 2009, Abbott developed a strategy for social responsibility based on four key areas representing the activities with the greatest social and environmental impact in which Abbott can or wants to make a difference:

1   'Innovate for the future': aiming to develop all production aspects in parallel and making scientific innovations in every line of business.
2   'Improving access to treatment': committing to guaranteeing easy access to those people who need it.
3   'Protecting patients and consumers': committing not only to protecting patients, but also to promoting the health and safety of its employees and the community it comes into contact with.
4   'Safeguarding the environment': protecting the environment by aiming to improve people's lives on a daily basis.

The Italian branch was set up in 1949 and with over 2,000 employees is one of the biggest in the world.

The company's headquarters and the production plant are in Campoverde di Aprilia (Latina); the plant is one of the company's most important chemical and pharmaceutical plants with a production and packaging factory for pharmaceutical products, two chemical production plants which produce basic pharmaceutical active ingredients and compounds, in particular anaesthetics and anti-HIV.

The high levels of conformity and performance excellence in its production and management activities is demonstrated by the numerous certificates obtained for Quality Management (ISO 9001), Environmental Management (ISO 14001), Occupational Health and Safety Management (OHSAS 18001) and Management of Safety in Plants with a High Accident Risk (UNI 10617), all received in 2006 and renewed in successive years. In November 2008, the Plant achieved EMAS registration as a demonstration of the on-going commitment by the company to environmental protection with specific commitments for reducing its environmental impact, gas emissions and increasing its energy efficiency.

In the last few years, ABBOTT has increased its commitment to the policy of continual improvement of its environmental performance in three areas, which it considers fundamental not only for the community, but also for its business:

- Climate change, with a particular commitment to reducing direct and indirect greenhouse gas emissions;
- Sustainable product management, with particular attention on reducing the environmental impact throughout the entire product life cycle by analysing the manufacturing phases, as well as the management of warehouses, distribution, use and disposal;
- Use of water resources with the aim of reducing water loss and improving resource management methods.

Abbott has dedicated particular attention to the resource of water since it is not only a fundamental part of the manufacturing of all its products, but also essential for anyone who uses its products. For this reason, the company has focused its efforts on a rational, efficient and sustainable use of this resource so it can contribute to improving the quality and quantity of water supplied to the community in which the company operates.

As early as 2004, Abbott had set for itself the global objective of reducing its water consumption by 40 per cent, which it achieved at the end of 2009 (two years earlier than its plan of 2011) with an approximate reduction in annual water consumption of four billion litres. This result was achieved by implementing a far-reaching programme aimed at conserving natural resources in the production process by creating a water management plan for all the Abbott plants in order to understand, analyse and optimise its methods of managing and designing new systems to limit water consumption.

The new challenge that Abbott set itself at the end of 2009 and committed to achieving by the end of 2015 is the additional reduction of water withdrawal (for all its plants) by 50 per cent against the figure for 2005.

Table 3.5 summarises the main objectives provided by the parent company for 2009–2015.

In planning the improvement for water resources management, Abbott Italia incorporated input from the parent company by making a major contribution to the objectives of rationalising its water consumption and combining the directives from Chicago with the findings that emerged from the critical environmental situation in the area where the production occurs.

For example, water resources management (water withdrawal and drainage) is a significant critical environmental factor for the Pharmaceutical Area in Latina

Table 3.5 Example of objectives set in Abbot Italia

Objectives 2009–2015		
Environmental aspect	*Goal*	*Benefit obtained*
Greenhouse gases	15% reduction in direct emissions of carbon dioxide	Reduction in 2015 in greenhouse gas emissions of up to 1,513,000 tons against 1,780,000 tons in 2005
Water withdrawal	50% reduction of water withdrawal	Reduction of drained water in 2015 to 340 gallons per $1,000 of revenue against data for 2005 of 680 gallons per $1,000 of revenue
Waste production	50% reduction of waste products	Reduction of waste production in 2015 of up to 2.8 tons per $1,000 of revenue against data for 2005 of 5.6 tons per $1,000 of revenue

and has been identified as a significant environmental aspect in the registration path for EMAS in Campoverde as discovered by the assessment of significant factors performed for the implementation of the environmental management system. In Abbot's case, one interesting, initial aspect concerns the ability of environmental management to combine the priorities of the group worldwide with the reality of the path to EMAS excellence undertaken on a local level by transforming the general objectives of the Head Office into specific targets conceived within the environmental management system and equipped with the necessary planning components by defining them precisely within the setting of environmental programmes envisaged by EMAS.

The environmental management system

The next step in the 'planning', or definition of policies, objectives and programmes is to create an organisational and management structure, consistent with the identification and assessment of the environmental aspects, the commitments outlined in the environmental policy, the objectives and goals set by the improvement programme as well as with the regulations which apply to the organisation identified during the initial environmental review.

The organisation needs to define, within its own general management system, a specific management, organisational and technical structure, the environmental management system (EMS), which is the 'heart' and driving force behind the organisation's activities and processes aimed at managing the environmental aspects that can effectively execute the improvement strategy in the environment. Once the organisational structure has been defined, it is necessary to understand the training needs for each figure within the environmental management system and define the operational methods to manage the significant environmental aspects properly as well as ensure the system functions correctly.

An analysis of the EMS definition in the ISO 14001 standard[10] makes it easy to understand why the design and implementation of an EMS do not always entail an organisational revolution, but merely a rationalisation and classification of some of the processes that are already in place before it is introduced into the organisation (take, for example, the operational methods for managing waste or the emission of pollutants into the atmosphere generated by the production process).

Without prejudicing the organisation's complete autonomy in adapting its structure to ISO 14001 or EMAS requirements in accordance with its own technical and management requirements, it appears necessary, however, to take a moment to consider some of the elements that need to be reviewed in the definition process of the system. In particular, an organisation must

- adapt its organisational layout by defining (and giving an adequate description of) the 'structure' of the environmental management system and the business functions involved by indicating the relevant tasks;
- involve personnel by finding suitable ways to raise awareness, train and increase competence in managing environmental aspects;

- define and implement effective work methods for the correct management of environmental aspects and a suitable response to emergencies;
- monitor its environmental performance, the functioning of the system and find effective ways to solve any discrepancies;
- define communication processes, both *top-down* and *bottom-up*, among the different company departments and towards interested external parties;
- document the system and record its performance.

Some guidelines for application are given for each of these activities.

Definition of roles and responsibilities within the field of environmental management

An essential element in guaranteeing the effectiveness of the environmental system is to establish a clearly defined organisational layout, consistent with the environmental problems that the organisation has to manage and adapted to the objectives it intends to pursue.

As previously indicated, every organisation defines the organisational layout of its own environmental management system in line with its characteristics and management approach. There are, however, a few general principles that the organisation can take into account in implementing its management system.

Firstly, responsibilities need to be allocated and roles defined for all the figures involved in some way in the management of environmental aspects or that create a direct or indirect environmental aspect through their activities.

In order to give all the functions and human resources working in the organisation, all the references and coordinates required to correctly carry out the activities required of them in the field of environmental management, a precise and detailed definition must be given for

- the roles of each figure in the organisation must cover in the environmental management;
- the responsibilities attributed to those figures concerning environmental aspects;
- the duties and tasks assigned for the environmental management system;
- the work methods each person must employ to complete these tasks and duties.

Particular attention must be placed by the organisation on the status quo between the responsibilities attributed and powers delegated to all the functions involved in the EMS in order to guarantee that they are able to fulfil their roles in the decisional and management processes concerning the environment.

The organisation may resort to different tools enabling it to specify the responsibilities, tasks and duties of environmental management for each function: organisational charts, responsibility grids, job descriptions, function charts, etc. These tools are valid support documents that may be useful to the organisation's operation.

The organisational chart is undoubtedly a very useful tool for providing a summary of the organisational layout of the company. It can take on different levels of detail: to represent the entire organisational structure in a single diagram or represent different areas of the company separately. It is advisable, however, to create a specific organisational chart that gives a clear picture of the roles and responsibilities within the organisation for environmental management with which to associate a job description detailing the tasks assigned to the different figures envisaged by this chart.

Secondly, the fundamental role taken on by top management to ensure the correct functioning of the management system must be emphasised. Management must, first and foremost, be able to express and convey its commitment to all personnel through the implementation of the principles defined in the environmental policy in order to strengthen awareness of the importance of these issues and the opportunity to act accordingly. In order to guarantee strong commitment, Management must appoint a representative designated to deal with all the activities related to environmental management with all the necessary powers and decisional responsibilities that it entails. The Management representative (or representatives), irrespective of other responsibilities in the organisation, must have a role, responsibilities and powers that are clearly defined in order to

- ensure that the environmental management system requirements are established, applied and maintained in compliance with the ISO 14001 standard or the EMAS Regulation;
- report on the performance of the system to the organisation's top management in relation to continual improvement.

In addition to a Management Representative, it is advisable to locate a person to be appointed as operational coordinator of the environmental management activities within the organisation. This figure, usually identified as Environment Manager or 'Management System Supervisor' must not, however, be conceived as a specialist function that alone has to guarantee all the activities linked to environmental management, on whom to 'offload' all the responsibilities and burdens entailed, but as a support and stimulus to Management (and therefore, to all the rest of the organisation's personnel) in environmental management.[11]

In some smaller organisations, for example, or those with less complex production processes, just one figure is identified within Management to cover these roles and act as Environmental Manager and Management Representative. In other larger organisations with more complex industrial setups, however, the Environmental Manager (who differs from the representative) is supported by a structure that is specifically dedicated to the operational management of the activities and processes causing direct and indirect environmental aspects. In these cases, a permanent work group can be formed of technicians and/or specialists who report functionally to the Environmental Manager and who deal with the operational management of the environmental aspects that he coordinates.

Box 3.9 Example of description of responsibilities for environmental management

---

Management Representative:

The Management Representative is responsible for the following:

- developing the Environmental Policy;
- identifying the Management System Supervisor;
- making means and resources available for the functioning of the Management System;
- approving the management system procedures;
- calling for and performing the Management Review;
- approving the improvement programmes and developing communication policies;
- verifying the planning of training activities.

The Environmental Management System Manager

The Environmental Management System Manager designs, carries out and maintains the management system through the following:

- the management (drafting, verification, archiving, etc.) of the documentation (procedures, operational instructions and registration documents) of all the management systems;
- the identification of the legal provisions and all the other requirements applicable to the company's activities and the periodic check on compliance with them;
- the identification and assessment of the environmental aspects associated with the company's activities and the processes and drafting of the initial environment review;
- the development of the report on the status of the management system which acts as the basis for conducting the Review Meeting;
- the update and development of the Improvement Programmes and the periodic check on their progress;
- collaboration in the planning and implementation of activities regarding training and instruction of personnel;
- the monitoring and measurement of environmental performances and activities affecting them;
- the planning and coordination of audits;
- the management of breaches of the management system.

(...)

Whenever the roles of Management Representative and the Environmental Manager coincide, it is both recommended and practical for this figure to be placed in the *Management team*. If the roles do not coincide, then the Environmental Manager (and the function that he coordinates at operational level) may report function-ally to the Representative's team. The location of the team within the organisation confers the prestige required to coordinate the management system, even when the upper levels of the management hierarchy are involved, in conjunction with the appropriate legitimisation and commitment required to motivate and involve all the personnel in carrying out the environmental policy.

In order to maintain the EMS, it is essential for the organisation to ensure the availability of adequate resources. This means that the organisation must guarantee the availability of the technical, financial and human resources needed to manage the environmental problems correctly and effectively.

Firstly, the organisation must have adequate knowledge, and technical and technological know-how to guarantee improvement in the environmental performances that it set itself as its main objective. Secondly, the economic and financial planning which is fundamental for normal business activity should be extended to include the budget aspects and requirements resulting from environmental management.

Lastly, it is essential that the human resources entrusted by the organisation with the implementation of the EMS and all the personnel involved in activities affecting the organisation's environmental performances are able to contribute to the achievement of the objectives that have been defined. Defining who does what (roles, responsibilities, duties and tasks), how to do it (work methods) and how to ensure that it can be done (training, information and communication) are essential aspects in guaranteeing an efficient and effective environmental management (see below).

Raising awareness, training and participation

An effective EMS can be achieved only if all the personnel, irrespective of the duties they perform and their function, are adequately informed and trained.

The most important objective concerning information and training activities is to raise awareness among personnel in order to actively involve them in the management of environmental aspects and the pursuit of the improvement objectives defined by the organisation, as well as guarantee that anyone carrying out tasks for the organisation itself or personally which may cause one or more of the significant environmental impacts identified by the organisation, has acquired the necessary skills.

The principles contained in the environmental policy, transferred to employees at all levels, must be experienced and implemented on a daily basis within their respective fields of operation.

This is a process of 'maturing' the organisation's culture, which requires time and gradual development since it affects individuals' behaviour. It is reasonable, therefore, as well as advisable to plan and carry out any training and activities for raising awareness in parallel with the activities around the implementation of the environmental management system.

The ISO 14001 standard and the EMAS Regulation place emphasis on the need to circulate environmental know-how among all the employees and, especially, on

- the importance of compliance with the environmental policy, procedures and environmental management system;

- the significant environmental impacts, whether real or potential, resulting from their activities and the benefits for the environment resulting from improvement in their individual performances;
- the roles and responsibilities for achieving compliance with the environmental policy, procedures and requirements of the environmental management system, including preparation for emergency situations and their ability to react to them;
- the potential consequences of deviations from the established procedures and operational instructions.

Employee training activities must be geared primarily towards promoting the process of change in behaviour through active ways of learning how to 'raise questions' and not just 'contribute to solving them'. Training must, therefore, respond to the employees' needs to learn in cognitive areas (*know-how*), operational areas (*know how to*) and behavioural areas (*know who you are*). For each of these areas tools must be provided, and educational and training activities implemented as well as checks on the learning and change. Different educational, information and practical training methods can be carried out based on learning requirements. These three areas of learning and personal development are complementary.

Education is essential for creating the organisational conditions needed to assimilate the culture of prevention and is aimed at transferring skills that are not tied to one specific field of activity (*know who you are*).

Information, to the extent that it may need to be reworked by those receiving it, is a simplified form of classroom training: it transfers contents which can be assimilated even if it does not develop advanced forms of interaction (*know-how*).

Practical training is a specific educational activity fulfilling the need to learn the correct practical use of tools (measuring devices, equipment) and procedures. During practical training, 'repetition and correction' sequences of the operational actions are developed. This kind of training is, therefore, an educational activity that pursues the learning objectives of *how to do*.

For each one of these areas, the company may develop appropriate tools to achieve its environmental objectives in terms of learning and change in employees' behaviour.

Box 3.10 Some environmental training tools

There are numerous different tools that can be used for training activities.

If the recipients are all employees, then theoretical classes can be used to transfer general knowledge and, where necessary, practical exercises to transmit specific skills.

A series of tools can be used for the classes, which encourage active participation by the attendees of classroom training. The use of *case studies* and so-called '*role playing*'

(*Continued*)

Box 3.10 Some environmental training tools (*Continued*)

are interesting examples. The latter entail simulations of real-life situations (such as the accidental spillage of a toxic, inflammable substance, for example) in which the participants are assigned a specific role (the person who caused the accident, the manager of the department involved, the Environmental Manager, the leader of the fire-fighting team, the first aid coordinator, the head of external relations, etc.) and are asked to adopt the correct behaviour in that situation. It is advisable to include an analysis of the management aspects connected to the event in the 'game' (in the example above, the occurrence of the accident may be an indication of a lack of management such as the incorrect application of the procedure regarding the handling of the spilled substance, etc.).

In order to ensure correct and effective management, it is crucial that employees are also trained with the group dynamics that occur in the organisation's activities in mind. It is quite common for situations involving environmental risks to be managed, not by a single person, but by a group of people who operate within the same area of activity: the same production department, the same vehicle, a common organisational function (maintenance or installation crews, etc.). In these cases, it is strongly recommended to implement an educational scheme aimed at groups of employees who operate in close quarters and consider them as a single recipient of the education activity (education of uniform groups).

For training employees with particular duties in certain skills, it may be worthwhile developing a job rotation programme, which will enable the specific skills of an individual to be enhanced by gaining a broader vision of the process through an analysis of the dynamics of the skill as a whole[12].

Lastly, the use of IT tools for self-learning could be considered. It is essential that in these circumstances the tools have a high-level of interaction, can hold the learner's attention for long periods of time and enable the individual to check his progress (through tests, for example).

Above all, in order to ensure that all personnel involved in activities that may cause a significant environmental impact reach an adequate level of awareness, the organisation may decide to train its employees on the following:

- the objectives and content of the ISO 14001 standard;
- the principles and commitments defined in the environmental policy;
- the organisation's environmental programme;
- the direct and indirect environmental aspects identified by the environmental review;
- the responsibilities, tasks and duties connected to environmental management (including emergency management);
- the technical and management characteristics of the EMS;
- the measurement criteria and systematic checks on environmental performances;
- the correct execution of procedures, operational instructions and methods of managing production processes and/or business activities;

- the possible repercussions on the environment caused by each individual's job and the consequences linked to the way in which each person perceives and performs his/her role within the organisation (for example, the negative consequences resulting from failure to apply procedures and the positive results from applying them correctly);
- the information channels and participatory tools for environmental management (e.g. how to report non-conformities) adopted by the organisation.

Environmental training should be based on the following principles:

- any training and update activity must involve the organisation at all levels, each one according to his/her own role in environment management (possibly differentiating the contents and its training methods according to the needs of the different figures involved: directors, workers, employees with special tasks, new recruits, etc.);
- this training activity (whether general or specific to each job, for example) must be performed systematically and continually, and be planned and documented;
- it must be aimed at creating skills accordingly, if necessary through appropriate qualification paths for particular functions (e.g. system manager, internal auditor).

In order to promote tangible participation and commitment to change behaviour, an employee training programme should not be limited to simply communicating knowledge, but to ensuring that mental and behavioural values and attitudes are assimilated. To achieve this, the organisation must firstly identify a figure (a person of function) within the organisational structure to entrust with the responsibility of planning and implementing any educational and training activities. The head of training, who may also be the Environmental Manager, should carry out and coordinate the following activities:

1 identify the training needs and requirements of personnel at all levels (making sure that the indications regarding these needs and requirements are understood through a systematic process);
2 locate the recipients for the educational/training activities;
3 choose the most suitable tools;
4 plan the educational and training activities (by defining a plan which includes the actions to be taken, the apportioning of responsibilities, the allocation of resources, the implementation timeframe and any methods for checking the results);
5 initiate the planned activities and check the results.

Figure 3.1 describes the diagram of training activities and Table 3.6 describes an example of a form of EMS that can be used to plan and record the training activities by the organisation.

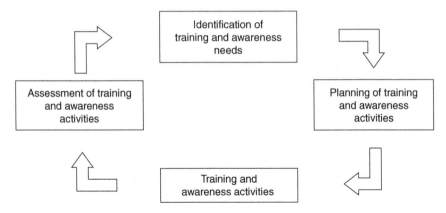

Figure 3.1 Diagram of training activities (source: Decision of European Commission 2013/131/EU).

Table 3.6 Example of a form for planning/recording of training activities

Compiled on:_____			
NO. OF EXPECTED PARTICIPANTS	**NO. OF ACTUAL PARTICIPANTS**	**TOPICS**	
	SIGNATURE		**Planned date:**_____ **Place:**_____ **Duration:**_____
	SIGNATURE		
	SIGNATURE		**Instructor:** ☐ internal ☐ external
	SIGNATURE		_____
	SIGNATURE		**Methods:** ☐ in office ☐ in the field
	SIGNATURE		☐ individual ☐ group ☐ incl./educ. ☐ w/o material
	SIGNATURE		Other_____
	SIGNATURE		**Manager:** _____

Once the most suitable training tools and methodologies for the organisation's needs have been identified, the classroom and practical training can start and be performed in the timeframe and by the methods indicated in the plan.

Having completed the training activities, it is advisable for the Environmental Manager to set up a system to verify the results of the training and education. The assessment of the effectiveness of the training activities gives an initial indication of performance improvement resulting from the development of staff skills and allows the validity of the tools used to be tested. The training activity can be deemed suitable if it has a positive influence not just on *knowledge*, but also – and above all – on *ability* and *behaviour*, which are key to improving performance. Checks on learning must be repeated continually on a long-term basis in order to ensure that training activities reflect changes in training needs. Checks on learning, for example, may be carried out by distributing and collecting questionnaires that incorporate direct observations by employees in the training sessions.

The classroom and practical training activities and checks on learning must be properly documented and recorded. The head of environmental training may be given the task of properly recording and filing all the documentation and creating personal records to track each employee's training path.

Defining and implementing the correct work methods for managing environmental aspects and emergency situations

One of the most important requirements of the environmental management system concerns the organisation's ability to define and apply work methods that guarantee the implementation of its principles for environmental policy in the field and the achievement of improvement objectives.

The organisation must, therefore, identify which operations and activities associated with the significant environmental activities are in line with its policy, objectives and goals. As a result, the environmental review results must be used as a starting point for identifying the operational activities with which the most significant aspects (direct and indirect) are associated and defining the most suitable actions and behaviour in order to ensure that these operations are carried out with minimum impact on the environment.

Once the 'mapping' of the relevant activities has been completed, the correct work methods need to be planned and executed, according to the specified conditions, by

- establishing and maintaining documented procedures to prevent situations in which the absence of such procedures could lead to discrepancies concerning the environmental policy, objectives and goals;
- defining the operational criteria in the procedures;
- establishing and updating the procedures regarding any significant environmental aspects (which can be identified) of the goods and services used by the organisation and by communicating any procedures and requirements to suppliers and contractors which directly concern them.

In order to guarantee that the procedures are effective and actually applied, it is important that their content is shared with the employees directly involved in the activities on which they focus by means of consultation tools for employees defined within the management system. Furthermore, the application of a new procedure and/or operational instruction[13] requires a trial period to test its effectiveness, level of acceptance by employees (through educational or training methods) and technical and organisational feasibility, so that any changes required can be identified and implemented in the meantime.

In general terms, it is advisable for the organisation to adopt

- operational procedures and instructions which define the methods of executing the activity both by the organisation's employees and by third parties acting on its behalf;
- procedures for procurement and tenders guaranteeing that suppliers and anyone acting on behalf of the organisation comply with its environmental policy;
- procedures for controlling the characteristics of the process;
- procedures for approving the processes and the maintenance of equipment used in carrying out the organisation's activities;
- procedures ensuring identification of and response to potential accidents and emergency situations and prevention and alleviation of the environmental impact which could occur as a result (the organisation must examine and review these procedures, when required, particularly after accidents or emergencies have occurred and set up periodic exercises, where possible);
- procedures aimed at communication and management of interaction with all external parties to the organisation from which an indirect environmental aspect could originate, that is management of the activity involving 'intermediate' parties.

To be more precise, some of the key procedures of operational control (often defined as 'operational instructions') may address the following areas:

- management of equipment, machines and plants;
- management of dangerous substances;
- maintenance, checks and controls (e.g. periodic checks on the efficiency of abatement plants of pollutants released into the atmosphere);
- design of new products and organisation of work;
- management of wastes;
- management of treatment operations for waste water;
- management of contractors;
- qualification of suppliers and contractors;
- management of other significant environmental aspects.

An important aspect, stressed by the ISO 14001 standard and the EMAS Regulation, concerns the management and supervision of suppliers and subcontractors. For example, the actions that an organisation can adopt to manage the relations with its contractors may concern

- the introduction of rules and performance requirements with regard to the environment in the terms of the contract (as well as conditions for the subcontract) and contractual clauses covering failure to respect them (e.g. exclusion of dangerous substances, use of specific machinery with high environmental performance; contractual clauses covering supervision of subcontractors' conduct);
- auditing of contractors and subcontractors to verify compliance with the environmental requirements in the service terms (e.g. an audit on maintenance services of thermal plants, documentary checks on declarations of standard compliance);
- setting up structures within the site and/or temporary structures within the organisation's worksites (and any relevant management procedures) to facilitate the correct behaviour of contractors and subcontractors operating there;
- the definition of internal procedures for the selection, qualification and control of contractors' and subcontractors' activities (e.g. procedures which envisage the presence of the organisation's personnel during the completion of technical services for direct surveillance);
- actions involving suppliers as a result of the outcome of audit, control and surveillance activities (e.g. corrective actions: notifications, official communications; punitive actions: decrease in qualification rating of the supplier, payment of penalties);
- the definition and sharing with contractors and subcontractors of the plans and procedures for the management of emergencies in the plants (code of conduct to adopt in the event of an emergency; training schemes for contractors and subcontractors on managing emergencies).

Table 3.7 shows an example of a questionnaire that can be used to collect data and information from suppliers in order to qualify them.

The procedures for operational control as defined by the organisation should be

- used for all activities requiring a clear definition of responsibilities, tasks and duties;
- properly distributed and made available where used;
- known by the personnel involved;
- periodically checked and updated;
- documented systematically.

There is a widespread conviction that writing down the work methods and detailing the operational criteria with which they will be applied in practice represents a useful tool for the organisation. A clear statement of the work methods enables the actions and operations carried out to complete a given activity of the organisation to be rationalised and standardised. The objective to pursue in clearly defining the EMS must be to achieve a level of documentation in proportion to the effective requirements of the organisation, above all

Table 3.7 Example of questionnaire for environmental qualification of suppliers

COMPANY'S NAME: _____

ACTIVITY PERFORMED: _____

DATE OF COMPLETION: _____

1. What are the most critical environmental aspects connected with your activities?

☐ Production of wastes	☐ Electromagnetic emissions
☐ Waste water	☐ Use of dangerous substances (chemical products, acid, oil, etc.)
☐ Air emissions and dust	☐ Water withdrawal and consumption

☐ Noise and vibrations	Presence of dangerous substances in your plant: ☐ PCB ☐ Asbestos ☐ CFC/HCFC
☐ Consumption of raw materials	☐ Other (_____)

2. Have you ever received complaints or been involved in disputes over the environment?

   ☐ YES
   ☐ NO

3. Do you possess environmental certification? (ISO 14001 / EMAS / Ecolabel)?

   ☐ YES
   ☐ NO

4. Do you carry out operational activities in the organisation's sites (for service providers)?

   ☐ YES
   ☐ NO

Notes:

_____

_____

_____

Company stamp and compiler's signature:

_____

with regard to its complexity and the problems in managing its environmental aspects. It should be borne in mind that

- an organisation can choose the level of formalisation that best suits it since there are no operational procedures or instructions bound by ties or requirements regarding the content, length and detail, other than that to reflect the true situation of the organisation and be suitable for it;
- in particular, a small organisation may legitimately rely on consolidated practices for some activities (implicitly or explicitly shared by all the operators even though not made official), which are, in fact, an integral part of the environmental management system.

The procedures should, therefore, be proportionate to the management requirements of the organisation. When deciding if the procedures are adequate, it is necessary to keep in mind the size and complexity of the operation, the nature of the environmental impacts associated with the operation itself and the competence of the operators charged with carrying it out. Simple diagrams, charts and grids can sometimes represent a simplified, but effective solution to provide the necessary guidelines.

It is possible that in setting up these procedures, significant connections to those already in place may emerge for quality systems or with regard to what is already being done in the organisation for occupational health and safety. Should this prove to be the case, it would be advisable for the organisation to exploit existing procedures in these different areas as far as possible and so avoid overlaps or inconsistencies.

Performance, monitoring and improvement measurement

The ISO 14001 standard and the EMAS Regulation indicate that the organisation should establish and maintain documented procedures for regularly monitoring and measuring the key characteristics of its activities and operations that may have a significant impact on the environment. This includes recording any information that enables the progress of the environmental performance, appropriate operational controls and compliance with the organisation's objectives and goals to be tracked.

The measurement and monitoring activity enables quantitative data to be collected which, when used as summary indicators, provide important information for assessing the organisation's performance, the effectiveness of the EMS and its ability to meet the environmental objectives.

We can, therefore, pinpoint two elements of the monitoring system, in addition to the audit, which the organisation must implement:

1 'management' monitoring
2 'performance' monitoring

The first category includes periodic monitoring of the implementation status of the objectives and the monitoring of the effectiveness of the controls, for example.

An organisation must, therefore, establish operational methods for effectively monitoring the level of achievement of the improvement objectives on a long-term basis. It is recommended that this verification take place every six months (and that at least one coincides with the Management Review), so that it can intervene in a timely manner should problems arise over meeting established deadlines.

Where important environmental parameters need to be monitored, the organisation must promptly define any monitoring activities and necessary controls to ensure optimum environmental performance (e.g. controls on the quality of waste water, emissions, waste management, periodic controls on equipment, plants, fire fighting systems, etc.) and check the implementation as well as the effectiveness (e.g. the use of certain fire fighting routines during periodic simulations).

The second category concerns the measurement of the organisation's environmental performance to verify that the goals set in the programme have been reached by using the performance indicators identified (for example, m^2 of asbestos roofing removed, hours of training performed per employee/function, etc.), and the operational criteria have been respected and accidents with environmental consequences have been monitored.

Box 3.11 provides details of possible indicators to use in measurement and monitoring activities.

The equipment and instruments used by the organisation for monitoring and surveillance must be calibrated and maintained, and the records showing fulfilment of this obligation must be kept according to the organisation's procedures.

If the measurement of the environmental parameters is carried out in an external laboratory (private or public, certified and/or accredited or otherwise), the organisation should guarantee certain requirements for work methods in the laboratory

Box 3.11 Useful indications for identifying monitoring indicators

On the one hand, management must measure and evaluate the performance of its environmental management system in order to keep track of and assess the adequacy of the actions carried out to manage the impacts of its activities on the environment, and on the other hand, it must respond to the need to communicate the terms of its commitment to external stakeholders and build on the results obtained in environmental protection. The measurement elements may cover

- what the environmental impacts are and how well the management system can handle them and improve continually;
- how effective the system is in reaching its set objectives or conforming to reference 'criteria' (e.g. ISO 14001, legal standards);
- what commitment has been made to improve the system and how 'widespread' it is;
- how well can the system react to 'unexpected events' in prevention management (NC, emergencies, etc.);
- how efficient the system is (costs and benefits);
- how it is perceived by (and what are the relations with) interested parties.

Some guidelines and suggestions are given below to help identify the best indicators to measure the functioning of the EMS:

1. **Performance guidelines**

   - measure environmental aspects (e.g. production of wastes);
   - select significant parameters (tonnes? hazard? critical areas?);
   - choose a reference term for the activity (production of tonnes? number of employees?);
   - make comparisons (past series, etc.).

2. **Results guidelines (or compliance)**

   - percentage of objectives reached;
   - indicators of 'distance' from reaching the objective;
   - indicators for 'progress status' of programmes;
   - indicators of 'distance' from reaching legal standards;
   - Non-Conformities (NC) detected;
   - ISO 14001 requirements fulfilled (or unfulfilled).

3. **Commitment guidelines**

   - Organisation (persons dedicated to environmental management, committees, how many times they meet, functions involved, etc.);
   - Training and personnel (persons trained, hours of training, learning assessment, 'spontaneous' NC, suggestions by personnel, etc.);
   - Auditing (number of areas subjected to auditing, trained and 'active' auditor, etc.);
   - Monitoring (how many process parameters are controlled, register updates, etc.);
   - Contractors and third parties (checks carried out, per cent of qualified suppliers, etc.).

4. **'Responsiveness' guidelines**

   - NC (how many resolved in set time?);
   - Emergencies and accidents (kept under control?);
   - Auditing (ratio of NC in the audit and 'spontaneous' NC, how many NC are repeated in different areas);
   - Personnel (how many suggestions received?);
   - External relations (how many complaints 'handled'?).

5. **Efficiency guidelines**

   - Investments;
   - Management costs (and cost savings);
   - Liabilities avoided (or could have been avoided);
   - Economic benefits and otherwise (e.g. motivation of personnel).

6. **Guidelines for consensus and participation by interested parties**

   - Number of complaints;
   - Number of violations encountered by controlling authorities;
   - Initiatives to disseminate certification;
   - Result of questionnaires on perception or satisfaction of environmental management among employees, customer satisfaction surveys containing references to the EMS, relations with institutions.

itself: if the test method is internal and not standard, then the laboratory must have it validated beforehand, namely it must have determined any errors (repeatable and reproducible) and, if applicable, recovered the analyte: the instrumentation used must be kept calibrated and any reference material indicated in the test report; this data must be made available if requested by the organisation. Furthermore, in accordance with the ISO/IEC 17025 standard, the minimum requirements for an environmental test report (which the organisation should verify) are the following:

- identification of the laboratory, report and person in charge;
- subject of the report and signature of the person in charge;
- parameters measured and for every parameter;
- the unit of measurement;
- the method used;
- the value measured, the threshold limit value permitted by current legislation;
- if applicable, the plan and sample method used;
- a score of conformity by the laboratory;
- any conclusions.

Monitoring of environmental performances is intended to monitor (and if necessary, confirm and scale down) the significance of the environmental aspects previously considered important for the organisation, identify any new ones and update the register accordingly.

It should be remembered that, for measurement and monitoring purposes, the identification and assessment of environmental aspects *must be repeated periodically* using the same objectives within the timeframe set by Management, namely every time significant changes in the environmental conditions inside or outside the organisation so require.

Whenever these changes are linked to modifications to 'parts' of the organisation, its production process or products and services, the environmental review will seek to identify the significant environmental aspects linked to these modifications and which may lead in part to this goal.

In accordance with the ISO 14001 standard and the EMAS Regulation, the organisation must define all responsibilities and powers for handling and analysing any NC required to decide actions to mitigate any impact caused and fix the activities, equipment or machines which caused the NC, thus avoiding any future repetition.

The term 'Non-Conformity' means the failure to fulfil one or more of the requirements defined by the organisation through its management system, in accordance with the reference standards (ISO 14001 or EMAS), legislation or applicable regulations which adversely affect its environmental performance. Take, for example, failure by workers to respect a given provision (e.g. incorrect management of a temporary waste deposit), failure to reach an objective, incorrect application of a legal provision (e.g. failure to carry out a periodic check on the quality of emissions) or the failure to meet a specific regulation requirement (e.g. not identifying external documentation).

The organisation should introduce a procedure that describes ways of identifying, documenting, assessing and handling NCs and managing corrective and preventive actions. The latter must be undertaken to avoid repetition of NCs due to systematic factors by eliminating the causes and introducing preventive measures.

Every corrective or preventive action undertaken to eliminate the cause of NCs, whether real or potential, must be commensurate with the importance of the problems and in proportion with the environmental impact detected. The organisation could, therefore, introduce a procedure that includes an operational procedure similar to the one below:

- notification of the NC through appropriate forms to be filled in by the workers in charge of carrying out the process;
- registration of the NC by the Environmental Manager;
- analysis of the causes of the NC, if necessary, in collaboration with other Functions within the organisation affected by the same NC;
- handling of the NC in accordance with the methods agreed with the Managers of the Functions involved and with the contribution of the person who issued the alert;
- introduction of the corrective or preventive action (if necessary) to avoid repetition of the NC;
- verification of the outcome of the action implemented (if negative, the procedure must be repeated).

It is important for the organisation to document any occurrence of NC situations (date it occurred, description, corrective or preventive action adopted, etc.) and keep records accordingly (see Table 3.8); such documentation is, in fact, an integral part of the information material that will be assessed during auditing.

The communication process in the environmental management system

Commitment to effective environmental management also calls for the implementation of adequate, systematic communication concerning environmental aspects.

The organisation's communication flow on the environment must be directed both internally and externally. The ISO 14001 standard and the EMAS Regulation stipulates that the organisation, with regard to its environmental aspects and the EMS, should

- guarantee internal communication at different levels and functions of the organisation;
- receive, document and respond to any request from interested external parties.

Table 3.8 Example of form for identification of Non Conformity

REPORT NO. _____		**DATED** _____	

Origin of non-conformity:

☐ From audit no. dated	☐ From notification dated	☐ From complaint dated	☐ Other _____

Type:	☐ NC	☐ Incident to prevent

Description

Analysis of causes and handling of non-conformity

Description of action:	☐ Corrective	☐ Preventive

Implementer of action	Completion of action implementation	Implementation check

Check on effectiveness of action

Date of check: _____	Signed by Env Manager _____

To encourage internal communication, the organisation should activate appropriate channels and tools and find ways to manage them, if necessary, by setting up a specific procedure. The information tools and channels must be efficient and effective (on the one hand, they must be able to ascertain if the requests originate from the 'right' people and, on the other hand, ensure appropriate and prompt information in reply).

The information and communication flow must be bidirectional, so that employees are not only informed, but are also able to make requests and suggestions, and to receive suitable, prompt *feedback*. In other words, they must be involved and participate in environmental management. In Box 3.12 some tools and methods are suggested to disseminate the organisation's environmental commitment and objectives.

Creating and maintaining relations and opportunities to interact externally on environmental topics, if organised correctly, can initiate a beneficial mechanism of information exchange with the organisation's stakeholders. External communication may occur through different channels and tools depending on the target audience:

- *institutional communications*, i.e. directed at institutions, ministries, public administration, bodies, control authorities, through meetings, participation in gatherings and programs to raise public awareness (take, for example, 'factory open days');
- *marketing communications* through participation in trade fairs/conventions, publications in specialised magazines, drafting of *corporate brochures or reports on the environment and sustainability*;
- *communications to suppliers* to present the organisation through the creation of descriptive leaflets or brochures describing the characteristics of the corporate management system and principles of environmental policy;
- *communications towards stakeholders* such as associations, the public, individuals through direct meetings, participation in public meetings, creation of informative brochures and leaflets, messages in the local press, etc.

Box 3.12 Tools for internal communication

The most common tools for internal communication are **display on notice boards** or **distribution with pay slips** in the form of a letter signed by the CEO in which the principles inspiring the organisation's intentions are stated.

Subsequently, it is advisable to present and describe the environmental objectives and action plan developed to achieve them through **information leaflets,** for example, which can **be distributed amongst employees and by organising meetings to present and discuss the programmes.**

Once the distribution of information has started, it must be constantly maintained by organising seminars for all personnel, for example, or selected groups of workers by sending **circulars** via internal post or by using **email** or the **Intranet,** both of which are becoming **increasingly widespread in organisations, as well as distributing pamphlets** or **other educational material,** etc.

The organisation, however, should not just concentrate on the outgoing flow of information (external communication), but should also be concerned with setting up tools and activating suitable channels to receive and manage all the *incoming* information required to run the EMS. The organisation can only reap the benefits derived from the strategic planning of external relations if it keeps the need to maintain 'bidirectional' communications and external relationships in mind.

To achieve this result, the organisation could create a complaints collection system in order to prevent any 'undesirable consequences' (claims, pressure on institutional figures, etc.) by activating a free-phone number, for example, producing questionnaires aimed as assessing environmental perception and the level of public consensus, or, more simply, by preparing information sheets with space for complaints, comments and suggestions to periodically send out to the community, mayor or representatives of environmental associations, etc.

It is recommended that any organisation intending to develop a communication strategy externally or from the outside creates (or identifies) a specific function with the mandate of collecting, analysing, processing, documenting and recording incoming information and creating, managing and making available any official outgoing information[14] to interested parties.

Documenting the system and recording its performance: maintaining and controlling documentation

The ISO 14001 standard and the EMAS Regulation indicate that the organisation should establish and maintain all information on paper or electronic systems needed to

- describe the fundamental elements of the management system and how they interact and provide directives on related documentation;
- record activities regarding environmental management and the control and monitoring of significant aspects.

The documentation envisaged should, therefore, include two types of documents:

1 so-called 'management' documents which describe EMS activities and act as a reference for carrying out these activities correctly;
2 'registration' documents aimed at showing that EMS activities have been carried out correctly and giving an updated picture of the environmental performance (as well as a 'reconstruction' with respect to the past).

It is important to emphasise that the objective to pursue in formalising the first type of documentation is to reach a level that is proportionate to the effective needs of the management system (and so that it can be assessed in the event of third party verification)[15]. The general criteria to adopt is that of pursuing the best correlation possible between the description given in the documentation and the effective operational reality of the organisation. Moreover, the level of formalisation and complexity of the management documents must be commensurate with the actual functional needs of the organisation and usage by workers. This means that it is strongly recommended that small organisations avoid creating documents or procedures which are excessively complex or elaborate, but are sufficient to describe the operational methods clearly and comprehensively (even just through simple action lists) which the different figures involved in the company must carry out to comply with the regulatory requirements. This approach is also increasingly appreciated and valued for third party certification in accordance with ISO 14001. It is clear that in these cases the verification of such requirements by third party certification bodies will mainly occur through observation of the workers' conduct whilst carrying out their jobs and the assessment of their knowledge of correct operational procedures through discussions or meetings with the workers themselves.

For the second type of documentation, it must be remembered that ISO 14001 and EMAS require the organisation to establish and maintain procedures for the identification, conservation and removal of environmental records. These registrations must include records of training and the results of audits and reviews. As mentioned, the organisation is given complete discretion and flexibility in defining its own documentation system provided that it guarantees effective management of the EMS.

A third category could be added: for 'operational' documents or Operational Instructions (OI), which describe in detail the operational methods for managing specific environmental aspects. These documents must, therefore, be created from actual requirements for managing the specific aspect. In order to ensure that these instructions are applied correctly and effectively, it is recommended that the workers themselves actively participate in the definition of the content. Furthermore, it is important to emphasise how the content of the operational instructions has to be proportionate as far as possible to the abilities and skills of the different users. To this end, the use of simplified language may be adopted by the company (even slang, if appropriate for the production area and local context) including figures, diagrams and various types of self-explanatory images that can be clearly understood and easily remembered. This solution is particularly suitable if there are foreign workers in the organisation who might otherwise be penalised by language barriers.

This said, there are some aspects of the system that the organisation needs be able to document. Table 3.9 shows, by way of example, some management and registration documents that can be adopted by the organisation when carrying out some system activities.

Table 3.9 System documents and registrations

Elements of the EMS management system	Examples of management documents	Examples of registration documents
4.1 General requirements		
4.2 Environmental policy	Environmental Policy	
4.3 Planning	P01 Identification and assessment of direct and indirect environmental aspects	
	IER Initial Environmental Review document	
	P02 Management of legal requirements	REG01 Register of legal requirements and relevant compliances
	Programme for environmental improvement	
4.4 Implementation and activities	P03 Management of human resources, information and training	REG02 Information, classroom training and practical training plan
	P04 Management of communications	REG03 Communications registration form
	P05 Management of system documentation	REG04 List of system documentation
	P06 Management and qualification of contractors	REG05 Questionnaire for environmental qualification of suppliers/contractors
	P07 Management of emergencies	
	OI01 Management of environmental documents for waste	
	OI02 Control of air emissions	REG06 Register of control results
	OI03 Control of transport of goods/waste in ADR	REG07 Checklist of controls on carriers
	OI04 Management of dangerous substances	REG08 Register of dangerous substances

Elements of the EMS management system	Examples of management documents	Examples of registration documents
4.5 Controls and corrective actions	P08 Management of performance and monitoring measurements	REG09 Register of monitoring and measurements
	P09 Analysis of NC and consequent CA and PA	REG10 Register of NC, CA and PA
	P10 Internal audit	REG11 Audit report
4.6 Management review	P10 Management review and planning	REG12 Review minutes

Whether talking about system documents or registration documents, they must both be monitored to ensure that

- they can be easily traced back to the activity, product or service they refer to;
- they are correctly filed, so they can be easily located and consulted, and are protected from damage, deterioration and loss.

In the case of system documents, in particular, the organisation should also make sure that

- they are examined and reviewed periodically, when necessary, and approved by authorised personnel;
- the latest editions of relevant documents are available in all places where essential operations for the effective (efficient) functioning of the environmental management system are performed;
- obsolete documents are promptly removed from all points of issue and use or otherwise assured against improper use;
- all obsolete documents retained for legal reasons and/or for documentation are suitably identified.

The environmental audit

One of the fundamental activities of the 'Check' phase of the Deming cycle is the internal audit.

After the implementation of the EMS, it will be necessary to assess its efficiency and effectiveness in guaranteeing the expected performance (both management and environmental) and its ability to achieve the objectives laid down in the environmental programme by applying what is defined in the system. Any organisation intending to implement an EMS must, therefore, plan adequate check and internal control methods, both for reaching an acceptable starting level for its environmental performance and for effectively monitoring the results produced by the 'virtuous circle' on continual improvement.

The operational scheme set out by ISO 14001 and the EMAS Regulation place considerable importance on the role of both the management and control of auditing activities of a correct and complete implementation of adequate environmental management systems. The standard defines the environmental audit as a 'systematic, documented, independent process designed to obtain audit results and evaluate them objectively to determine the extent to which the criteria for the environmental management system established by the organisation have been respected'; a similar definition is given in the EMAS III Regulation: 'a systematic, documented, periodic and objective evaluation of the environmental performance of an organisation, management system and processes designed to protect the environment'.

The organisation sets itself the objective of performing verification through the auditing activities:

1   of 'merit', of the environmental performance, of compliance by the EMS with the criteria and principles guiding it, the appropriateness of the system for the operational, technological, organisational and management characteristics of the organisation, as well as its ability to achieve the improvement objectives established;
2   of 'method', of the correct application of the EMS and compliance of effective conduct with the regulations established.

On the basis of the reference definitions, it is clear that the assessment must be; systematic, that is, based on definite, recognised methodologies; objective, that is, resulting from objective findings which can be verified and reproduced in a systematic auditing process; documented, that is, based on existing documents guaranteeing the traceability of the findings and consequently, the conclusions of the audit on which they are based and periodic, that is carried out with regularity planned to start and maintain a cycle of continual improvement over time.

Even though the main aim of this paragraph is to deal with the topic of internal audits, also known as 'first tier' audits, it must be pointed out that there are two additional types of audit: second tier audits carried out by anyone with an interest in the organisation (such as audits performed by customers on their suppliers, for example) and third tier audits performed independent external auditors (such as those for the release of environmental certification by accredited bodies, for example).

Many industrial companies now perform audits systematically (in the past they were mostly used by large, complex companies of Anglo-Saxon origin). The systematic auditing activity has been instrumental in creating a trend in performance improvement enabling all organisations to exploit the benefits resulting from this activity in terms of

•   the identification of possible areas for improvement and necessary corrective actions;
•   the availability of a complete, adequate, updated information source useful to Management in the decisional process and assessment of the organisation's performance;

- facilitating the comparison and distribution of information within the company;
- the increase in the level of involvement, participation and cultural growth of all personnel;
- the availability of a support tool for managing relations with external contacts (controlling authorities, shareholders, financers, insurers, customers, suppliers, public opinion, etc.).

It is becoming increasingly more common to see audits being implemented in which the basis for the audit (that is, the reference against which the findings are compared) is not just the reference standard, but other requirements as well, such as environmental laws that apply to the organisation. In these instances, the audit becomes a true check on legislation or a 'regulatory audit'. The practice of conducting periodic regulatory audits in conjunction with or closely linked to audits on the EMS operation is becoming increasingly widespread. This trend has been reinforced, above all, by the publication in 2004 of a new version of ISO 14001 introducing a new paragraph (4.5.2 Evaluation of legal compliance) that requires the organisation to carry out and record periodic checks of compliance with legal requirements. From the onset, the trend among organisations has been to respond to this requirement by conducting periodic regulatory audits, along with other methods and tools, which sometimes coincide with the internal audit on EMS. This interpretation was reiterated by the ISO 14004 standard published in 2005, which provides a guide to interpreting the ISO 14001 standard. This standard indicates auditing as a method for conducting periodic evaluations of legal compliance. This aspect was also confirmed by the recent issue of Regulation 1221/2009 (EMAS III), which, unlike the previous version of the Regulation, states that the internal audit is aimed at 'the assessment of the management systems in place and determining conformity with the organisation's policy and programme which must include compliance with applicable legal requirements relating to the environment' (see also para. 2.6).

In addition to the indications given in the ISO 14001 standard and EMAS Regulation, the main reference standard for conducting environmental audits is ISO 19011, published specifically for this reason and entitled 'Guidelines for quality and/or environmental management systems auditing'. The standard has three main chapters that deal with the methods for planning audits, conducting auditing activities and indicate the requirements of competence of the auditors.

If it is true that the fundamental objective of implementing an EMS is the planned management of environment aspects linked to an activity, then the programming of an audit that is correctly set out and developed is an essential element in fulfilling this objective.

From a management point of view, the ISO 14001 standard and EMAS require that the organisation establishes and maintains procedures for periodically conducting audits whilst taking into account the results of previous audits and the environmental importance of the activity to be audited.

Box 3.13 Auditor principles according to the ISO 19011 standard

Ethical conduct: is the basis of the competences of anyone conducting an audit characterised by such qualities as trust, integrity, confidentiality and discretion.

Impartial presentation: obligation to report the audit results faithfully and accurately.

Adequate Professionalism: to ensure that the audit is effective and provides indications enabling the organisation to pursue continual improvements in its management system, the auditors must possess the necessary professional competences.

Independence: the audit must be conducted by independent parties, that is, must demonstrate that the auditors are independent of the activities they audit and exempt of conflict of interest.

Evidence based approach: the audit results are based on objective and verifiable findings. They can be gathered through document checks, interviews and observations.

These procedures should, in particular, define the ways to

- train internal auditors and/or select external auditors;
- set up a team of auditors;
- plan, program and conduct the audit;
- report and use the results for the EMS review by Management.

Training internal auditors or selecting external auditors is an important step in guaranteeing the successful outcome of the audit: the reliability of the process and the authenticity of its results are, in fact, linked on the one hand, to the independence and impartiality of the auditors' judgment and, on the other, to their competence. In general, large companies with multiple sites are successful in guaranteeing teams of competent, independent auditors by involving various contacts of the environmental management system in auditing activities at the other sites where they are not involved in operations. This activity, which is also known as a 'peer audit', ensures a certain level independence by the auditing party who is also competent through his/her role as an EMS reference at another own site. The 'peer audit' can be applied to two or more sites belonging to different organisations. This type of audit is definitely less widespread than the first because many companies are not confident in being audited by parties belonging to other companies even if from different sectors.

Auditing activities must also be adequately prepared and correctly planned by identifying the objectives and the scope of each audit (or audit cycle).

Box 3.14 Competencies for auditors according to the ISO 19011 standard

---

Personal characteristics

- respectful of ethical principles: just, truthful, sincere, honest and reserved;
- open-minded: willing to consider alternative ideas and points of view;
- diplomatic: tactful in approach to others;
- keen spirit of observation: actively conscious of activities and surrounding environment;
- discerning: insightful of situations and capable of understanding them;
- versatile: ready to adapt to different situations;
- tenacious: perseverant, concentrated on the objectives to be achieved;
- resolute: capable of reaching conclusions quickly based on logical analyses and thinking;
- self-assured: capable of acting and behaving independently whilst interacting effectively with others.

Principles, procedures, auditing techniques

- apply the principles, procedures and auditing techniques;
- effectively plan and organise the work;
- start the audits within the agreed timeframe;
- give priority to and concentrate on significant aspects;
- collect information through effective interviews, by listening and observing, reviewing documents, records and data;
- understand the appropriateness and the consequences of using sampling techniques in the audit;
- check the accuracy of the information collected;
- confirm the sufficient quantity and appropriateness of the audit findings to support the results and conclusions of the audit.

Management system and reference documents

- application of management systems to different organisations;
- interaction between elements of the management system;
- regulations regarding management systems for quality or environmental management, applicable procedures or other documents relating to management systems used as auditing criteria;
- recognition of differences and priorities in reference documents;
- application of reference documents to different auditing situations.

Organisational situations and applicable laws

- size, structure, functions and interrelations of the organisation;
- general corporate processes and relative terminology;
- local, regional and national rules, laws and regulations;
- contracts and agreements;
- international treaties and conventions.

(Continued)

Box 3.14 Competencies for auditors according to the ISO 19011 standard (*Continued*)

Science and environmental technology

- impact of human activities on the environment;
- interaction of ecosystems;
- environmental elements (e.g. air, water, soil);
- management of natural resources (e.g. fossil fuels, water, flora and fauna).

Environmental and technical aspects of current operations

- sector-related terminology;
- environmental aspects and impacts;
- methods of assessing the significance of environmental aspects;
- critical characteristics of operational processes, products and services.

The ISO 14001 standard does not have any fixed rules regarding the frequency with which audits should be conducted. In contrast, the EMAS Regulation indicates that an audit cycle shall be completed at intervals of three years or every four if the derogation provided for in Art. 7 of the Regulation is applied to small organisations with less significant environmental impacts.

The audit cycle consists of a period in which all the areas/activities/elements of an organisation are subjected to an audit. As a result, programming becomes very important in responding to the requirement of establishing an audit cycle to ensure the verification of all areas involved in the EMS in the reference period.

In some cases, for example in the 'start-up' phase of management systems, it could be worthwhile planning more frequent audits, or at least with intervals of less than a year, to demonstrate the Management's commitment to workers and guarantee greater control designed to get the system 'up to speed' more rapidly. Whatever the case, the organisation, in fixing the schedule for the audits best adapted to its characteristics, must consider the following:

- the nature, size and complexity of the activities;
- the significance of the environmental impacts associated;
- the importance and urgency of the problems identified in previous audits;
- the previous environmental problems.

In organisations with more complex organisational, management and/or operational setups, the auditing activities may be structured in a series of specific audits which are developed in a set timeframe and set out in relation to the goals of the audit. In that case, once the necessary assessment has been carried out on the basis of the above-mentioned elements, the organisation may decide to carry out more frequent checks on some areas/activities/elements identified as being particularly problematic.

In short, before conducting the audit, the organisation must have

- trained the internal auditors or selected external auditors;
- planned the intervals of the audit cycle;
- defined the audit team, which may call on support from the organisation itself, any working tools required (worksheets, checklists, protocols, questionnaires, etc.).

At this point, the actual planning and execution phase can start of one or more audits depending on the programme (Table 3.10).

a. Planning and understanding the management systems

This is the preliminary phase of the onsite work by the audit team and includes the definition of the work calendar, the collection and analysis of information about the relevant activity and the necessary documentation (e.g. policy and programme, management procedures, applicable legislation, general documentation – organisational charts, process sheets, layout) with particular reference to the results of previous audits. The Audit Plan (Table 3.11) is set out in this phase and proves to be an essential tool of the successful outcome of the activity since it enables schedules and resources to be well organised. The key elements of the plan are: the objectives of the audit, the date and place where the audit will be conducted, details of the activities and their duration, the personnel from the organisation involved and the documents to make available during the audit.

Every audit includes an opening meeting with the organisation's Management and, if necessary, with the heads of any processes and activities undergoing the audit, in order to confirm the audit plan, provide a short summary of how the activities will be carried out and confirm the communications channels. If the auditors are employees of the organisation or the organisation is limited in size, then the meeting will be less formal. If the auditors involved are employees of external companies recruited especially for the audit, then the conditions of confidentiality usually in force in the company concerning any information acquired during the audit should be confirmed in the meeting along with confirmation of any individual apparatus required by the auditors for the inspection of the production areas.

b. Collection and assessment of findings

The objective in this phase, which is at the heart of the audit, is to acquire all the elements necessary for the collection of evidence needed to evaluate the EMS.

The findings of the audit form the basis of the documents with which the team of auditors establish the conformity of the existing activities with the applicable

Table 3.10 Examples of an audit programme

Audit programme

Year: _____

Subject of audit	Reason for audit	Audit team	Personnel involved	Jan.	Feb.	Mar.	Apr.	May	Jun.	Jul.	Aug.	Sep.	Oct.	Nov.	Dec.
Paragraphs 4.2, 4.3.1	Verification of the methods for identifying and assessing the environmental aspects and content and distribution of the Environmental Policy	Auditor A	EMSM		X										
Paragraphs 4.3.2 and 4.5.2 of the ISO 14001 standard	Completeness of the identification of legal requirements and search for evidence of application thereof, execution of periodic verification by the organisation	Auditor A Auditor B	EMSM Management				X								
Paragraphs 4.4.6 and 4.5.1	Verification of production department, warehouse and purification plant. Verification of monitoring and measurement activities	Auditor B	EMSM Head of Production			X						X			
Etc.	Etc.														

Date _____   Signature Department Manager _____

Table 3.11 Example of Audit Plan

AUDIT PLAN

Organisation:

Objective of Audit:

Date of Audit:

Members of Audit Team   Team Leader:

                                                             Auditor:

Agenda:

1° Meeting (1/2 day)

Time	Activity	Corporate functions to be involved
9:00 – 9.30	Opening meeting	EMSM[1] – Head of Prod., Management
9:30 – 10:30	Inspection of production plant and area outside the works	EMSM – Head of Prod.
10:30 – 11:45	Analysis of documentation: Initial Environmental Analysis, User Guide	EMSM
11:45 – 13:00	Analysis of documentation and compliance with management of emergencies, firefighting	EMSM, Firefighting team leader, Maintenance Manager
13:00	*Team briefing*	

2° Meeting (1/2 day)

Time	Activity	Corporate functions to be involved
9:00 – 9:15	Opening meeting	EMSM – Head of Prod.
9:15 – 10:00	Choosing and managing suppliers and contractors	EMSM – Head of Procurement
10:00 – 11:00	Objectives for monitoring, measurement and improvement	EMSM – Management Representative
11:00 – 12:00	Management of regulatory conformity and spot checks of applicable compliance	EMSM – Head of Prod.
12:00 – 12:40	Analysis of findings emerging from audit and drafting of report	
12:40 – 13:00	Closing meeting and submission of report	Project Mgr – HSE Mgr/HSE Ofc.

Please make a copy of the Initial Analysis, User Guide, Environmental Programme and all the Environmental Management System procedures available during the audit.

[1] Environmental Management System Manager

laws, regulations, corporate procedures and any management standards, as well as the degree of fulfilment of the objectives fixed in the policy and improvement programme.

Three main methods of voluntary evidence can be identified for the collection of evidence: interviews with personnel, document analysis and direct observations on-site (inspections of working conditions and of the plants).

When conducting the audit, the audit team can make use of a checklist as an auxiliary tool to verify management and regulatory aspects of the system that has been implemented.

Once the evidence has been collected, it is organised and analysed by the audit group who form an opinion and evaluation on the performance of the environmental management. The findings are also analysed with regard to the programme to decide whether the observations made can be used to define a work programme aimed at improving the performance of the EMS.

c. Preparation of report and follow up

The audit results are summarised in a final report (Table 3.12) with an evaluation of the efficiency and effectiveness of the management. The report is presented to the Management of the organisation, usually during the Review.

Any adjustment/improvement plans suggested by the team of auditors on the basis of the audit results may be resolved immediately, depending on the type and degree of urgency, through suitable corrective actions carried out in accordance with the organisation's normal procedures or be merged with any actions planned for the subsequent period.

The phase in which the findings are taken on board and resolved is called the 'follow up'. This phase is extremely important since it allows the system to bring about improvements with regard to the indications laid out by the auditor during the audit.

Lastly, it must be emphasised that the operational or management aspects implemented or modified subsequent to the audit will become elements to check during the next audit.

Management review

As seen, the definition of responsibilities is a fundamental step in structuring an environmental management system. In particular, the figures that form top management have important strategic and decisional responsibilities. These figures must firstly define the policy principles, fix the objectives and decide the programmes by guaranteeing adequate resources. In addition to this, Management must also supervise the handling and correct functioning of the EMS through the promotion, supervision, check and review of the objectives, programmes and system itself.

Table 3.12 Example of structure of audit report

Year: _____		Audit n°:_____		
Carried out on: _____		Type of audit: ☐ ordinary ☐ extraordinary		
Head of Audit Team:				
Members of Audit Team:				
Areas/functions to be audited:				
Area	**Area Supervisor**	**Other figures involved**	**Date**	**Time**
Objective of audit:				
Description of process and audit criteria:				
Findings and NC/observations found:				
Audit Conclusions:				

In light of this, the organisation's Management must, first and foremost, review the management system periodically in order to evaluate the adequacy and efficiency of initiating the policy and programmes.

In line with continual improvement, the Review is essentially aimed at identifying which areas of the management system present margins for improvement. Once the critical points have been narrowed down, the organisation's

Management can redefine the objectives and/or the components of the EMS in order to pursue any opportunities identified for improvement.

The Management review must be conducted without limitations and be extended to all environmental management activities. Particular attention should be paid to the review of the policy, objectives and programmes.

The review process allows Management to ensure, first and foremost, that the commitments expressed in the policy are up-to-date with regard to any changes in the assessment of the environmental aspects. Secondly, an assessment can be carried out to determine if the performance improvement objectives have been fulfilled, the objectives are consistent with the commitments undertaken and the means and time limits meet actual requirements.

The review will identify any needs or opportunities for updates and improvement of the policy, objectives, programmes and the system. These requirements may derive from:

1   evidence of non-conformities of

    a   performances with regard to specific objectives quantified in the programme;

    b   compliance with corresponding laws or regulations;

    c   the EMS for the improvement objectives (adequacy and effectiveness of the organisational and management structure; correctness of methods to execute the activities; effectiveness of raising awareness; information and training, etc.).

2   internal changes in the organisation: take, for example, the introduction of a new production technology which modifies environmental aspects;

Box 3.15 Management review: input and output elements

Input elements:

- results of internal audit and assessment of compliance
- communications from interested third parties including complaints
- environmental performance of the organisation
- degree of achievement of objectives and goals
- status of corrective and preventive actions
- status of progress of actions indicated in previous reviews
- change in surrounding situation including changes in applicable laws
- recommendations for improvement

Output elements:

- amendments to the Environmental Policy
- amendments to the environmental programmes, objectives, targets
- amendments to other elements of the EMS

the achievement of an objective which changes the priority of actions; the start-up of a project for a new activity, product or service; a change in the organisational structure of the organisation, etc.

3   changes due to external factors: for example, the introduction of a new regulatory law on the environment; the availability of new production technology on the market enabling reduction of a specific impact; requests of various kinds from stakeholders, etc.

Companies often need better support tools providing brief input guidelines for the Review. In many cases EMS analysis and assessment methods are developed by collecting concise guidelines, which can help the Environmental Manager and Management when making decisions during the Review. The 'MaRe' (*Management Review*) software is an example of an operational tool developed as an experiment by the IEFE Bocconi (the Italian Institute of Political Economics of Energy and the Environment) in the framework of the Observatory for Environmental Management Systems with the aim of supporting the System Manager in collecting and assessing data and indicators through which to report, in the Review, on the effective functioning of the System, its continual adaptation to changing internal conditions and lastly, the response to external requests and solicitations.[16]

The review is carried out in periodic interfunctional meetings managed by the top function in the organisation (e.g. the Managing Director). It is worthwhile defining the intervals and methods for conducting the meeting in advance and describing them in an appropriate procedure.

With regard to the frequency of the meetings, they generally need to take place at least once a year and be convened whenever abnormal or emergency situations occur which call for important decisions and immediate action. The review should also follow the completion of EMS audit: the audit results and reports can, in fact, form an important information base – detailed, objective and documented – to be used by the organisation's management to assess whether the measures adopted are adequate and comprehensive, and whether the overall EMS is able to fulfil the policy and programmes defined.

With regard to the method of conducting the Review, the person in charge should fix the date of the meeting after consulting top management and summon the participants in writing in good time. In addition to Management (or its representative) and the Management System Manager, the key figures involved in environmental management, the mid to top level managers of the organisation with specific tasks concerning the environment (e.g. Head of Production) and any employee representatives should also attend the meeting.

There are many ways with which the organisation can implement the decisions taken during the meeting. The review often offers the opportunity to define new objectives and new improvement programmes which are agreed upon and planned during the meeting and subsequently defined in detail. Once the previous 'management cycle' have been concluded with the audit (and the results obtained have been reviewed), a new management cycle can be initiated during the management review by planning future activities.

Internal audit: the case of WEPA-Lucca

The WEPA Group started in Germany in 1948 as a family-run business. Today, under the guidance of the same family, it has become one of the biggest European manufacturers of tissue paper products such as toilet paper, kitchen rolls, tissues, napkins, etc. The WEPA Group is an organisation with over 2,500 employees and revenue that exceeds 950 million Euros, which has tripled in the last five years.

The Group has an annual production capacity of about 615,000 tonnes of paper thanks to 17 continuous machines in different European plants. It has five factories in Germany, which cover 60 per cent of production, 25 per cent of which is in Italy, whilst the remaining production is covered by three factories in France, Spain and Poland. Figure 3.2 describes the distribution of WEPA factories in Europe. About 60 per cent of revenue is generated by production of toilet paper, which, added to revenue for kitchen rolls, reaches 80 per cent.

The paper is produced by using both virgin fibre and recycled paper. The production process covers all the phases of production of tissue paper from the production of paper reels from virgin fibre to transformation into the finished product through the final phase of processing known as 'converting'. The main raw material (cellulose) is purchased from suppliers. WEPA mainly works for large distribution chains and markets its products through noted distributors such as Coop, Esselunga, Lidl, Auchan, Carrefour and other large distribution brands, better known abroad, such as E.Leclerc, Schlecker, Edeka.

WEPA-Lucca is a division of the group which heads five factories in the paper manufacturing area in the Province of Lucca, the most important industrial area in Europe for production capacity. In the area around Lucca, there are three plants for production (Porcari, Pian della Rocca, Fabbriche di Vallico) and two for 'converting', in which reels of paper are transformed into the finished product (Carraia, Salanetti). These plants and another located in Cassino form WEPA Italia, which has 639 employees. The production plants in the Lucca area have been certified to the ISO 14001 standard since 2005 whilst the two 'converting' plants are aiming for certification by 2010.

The path for certification to ISO 14001 of the production plants was started in 2002 with participation in a EU-funded project called PIONEER[17], jointly financed by the European Commission. The project was headed by the Province of Lucca with other partners, such as the Industrial Association of Lucca, the Chamber of Commerce of Lucca and other scientific partners such as the Scuola Superiore Sant'Anna in Pisa and the IEFE Institute of the Bocconi University. PIONEER's aim was to carry out an experiment by applying the EMAS regulation over an area taking in the entire paper manufacturing district around Lucca and set out a methodology for this sector which would go on to be a precursor of initiatives and actions earning international and national recognition, such as article 37 of the EMAS III Regulation entitled 'cluster approach' or the Position of the Italian EMAS Committee for Cluster Environment. The project enabled about 20 businesses connected to the paper manufacturing sector to achieve EMAS

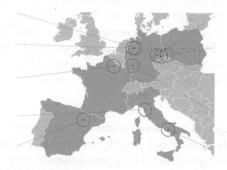

Figure 3.2 Distribution of WEPA factories in Europe (source: Authors' own).

registration or certification to ISO 14001 and the district to obtain the EMAS Committee award of the Cluster Certificate.

The WEPA group has already indicated auditing in its Group Policy as one of the objectives to pursue. The objectives of the Policy include the following:

- power of innovation
- leadership in costs
- orientation to a European dimension & development
- Customer Service Excellence
- concentration on marketing brands
- auditing and eco-labels
- respect for corporate values and culture
- long-term corporate orientation

Auditing for the group, therefore, is indicated not just as a tool, but also as a real 'strategic objective' for improving the whole organisation. By following in the footsteps of the parent company, the auditing activity carried out in the three certified plants around Lucca has taken on more interesting organisational aspects.

Firstly, it should be noted that the audit team is made up entirely of internal personnel. Each of the three plants (Porcari, Pian della Rocca, Fabbriche di Vallico) has its own Environmental Management System Manager (EMSM) who, in some cases, also covers the role of Health and Safety Services Manager (HSSM) and Head of Production. Furthermore, from an organisational point of view, there is also an 'HSE Coordinator' who oversees and coordinates the EMS activities of the three plants and promotes integration of the System in the two 'converting' plants undergoing certification. WEPA Lucca has decided to set up an audit group in which all the EMSMs take part. The personnel involved have participated in a course for internal auditors whilst their knowledge of the production cycle and the inherent environmental aspects is guaranteed through their work experience. As mentioned in the previous paragraph, there is a risk that, by using internal resources to conduct the audit, the audit team may not be sufficiently independent with regard to the focus of the audit.

This aspect has been resolved by creating a 'peer audit' between the different certified plants. In particular, the annual audit of each plant is conducted by the EMSM of another plant who is not involved in the running of the plant undergoing the audit (Figure 3.3). The system offers a series of advantages, for example:

- the EMS managers of the various plants can contribute to the running of the plants in which they are not directly involved by picking up on any nonconformities during the audit or suggesting ways to improve management of certain environmental aspects;
- the audit is an opportunity to see how colleagues in similar roles from other plants in the Group deal with certain problems which the auditor has to deal with on a daily basis in the plant where he acts as System Manager;
- on the assumption that the problems to be solved are similar, a system of 'peer audits' will enable reciprocal growth and improvement in the management of all three plants;
- the organisation is able to maintain the EMS without calling on external consultants;
- a strong team is consolidated over time, which conducts audits that will be the foundation for extending the approach to other plants.

A current evolution is proving particularly interesting in relation to this final point. Since the experience of peer auditing has proved to be so positive, the mechanism is now being gradually extended. In addition to the three plants with certification to ISO 14001, WEPA Lucca is introducing other potential EMSMs into the peer auditing system from the two converting plants that will obtain certification by 2016. A similar evolution will occur soon with the involvement of the EMSM from the Cassino plant (already certified to ISO 14001).

The peer audit system incorporated in WEPA Lucca involves three EMSMs from plants that are, however, as previously mentioned, coordinated and supervised by the HSE Coordinator (Health, Safety and Environment) of WEPA Italia. This figure does not actually conduct the audits, but ensures that the activity is carried out with a uniform approach including a complete check on all the requirements undergoing the audit and therefore, that all the activities lead to the fulfilment of the objectives established.

The HSE Coordinator performs this function in the audit by providing the same tools (such as the checklist shown in Table 3.13), for example, to the auditors, or by coordinating the drafting of the audit reports and the layout of the findings so that they can be compared to each other.

The audit results and the subsequent follow-up phase are managed jointly in WEPA Lucca. All the auditors involved in the activity have the opportunity to

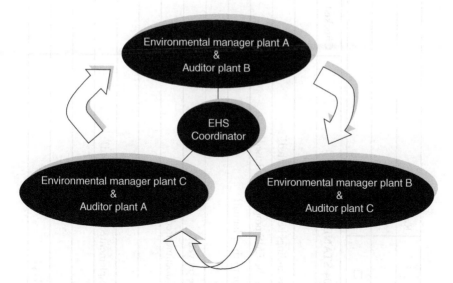

Figure 3.3 Organisation of peer audits in the plants for WEPA Lucca with ISO 14001
certification (source: Authors' own).

discuss the findings from all the plants and look for common solutions. This joint
follow-up activity enables the auditors who have been involved in peer audits for
several years to build on their ability by discussing the findings by other auditors,
and the auditors who are just starting out in the group (e.g. the future EMSMs
from the converting plants undergoing certification) to understand the way the
audits are conducted and closed.

The good practice of peer auditing, which started in the three certified
plants in the paper industry district of Lucca, has been rapidly extended not
only to all the Italian plants, but has also been adopted as a model by the
Group. Through coordination by its central headquarters, the WEPA Group
is setting up an audit team on health, safety and the environment for the
entire Group. The future audit team formed by employees with different skills
selected from all the plants will be given the objective of conducting audits in
plants Europe-wide.

The case discussed in this paragraph demonstrates how auditing can be organised by using internal resources within an organisation to guarantee compliance
with the requirements stipulated in the reference standards. The results achieved
are considered by WEPA Lucca to be an improvement on the previous methods
used for conducting audits. In particular, not only the number of non-conformities,
but also the planning and management methods of the corrective actions set out
jointly in the follow-up phase have meant an increase in the effectiveness of the
Environmental Management System.

Table 3.13 Audit checklist example

Organisation:		Report No.:
Site:		Date:
Type of audit: Preliminary: ☐ Certification: ☐ Periodical: ☐ Complete review: ☐		Auditor:

N°	Par	CHECKLIST – UNI EN ISO 14001: 2004 STANDARD	Checked
		PREVIOUS AUDIT	
		Have the corrective actions established in connection with the previous findings been implemented?	
		Is the RINA certification logo used in accordance with the Rules and is the EMS properly publicised?	
		Have modifications been made to the EMS documentation, in particular to the Manual?	
		Has the system been implemented for at least three months?	
		Is the internal audit system fully operational and can its effectiveness be proved?	
		Has at least one management review of the system been performed and documented?	
	4	**Environmental Management System Requirements**	
	4.1	**General requirements**	
		Is the Environmental Management System established, documented, implemented and maintained?	
		Has the organisation defined and documented the scope of its EMS?	
	4.2	**Environmental policy**	
		Has the Top Management defined the organisation's environmental policy?	

		Has the Top Management ensured that the organisation's environmental policy within the defined scope of its EMS
	a)	is appropriate to the nature, scale and environmental impacts of the organisation's activities, products and services?
	b)	includes a commitment to continual improvement and prevention of pollution?
	c)	includes a commitment to comply with applicable legal requirements and with other requirements to which the organisation subscribes which relate to its environmental aspects?
	d)	provides the framework for setting and reviewing environmental objectives and targets?
	e)	is documented, implemented and maintained?
	f)	is communicated to all persons working for or on behalf of the organisation?
	g)	is available to the public?
4.3		**Planning**
4.3.1		**Environmental aspects**
		Is a procedure(s) established, implemented and maintained to
	a)	identify the environmental aspects of its activities, products and services, within the defined scope of the EMS,
	–	which it can control? (direct aspects)
	–	which it can influence? (indirect aspects)
		In identifying these aspects, does the organisation take into account new or planned developments or new or modified activities, products and services?
	b)	determine those aspects that have or can have significant impact(s) on the environment (significant environmental aspects)?

(Continued)

Table 3.13 Audit checklist example (*Continued*)

N°	Par	CHECKLIST – UNI EN ISO 14001: 2004 STANDARD	Checked
		Is the above information documented and kept up to date?	
		Does the organisation ensure that the significant environmental aspects are taken into account in establishing, implementing and maintaining its EMS?	
	4.3.2	**Legal and other requirements**	
		Is a procedure(s) established, implemented and maintained to	
		a) identify and have access to the applicable legal requirements and other requirements to which the organisation subscribes related to its environmental aspects?	
		b) determine how these requirements apply to the organisation's environmental aspects?	
		Does the organisation ensure that these applicable legal requirements and other requirements to which it subscribes are taken into account in establishing, implementing and maintaining its EMS?	
	4.3.3	**Objectives, targets and programme(s)**	
		Are documented environmental objectives and targets established, implemented and maintained for each pertinent function and level?	
		Are the objectives and targets, where practicable, measurable?	

Distinguishing features of the EMAS path with regard to organisation requirements

The last version of EMAS Regulation considers EMAS registration to be the end of the journey along the path towards excellence in environmental management in contrast to other types of certification (including ISO 14001), which are seen more as intermediate steps. There are many new components contributing to this vision.

First and foremost, although EMAS III continues to be founded on the environmental management system introduced by the ISO 14001 standard, it also integrates a series of distinguishing features into it starting with the reinforced compliance mechanism for the environmental regulation.

Indeed, the focus on this aspect emerges quite emphatically from numerous points of the new Regulation. Article 2, for example, defines 'compliance with regulatory obligations' for the first time as full implementation of the requirements that apply to the organisation seeking registration, including permit conditions. Moreover, it is made clear that the initial environmental review (explicitly mentioned in the text as compulsory for EMAS registration) must provide not only a comprehensive picture of the obligations of applicable laws, but also describe what the organisation does to ensure conformity. The Regulation requires, in fact, that organisations present material or documentary evidence that demonstrates compliance with all the regulatory obligations relating to the environment.

Focus on compliance with regulations also emerges from the requirements regarding the tasks of internal auditors, in particular, the need to assess the management system to verify conformity, as well as compliance with the organisation's environmental policy and programme, in relation to the applicable regulatory requirements. It is, therefore, quite clearly indicated that the internal audit must also include compliance with laws.

The recurring emphasis on the guarantee of regulatory conformity by EMAS organisations has led to the compiler of the new Regulation to also include new 'legal requirements and permit limits' in the list, albeit non-exhaustive, of environmental aspects included for consideration on the path to EMAS as shown in Annex I point 2 (in addition to the 'use of additives and auxiliaries as well as semi-manufactured goods'). It is clear how this inclusion has been dictated by the desire of the Commission to emphasise the importance of conformity itself, rather than the idea that it actually represents an environmental aspect which would also be methodologically misleading if compared to the same definition of aspect ('an element of an organisation's activities, products or services that has or can have an impact on the environment'). The presence of regulatory constraints, however, can and must be reasonably used as a factor for assessing the significance of a given aspect (as indicated in Annex I point 2, moreover) and for gleaning information as to how to use it (take, for example, conditions in permits for air emissions or regulations for waste products).

Lastly, it should be noted that EMAS III also considers regulatory conformity to be a fundamental point in the content of external communications. The initial 'recitals' state that 'the organisation should produce and make publicly available periodic environmental statements and environmental performance reports providing the public and other interested parties with information on their compliance with applicable legal requirements relating to the environment and their environmental performance' and even that the 'updated environmental statement', no matter how short, must at last contain 'updates of the last validated environmental statement, only with regard to an organisation's environmental performance and compliance with applicable legal obligations relating to the environment'.

To counterbalance the considerable commitment required of organisations in terms of concrete assurances and long-term maintenance of regulatory compliance, a request to the Member States was introduced in Article 32 of the new Regulation asking for assistance in fulfilling the regulatory obligations by facilitating access to information about such obligations and activating communications channels (for example, to obtain explanations) among organisations interested in EMAS and the authorities responsible for enforcing the obligations.

This role could be assumed directly by the competent authorities or by other support institutions correctly identified by the Member States. There is an obvious connection in this sense to the European Commission's Environmental Compliance Assistance Programme for SMEs (ECAP) which in a strange game of give-and-take, indicates EMAS as one of the most effective tools for supporting small organisations in keeping up-to-date on (and fulfilling) legal requirements.

Lastly, it is worthwhile noting that strengthening the mechanism for establishing an organisation's compliance with all the applicable legal requirements has, according to the directive of the EMAS III Regulation, a very clearly stated objective that should not be underestimated by national governments: 'the credibility of EMAS, in particular, to enable Member States to reduce the administrative burden of registered organisations by way of deregulation or regulatory relief'.

A particularly important modification introduced by EMAS III concerns the environmental review phase. In cases of dynamic changes of company structures (very frequent in real life), the Regulation states that when a registered organisation sees the need to implement substantial changes, it must perform an *ad hoc* environmental review of all relevant environmental aspects and impacts and, as a result, update the initial environmental review, modify the environmental policy, environmental programme and environmental management system and revise and update the environmental statement accordingly.

The Regulation applies the definition 'substantial change' to any change in an organisation's operation, structure, administration, processes, activities, products or services that has or can have a significant impact on an organisation's environmental management system, the environment or human health (article 2, point 15). It is clear, therefore, that, by law, these cases include any types of change requiring a request for extensions or a new permit. It is equally clear that the organisation cannot be limited to these cases. A factor with which it is possible to define what is 'substantial' can refer to significant environmental aspects: every change concerning the aspects that the organisation has identified as more important or altering the level of significance of its environmental aspects should be treated as a 'substantial' change. Obviously, this is inferable from the evaluation of the impacts connected to the change, and so the organisation should carry out a preventive environmental review anyway, albeit in a simplified form, of the changes it intends implementing, as provided by the ISO 14001 standard with regard to 'management of changes' of the environmental management system.

In the case of environmental review, moreover, the EMAS Regulation focuses on one of the essential criteria for correctly evaluating an organisation's environmental aspects. In addition to mentioning, as seen before, the 'importance for interested parties' and the 'views of interested parties' among the input for defining the evaluation criteria, EMAS III makes it quite clear that organisations should focus on any situations considered critical by stakeholders, stating that they 'shall be able to demonstrate an open dialogue with the public and other interested parties including local communities and customers with regard to the environmental impact of their activities, products and services in order to identify the public's and other interested parties' concerns'. The text in the conventional approach to EMAS Regulation does not indicate how this can be done, but it seems fairly obvious to look for solutions such as the following:

- direct consultation (e.g. questionnaires) or indirect consultation (e.g. surveys conducted in the area by third parties) of the local community and social stakeholders;
- measuring awareness in the local community based on the number of direct complaints received or petitions submitted to the competent authorities;
- using assessments carried out on the criticality of environmental issues in the area involving public participation (such as the Local Agenda 21 Forum);
- the transposition of community themes by consulting the media (e.g. newspaper articles on the environmental aspects of the company or the area); etc.

With regard to the management system, it should be pointed out that the new Regulation merges the system requirements deriving from the ISO 14001 standard and the other elements which organisations applying the EMAS system need to consider (previously included in an Annex) into a single Annex (Annex III), thus improving the effective integration and highlighting the distinctive features of the EMAS scheme, at the same time.

In addition to the role of initial environmental review and the importance of legal conformity, continual improvement and transparent, widespread communication (as shown below), Annex II focuses, in particular, on training and the involvement of the organisation's personnel whose on-going active participation continues to be a prerequisite and essential resource both for the functioning of the system and improvement of the environmental performance. Following this logic, in addition to including the provisions in Annex IB point 4, the new text, in fact, makes some of the guidelines for the participation of personnel in the EMAS framework compulsory as already recommended in the 2001/680/EC Act. Take, for example, the requirements to define concrete measures designed to involve employees in the process such as the so-called 'suggestion book' system, activate project-based group work or set up environmental committees, ensure that Management provides actual feedback to employees and guarantee the involvement of any employee representatives within the organisation. It is clear from a reading of the 'additional issues' in Annex II that it is not simply a question of informing or training employees on environmental matters (a requirement that is fully met if the indications of ISO 14001 are implemented), but rather of devising initiatives and tools which enable all employees to play an active, proactive role in the system.

In other words, these initiatives for 'employee involvement' are suggested by the Regulation to allow the EMAS-registered organisation to effectively achieve actual employee participation in the functioning of the environmental management system. EMAS III, indeed, stipulates that employees shall be involved in the process aimed at continually improving the organisation's environmental performance through

- the initial environmental review, the review of the status quo and in collecting and verifying information;
- the establishment and implementation of an environmental management and audit system improving environmental performance (resulting in the need to gather ideas and suggestions by employees on 'how' to improve);
- environmental committees to gather information and to ensure the participation of environmental officer/management representatives and employees and their representatives;
- joint working groups for the environmental action programme and environmental auditing;
- the elaboration of the environmental statements (obviously not considering employees merely as recipients or potential 'readers' of the statement).

Lastly, it must be pointed out that the European Commission's *User Guideline* focuses the attention of those organisations interested in EMAS on reward mechanisms and incentives (even financial) for active and proactive employees in order to increase the level of involvement and participation in the management system's activities.

In addition to the above-mentioned new components, there are some minor explanations regarding individual elements of the environmental management system, which were already consolidated by the practical application of many verifiers, especially in Italy (which probably motivated the changes in the Regulation). By way of example, the following explanations can be cited concerning:

- objectives and programmes: emphasis is placed on the fact that an organisation's programmes can be based 'on local, regional and national environmental programmes' and that, in any case, the 'means to achieve the objectives and targets cannot be considered environmental objectives';

- the management of suppliers: 'The organisation should endeavour to ensure that the suppliers and those acting on the organisation's behalf comply with the organisation's environmental policy (a requirement apparently expressed more restrictively in comparison to ISO 14001) within the remit of the activities carried out for the contract';
- the audit and review: the need to plan and start, but not to complete, an audit program (which must at least address the most significant environmental impacts) is referred to for first-time registrations as is the need to carry out at least one management review.

EMAS seems to focus on the results that it can guarantee rather than on the way the environmental management system is implemented. A great deal of attention is dedicated by EMAS III to the subject of environmental performance, appropriate benchmarks and the organisation's ability to improve them.

The considerable emphasis placed by the EMAS Regulation on the subject of performance is also denoted by the requirements linked to its improvement. The organisation's ability to effectively commit itself to the continual improvement of environmental performance is one of the key points insisted on by the European Legislator to strengthen the credibility of EMAS.

Indeed, the new EMAS III Regulation makes the check on continual improvement of the organisation's environmental performance one of the objectives for verification – namely, one of the minimum requirements that the verifier must check in order to maintain registration. Thus, 'continual improvement' (the definition of which, for some unknown reason, has been removed from the new Regulation) is promoted to a bona fide requirement with which the organisation must comply to avoid facing a non-conformity, which could preclude obtaining or maintaining registration. One of the conditions of failure to comply with the EMAS III requirements which can impede the granting or renewal of registration is, in fact, 'the comparison of the achievements and targets with the previous environmental statements and the environmental performance assessment and assessment of the continuous environmental performance improvement by the organisation'.

Obviously, the measurement of 'continual improvement' must be interpreted, as in the past, in a reasonable, not overly rigid manner. The term 'continual' is intended as a path marked over the years by progress in the measurable results of the environmental management system with regard to the organisation's management of its significant environmental aspects, to be measured above all by the policy and its objectives and targets. Furthermore, it is clear that 'progress' of this type in the results does not necessarily have be immediately apparent in all sectors of activity or for all environmental aspects, but must refer to the organisation's global results and can be highlighted by just a few of the indicators for measuring environmental performance and not necessarily all of them. There can also be cases of 'sporadic' progress (typical of investments in new technology), or areas in which the organisation has already improved its performance in the past and in which the margins for improvement are obviously lower: in cases such as these, it is understandable that the organisation's aim is to maintain a stable performance and strengthen past efforts whilst it pursues improvements in other areas.

Lastly, the importance attributed by EMAS III to performance and continual improvement is made quite clear by the introduction of the obligation by the organisation to report on the progress of its environmental performance through a set of predefined guidelines.

The new Regulation includes the obligation to provide a summary of available data on the environmental performance in the environmental statement showing details of the type and methods of how the indicators of environmental performance to be used are created. The so-called *core indicators* defined in Annex IV focus on six key environmental areas – energy efficiency, material efficiency, water, waste, biodiversity and emissions – and they can be applied to all types of organisations with the aim of comparing the performances of organisations even if from different sectors. It is quite natural to think that the European Commission considers core indicators to be the key tool for reporting the results achieved in terms of progress of the environmental performance and registered organisations are expected to be able to demonstrate a continual improvement mainly through these indicators.

External communication is the last area in which some clear progress has been made in the new Regulation and with respect to ISO 14001, as well.

Above and beyond the specific tool that EMAS dedicates to communication with stakeholders (the environmental statement, dealt with in the following paragraphs), the role of the latter seems to have been strengthened overall by the new Regulation, above all by ensuring the credibility of registration. Take, for example, Art. 14 point 1, in which the Regulation establishes that one of the conditions required for renewing registration (in addition to legal conformity) is the absence of claims regarding interested parties or at least the positive outcome of such complaints. This condition could cause considerable discretional problems in interpreting situations involving local conflict.

The most important new element in communication, however, is the attempt (strongly championed by registered businesses) to unlock the full potential of the EMAS logo which is clearly intended as a marketing tool: 'the logo should be an appealing communication and marketing tool for organisations, which raises the awareness of buyers and other stakeholders to EMAS'.

To this end, the EMAS Regulation introduces a revolutionary simplification of the rules which regulate the use of the logo by envisaging one single version and eliminating the existing restrictions (thus allowing its use with any validated information including advertising) with the exception of the need to avoid any possible confusion with environmental product labels and the ban on use with comparative statements regarding other activities or other services. Any environmental information published by a registered organisation can contain the EMAS logo provided that such information refers to the latest environmental statement or to updated environmental statement of the organisation from which it has been drawn and an environmental verifier has validated it (for the specific use intended by the organisation) after ensuring that the information is

- accurate;
- substantiated and verifiable;
- relevant and used in an appropriate context or setting;
- representative of the overall environmental performance of the organisation;
- unlikely to result in misinterpretation;
- significant in relation to the overall environmental impact.

In addition, the 'liberalisation' of the use of the logo for promotional purposes with no reference to a specific registration should be pointed out: the EMAS logo without a registration number and with no indication of the user's registration may, in fact, be used (both by Bodies overseeing the scheme and by other stakeholders) for EMAS-related marketing and promotional purposes.

The environmental statement

One of the main objectives required by the community legislator through the Regulation is to promote the start of relations between the organisation participating in the Scheme and its stakeholders. This process must be founded on trust, dialogue and transparency. The key element in any relation built on trust between two parties is the willingness to provide clear, comprehensive and above all true information. The preparation of the environmental statement in accordance with the Regulation's requirements, the acceptance of the verification and validation mechanism of the information contained within it, the commitment to its continual update and its dissemination to the public should not be seen by the organisation as simply the last steps in obtaining registration, but rather as a sign of this willingness.

It is important, therefore, that the organisation is aware of the importance of this 'step' required by EMAS and views the environmental statement as a true instrument for external communication and as such, in need of a 'planned' approach. Consequently, the organisation must identify the strategic objectives it intends to achieve and select the main recipients of the document through an appropriate choice of language, the methods to make it publicly available and the most suitable content in full compliance with Regulation's requirements.

For each of these aspects, the Regulation limits itself to providing general guidelines in the belief that the organisation alone can best describe the environmental situation that characterises it and the actions taken to improve its performance. In the logic of the Regulation, leaving a wide margin of discretion and creative presentation to the organisation is also a way of making it take ownership and become more 'open' in its dialogue with the public.

Objectives and key characteristics

The environmental statement is a series of information about the organisation and its activities, the impact these activities have on the environment, the methods adopted to achieve the best environmental performance and the relevant results as well as the announcement of future objectives and programmes. This information must be updated each year and the changes validated by an environmental verifier. There are several aspects that characterise the document.

The first aspect concerns the communication objectives that the organisation can achieve through the environmental statement. The Regulation attributes a role to this tool that seems to go beyond that of just a one-directional communications channel by the organisation to the outside. In fact, in addition to affirming that the environmental statement serves to 'give information to the public and other people involved about the environmental impact and performances of the organisation and also on the on-going improvement of environmental performance', the Regulation also adds that 'it is also a vehicle to respond to the stakeholders' requirements…'. It is this bi-directionality, if correctly pursued, which makes the document not just an information channel, but also an important means of dialogue with the public.

A second aspect concerns the possibility of using the environmental statement as a tool for communication to fulfil the information needs of different groups of stakeholders. In defining a communication strategy, the greatest problem that a company has to face is the diversification of the public it addresses, all with very different technical competence, scientific knowledge and background in the environment. This makes it that much more difficult to develop a communications strategy that is specific and effective for the entire audience: it is clear, for example, that basic technical information on the chemical process of an industrial plant is quite comprehensible to a 'specialised' audience, but not to the residents living in the vicinity of the company.

There are different types of recipients, therefore, who have well defined identities in terms of perception of the information contained in the statements, each of whom require a different linguistic, explanatory and content-related approach.

Whilst acknowledging that there are numerous, diversified stakeholders in the company, it is important not to forget that, according to the Regulation, the main recipient of the statement is the 'public' in the sense of the 'community', or a combination of citizens-consumers-users. In terms of communication strategy, the requirements for clarity and coherence, on the one hand, and conciseness on the other can be interpreted as suggestions aimed at capturing the attention of the reader who may not necessarily be particularly knowledgeable, open or interested in interacting with the organisation on environmental issues, as well as avoiding weighing down organisations, in particular small to medium businesses, with the burden of a complex document.

The importance given to communications aspects by the Regulation is shown by the reference to the way the statement is made available: the organisation is encouraged to use 'all methods available' with specific reference to use of electronic publication. The indication by the Commission also highlights how the environmental statement must be considered as a series of information and not merely as a paper document, which is just one of many ways of disseminating the information contained in it.

The key strategic factor in a communications strategy is the type of information it provides, which depends on the message it intends to transmit and the recipient to whom it is addressed.

In this respect, the question could be asked to what extent the definition of the content of the environmental statement is left to the discretion of the organisation.

The EMAS Regulation lists the minimum required content of the document and leaves ample margin in defining the level of detail and extent to which it is handled and publicised.

- a clear and unambiguous description of the organisation registering under EMAS and a summary of its activities, products and services and its relationship to any parent organisations as appropriate;
- the environmental policy and a brief description of the environmental management system of the organisation;
- a description of all the significant direct and indirect environmental aspects that result in significant environmental impacts of the organisation and an explanation of the nature of the impacts as related to these aspects (Annex I.2);
- a description of the environmental objectives and targets in relation to the significant environmental aspects and impacts;
- a summary of the data available on the performance of the organisation against its environmental objectives and targets with respect to its significant environmental impacts. Reporting shall be on the core indicators and on other relevant existing environmental performance indicators as set out in Section C;
- other factors regarding environmental performance including performance against legal provisions with respect to their significant environmental impacts;
- a reference to the applicable legal requirements relating to the environment;
- the name and accreditation or license number of the environmental verifier and the date of validation.

Notes

1 For organisations that have already carried out an initial review of their set-up and impacts on the environment, the objectives of the initial environmental review translate into an update of the document records of the results of the initial environmental review (these results are discussed in depth in point 6 of this chapter) in other words, in an activity where the process of identifying and assessing the most significant environmental aspects is revised.

2 It is important to understand the context because it can facilitate the process of assessing the most significant environmental aspects by providing data and information on the sensitivity and criticality of the territory in which the organisation resides and operates and, serve as a result, as a reference in defining its objectives and priority for actions. The more frequently these activities are performed in an enclosed are, the more uniformly this area can be classified (districts, industrial areas, tourist areas...). EMAS II recognises that in the latter case the environmental classification of the area can constitute an essential reference point in allowing the organisations operating in that area to identify the important environmental aspects and the subsequent definition of actions to take as a contribution by the organisation to achieve goals to improve environmental quality which have been established for the area. Furthermore, there are organisations operating in areas with boundaries, but covering a wide, uneven territory that is also the site for several different types of businesses (for example, a public entity for gas, electricity and remote heating distribution, or even local authorities – councils, provinces, etc.). The analysis and classification of the environmental context is essential for these organisations to correctly identify, measure and assess the environmental aspects.

3 It is clear that two identical environmental aspects (like, for example, the emission of two identical quantities of sulphur dioxide from two smokestacks) have a different degree of significance depending on the characteristics of the organisation (e.g. in the case of an industrial site, the local ecosystem on which they have an impact). The sulphur dioxide (direct environmental aspect) emitted from a smokestack of a factory situated in a densely populated area in the middle of the Po Valley plain will have a much higher impact than that emitted from a factory situated in a scarcely populated, well ventilated area. It is quite clear that the consequence of the impact caused helps to assess the significance of a particular environmental aspect.

4 In the case or complex production processes, the activities can be grouped in uniform categories – according to predefined, explicit or reproducible criteria – which can vary according to: the unique nature of the process (e.g. activities characterised by similar operations, functionally connected or logistically adjacent); the management/ organisational characteristics of the organisation (e.g. activities which are transversal to the process, but managed jointly); the criticality with respect to the environmental subsystems (e.g. activities which give rise to environmental impacts with comparable characteristics).

5 This is the case, for example, of production processes that do not generate odours; emission-free activities by service companies, etc.

6 Please note that the concept of 'significance' and 'importance' are considered to be synonyms in the document.

7 In the case of organisations that already have a management system and are committed to following the environmental analysis, this entry must be applied with reference to an assessment of the management and control methods based on consolidated indications of effectiveness.

8 In order to assess legal compliance it may be advisable to apply a *gradual* approach based on how long the management system has been in place: initially the organisations could place high significance on all the aspects for existing set parameters (i.e. with fixed legal limits); secondly, with a better understanding and awareness of environmental interactions and the adaptation of the control and monitoring systems, the organisation could become more selective of the assessment being used, for example, criteria of significance linked closely to the legal limits. This allows it to concentrate its attention on the more sensitive parameters by excluding the ones which are no longer significant since they are under control and systematically below the legal limits.

9 More complex systems may envisage individual quantitative assessments for each criterion (as well as the expansion of such criteria based on unique features specific to

the organisation) by the application of functions (e.g. the sum function) that allow a set of values F/II/IE to be reached. The same systems may also envisage application methods of different incidences to the three assessment axes in order to identify the priority of actions.

10 Part of an **organisation**'s management system used to develop and implement its **environmental policy** and manage its **environmental aspects**.

11 With regard to EMAS, in particular, with the publication of the accompanying User Guideline by the competent EC bodies, the figure of System Manager has become virtually compulsory: "*A person responsible for the EMS must be appointed by the organisation manager. The role of this person is to make sure that all the system requirements are in place and updated as well as to keep the general management team informed about the system operation, strengths, weaknesses and improvements needed for future actions*".

12 The transfer of skills should also entail support (*coaching*) by experts who deal with on-site training.

13 According to the definition of the *EMAS User Guideline*: '*Working instructions must be clear and easy to understand. The content should contain: relevance of the activity, environmental risk associated to that activity, specific training for the staff in charge of it, and supervision of the activity*'.

14 A particularly effective way of collecting and/or making important environmental information available to the public is to publish it on the Internet which offers notable advantages in terms of punctuality, accessibility and comprehensiveness of external communication.

15 This is true, for example, for drafting an Environmental Management System Manual, a tool required by regulations governing quality system certification. Many organisations have chosen to adopt this document because it can prove useful to the functioning of the EMS and how it is documented. Some organisations do not recognise this need and have not adopted a manual. In cases like these, even though the ISO 14001 standard does not include the use of a document with these characteristics, it is advisable for the organisation to adopt support documentation, even if extremely simplified or schematic, which clearly describes the EMS. It should also be remembered that the current edition of the *EMAS User Guideline* of the EC clearly includes a 'User Guide for Environmental Management' ('*this document contains the environmental policy, environmental protocols and actions, responsibilities distribution among the staff*'), even though it specifies that it is useful for providing a representation of the system and the roles and tasks of the people involved and does not necessarily have to include a lengthy or complex reporting structure.

16 For further details, refer to Iraldo, 2009.

17 For further information, refer to: www.life-pioneer.info.

References

Boiral, O., 2007. 'Corporate greening through ISO 14001: a rational myth?' *Organisation Science*, Vol. 18, 127–146.

Bracke, R., Verbeke, T., Dejonckheere, V., 2008. 'What Determines the Decision to Implement EMAS? A European Firm Level Study'. *Environmental and Resource Economics*, 41, 499–518.

Darnall, N., Jason Jolley, G., Handfield, R., 2008. 'Environmental Management Systems and Green Supply Chain Management: Complements for Sustainability?' *Business Strategy and the Environment*, 17, 30–45.

Fryxell, G.E., Lo, C.W., C., Chung, S.S., 2004. 'Influence of motivations for seeking ISO 14001 certification on perception of EMS effectiveness in China'. *Environmental Management*, 33, 239–251.

German Federal Environment Agency, 'EMAS in Germany Evaluation, 2012', 2013, Available at: http://www.emas.de/fileadmin/user_upload/06_service/PDF-Dateien/ EMAS_in_Germany_Evaluation_2012.pdf.

Granly, B.M., Welo, T., 2014. 'EMS and sustainability: experiences with ISO 14001 and Eco-Lighthouse in Norwegian metal processing SMEs'. *Journal of Cleaner Production*, 64, 194–204.

Gravonski, I., Ferrer, G., Paiva, E.L., 2008. 'ISO 14001 certification in Brazil: motivations and benefits'. *Journal of Cleaner Production*, 16, 87–94.

Grolleau, G., Mzoughi, N., Thomas, A., 2007. 'What drives agrifood firms to register for an environmental management system?' *European Review of Agricultural Economics*, 34, 233–255.

Heras, I., Arana, G., 2010. 'Alternative models for environmental management in SMEs: the case of Ekoscan vs. ISO 14001'. *Journal of Cleaner Production*, 18, 726–735.

IEFE Bocconi, Adelphi Consult, IOEW, SPRU, Valor & Tinge, 2006. EVER: Evaluation of eco-label and EMAS for their Revision'– Research findings', Final Report to the European Commission – Part I-II, DG Environment European Community, Brussels, 2006. Available at: www.europa.eu.int/comm/environment/emas.

ISO, 'Continual Improvement Survey 2013', Final Report and analysis, 1 February, 2014. Available at: file:///Users/mariarosa/Desktop/iso_14001_survey_2013_-_final _report_and_analysis.pdf

Johnstone, N., Labonne, J., 2009. 'Why do manufacturing facilities introduce environmental management systems? Improving and/or signaling performance'. *Ecological Economics*, 68, 719–730.

Kassolis, M.G., 2007. 'The diffusion of environment management in Greece through rationalist approaches: driver or product of globalisation?' *Journal of Cleaner Production*, 15, 1886–1893.

Lannelongue, G., Gonzalez-Benito, J., 2012. 'Opportunism and environmental management systems: certification as a smokescreen for stakeholders'. *Ecological Economics*, 82, 11–22.

Marazza, D., Bandini, V., Contin, A., 2010. 'Ranking environmental aspects in environmental management systems: a new method tested on local authorities'. *Environment International*, 36, 168–179.

Milieu Ltd., RPA Ltd., Study on the Costs and Benefits of EMAS to Registered Organisations, Final Report for DG Environment of the European Commission under Study Contract No. 07.0307/2008/517800/ETU/G.2, 2009. Available at: http:// ec.europa.eu/environment/emas/pdf/news/costs_and_benefits_of_emas.pdf.

Neugebauer, F., 2012. 'EMAS and ISO 14001 in the German industry — complements or substitutes?' *Journal of Cleaner Production*, 37, 249–256.

Nishitani, K., 2010. 'Demand for ISO 14001 adoption in the global supply chain: an empirical analysis focusing on environmentally conscious markets'. *Resource and Energy Economics*, 32, 395–407.

Price, T., 2007. 'ISO 14001: transition to champion'. *Environmental Quality Management*, Vol. 16, 11–23.

Qi, G.Y., Zeng, S.X., Tam, C.M., Yin, H.T., Wu, J.F., Dai, Z.H., 2011. 'Diffusion of ISO 14001 environmental management systems in China: rethinking on stakeholders' roles'. *Journal of Cleaner Production*, 19, 1250–1256.

Salomone, R., 2008. 'Integrated management systems: experiences in Italian organisations'. *Journal of Cleaner Production*, 16, 1786–1806.

Singh, N., Jain, S., Sharma, P., 2014. 'Determinants of proactive environmental management practices in Indian firms: an empirical study'. *Journal of Cleaner Production*, 66, 469–478.

SSSUP – Scuola Superiore Sant'Anna, 'The implementation of the EMAS Regulation in Europe: level of adoption, benefits, barriers and regulatory reliefs'. Brave Project – Survey on European EMAS organisations, 2013. Available at: http://www.braveproject .eu/wp-content/uploads/2013/03/Report-survey-europa -rev-19122013.pdf.

Zhang, B., Bi, J., Yuan, Z., Ge, J., Liu, B., Bu, M., 2008. 'Why do firms engage in environmental management? An empirical study in China'. *Journal of Cleaner Production*, 16, 1036–1054.

4   The environmental certification of products

The literature framework in the field of environmental certification of products

Our sense of quality of life and its underlying economical, social and cultural values ultimately depend on the structure of our systems of production and consumption and, more specifically, on how the markets can guarantee the achievement of such desirable objectives. Since the first global conference on human environment (Stockholm, 1972), scientific and political debates have considered systems of consumption and production as a potential threat to human survival: climate change, loss of natural resources, extinction of species and environmental damage caused by emissions and waste could in fact result from unsustainable patterns of consumption and production.

Therefore, the role of consumers in such a scenario becomes crucial in guiding the production paths (Leonidou et al., 2011; Carrete et al., 2012), since these can directly influence the environmental impact of a product in the phases of use and end-of-life (way of functioning, separation of waste, collection, recycling) and exert pressures on producers to take environmental criteria into account starting from the design and production processes (by requesting environmentally friendly products).

Ecological behaviours in purchasing choices have been deeply investigated by marketers and scholars, especially by focusing on the potential predictors of green choices. A relevant amount of literature has analysed the impact of internal factors such as attitude on environmental concerns (Paco et al., 2009; Ramayah et al., 2010; Aman et al., 2012), knowledge on product environmental impacts (D'Souza et al., 2007; Moisander, 2007; Ha and Janda, 2012), etc. Other streams of research focused on the effect consumer demographic characteristics have on the probability of choosing green products (Tikka et al., 2000; Mostafa, 2007; Chen and Chai, 2010), the role of trust towards external stakeholders (Darnall et al., 2012) and the reasons leading consumers to choose eco-labelled products (Loureiro et al., 2001; Brécard et al., 2009; Perrini et al., 2010).

Scholars and marketing practitioners have developed several models to investigate environmentally friendly behaviour (Kalafatis et al., 1999; Gotschi et al., 2010; Abdul Wahid et al., 2011; Aman et al., 2012). For instance, Ajzen developed the Theory of Planned Behaviour focusing on self-interest-based and rational choice-based (1988, 1991). On the other hand, Stern (1992) has proposed the Value-Belief-Norm (VBN) Theory focusing on values and moral norms (López et al., 2012). In particular, this theory is based on the principle that pro-social attitudes and personal moral norms are predictors of environmentally friendly behaviour (Jackson, 2005 as referenced in Martiskainen, 2007).

An effort to integrate different theories in order to predict environment significant behaviour had been made by Stern (2000) and Guagnano et al. (1995) through the development of the 'Attitude Behaviour Context' (ABC) theory. According to Stern (2000), to understand any specific environmentally significant behaviour requires empirical analysis. The role of environmentalist predispositions can vary greatly with the behaviour, the actor and the context (Stern, 2000). According to Stern (2000), behaviour is a function of the organism and its environment; while based on Guagnano et al. (1995), behaviour (B) is an interactive product of personal-sphere attitudinal variables (A) and contextual factors (C).

Stern (2000) was one of the first to provide an overview of the external variables that influence pro-environmental behaviour, i.e. contextual forces or external forces. These include interpersonal influences, community expectations, government regulations, the physical difficulty of specific actions and other features within a broad social, economic and political context. According to Stern (2000), these contextual forces are activated when an individual believes that violating them would have an adverse impact on things they value, and that by taking action, they would bear the responsibility for those consequences. There are several examples of the role of contextual forces in the environmental literature. For example, Blake (2001) shows how contextual forces can interact with social psychological and social-cultural factors to shape pro-environmental attitudes. These attitudes can be defined as a person's tendency to be concerned about the natural environment (Bamberg, 2003).

Of these contextual forces, social norms are important determinants of pro-environmental attitudes. Social norms arise when individual actions cause a potentially negative side effect for other members of a community (Coleman, 1990) and play the role of restricting selfish impulses in favour of collective outcomes (Biel et al., 1999). Social norms imply that people should adopt a certain behaviour or not manifest a proscribed one; the violation of these norms is met by sanctions (Biel and Thøgersen, 2006). A positive correlation between social norms and pro-environmental attitudes has been reported for correct waste-handling (e.g. Heberlein, 1972), participation in a recycling programme (e.g. Thøgersen, 2003) and consumer purchases of environmentally friendly products (Heberlein & Black, 1976).

The importance of internal variables in influencing pro-environmental behaviour has also been stressed (Hornik et al., 1995; Grob, 1995). Knowledge of the environment is a key factor contributing to a long-term commitment to pro-environmental behaviour (Hornik et al., 1995). Several authors underline that the most informed people are more likely to adopt a specific pro-environmental behaviour. For example, Oskamp et al. (1991) discovered that general knowledge regarding conservation played a significant role in environmentally responsible behaviour in the United States. Grob (1995) underlines that being aware of how a phenomenon could impact on the environment and its potential consequences were a key factor behind the long-term commitment to pro-environmental behaviour. In his work he shows how recognition of the consequences of environmental problems is directly linked to environmental attitudes.

While, environmental knowledge could be regarded more as having knowledge of the importance of a good environment, awareness of the consequences, could be seen as being aware of the activities endangered by the ineffective preservation of the environment. Thus, Cottrell (2002) tested how awareness of the consequences could influence recycling attitudes.

However, the absence or the scarcity of information (*information asymmetries*) about the environmental impact of a product has limited consumer uptake of green products. In detail, if producers do not provide complete, correct and easy-to-understand information on the life-time environmental performance of their products, and if it is costly and time-consuming for consumers to acquire that information, this asymmetry may lead to greener products not being bought.

This problem is especially caused by misleading claims on environmental performance of products on the final market, which is clearly preventing consumers from fully deploying their potential in terms of green products demand. In detail, this problem has two facets:

- on the one hand, companies are increasingly and significantly making use of green claims in advertising their products;
- on the other hand, consumers often believe that these claims are not reliable and, because of this, they are not orienting their purchasing decisions towards greener products.

There is considerable evidence showing that this is increasingly happening in the EU market. The last decade has witnessed a remarkable increase in advertisements containing environmental claims, as companies have become eager to appeal to the growing number of environmentally conscious consumers. This has led to a wide dissemination of green messages on the market, as shown by a series of recent studies.

A 2009 study carried out by Testa et al. (2011) analysing the dissemination and characteristics of green advertisings in Italian newspapers between 2007 and the first half of 2008, found that out of 13,490 advertisements in the sample, 1,314 were messages with an explicit environmental content, equal to 9.8 per cent of the total. The survey showed an increase of 3 percentage points compared to what was reported in a previous survey in 2001.

Moreover, the *2010 DEFRA Assessment Report on Green Claims in Marketing* shows that in the UK green claims have been subject to a notable and rapid growth in their number between 2006 and 2007/8 (during which time they roughly tripled in number), although they have since fallen back, coinciding with the worsening economic cycle.

These results are consistent with the findings of the 2011 ADEME (French Environment and Energy Management Agency) study '*Publicité et Environnement*': although the number of environmental advertising campaigns was lower in 2011 if compared with 2010 (due to economic downturn), the number of visual supports used for internet and paper campaigns was higher, reaching therefore a larger public.

The results of the previously mentioned studies clearly show an increase in the use of green claims in advertising in the last decade.

However, despite the increasing importance of environmental marketing, consumers remain sceptical about environmental claims made in advertisements. A 2008 survey[1] by *Burst Media* shows that only around 20 per cent of the respondents say they 'always' believe green claims made in advertisements. The remaining part is composed by sceptical consumers, many of them declaring that they need to further investigate claims. More precisely, 41.6 per cent of sceptical consumers frequently or occasionally research the claims made in green advertisements.

Furthermore, a survey by the 2011 GFK *Green Gauge Report* found that 39 per cent of consumers say business claims about the environment are not accurate. And, still, around 60 per cent of the 2011 respondents said business and industry are not fulfilling their responsibility to the environment.[2]

If we investigate the main motivations behind consumers' scepticism toward companies green claims, we find that the lack of credibility together with unclear messages rank first.

According to the *2010 National Geographic Greendex* online survey, which involved approximately 1,000 consumers in each of the 17 investigated countries, both developed and developing, when asked to what extent 10 different factors discourage them from buying more environmentally sound products, the largest proportion across the 17 countries said the reason is that *companies make false claims about the environmental impacts of their products*.[3]

In addition, according to a 2009 survey by the British *Consumer Focus*, 64 *per cent of consumers found it difficult to understand claims* and to know which products are better for the environment.[4]

For instance, confusion and lack of clarity are believed as being significant by consumers. A 2012 study by *Greener Package*[5] found that consumers are increasingly frustrated by the information provided. More in detail, 26 per cent of the respondents reported that there isn't enough environmental information in companies' advertising (compared to 20 per cent in 2010), and 20 per cent reported that they are confused by all the different environmental claims (12 per cent in 2010) and that they don't know which products are best for the environment (22 per cent vs. 17 per cent in 2010).

One of the most effective instruments to prevent misleading claims and to guide the consumers' choices is undoubtedly eco-labels. Eco-labels can be defined as claims stating that a product has particular environmental properties and features (De Boer, 2003). Consumers often rely on advertising and other corporate messaging to inform their choices. Today, *greenwashing* is undermining confidence in such advertising (Peattie & Crane, 2005). Surveys carried out at EU level provide evidence that confidence is progressively decreasing, with low percentages of consumers trusting green information coming from businesses (Eurobarometer, 2011). Without confidence in the advertising claims, consumers are reluctant to exercise the power of their green purchasing, as they no longer know who or what to believe. This significantly damages the virtuous circle of companies promoting their green products and consumers choosing them over non-green products, which is what encourages companies towards investing greater resources in efficiency and competitiveness, meanwhile reducing their environmental impacts (Iraldo et al. 2013).

In a recent research, Testa et al. (2013) showed the significance awareness and knowledge of eco-labels (such as the EU Ecolabel and Forest Stewardship Council) to determine the choice of adopting an ecological behavior by consumers; specifically, the higher the consumer's awareness and information on a product's superior environmental performance, the higher the probability that he/she will buy paper and home cleaners with a reduced impact on the environment. Their results, therefore, confirm the ability of eco-labels to support the development of 'green purchasing' (Perrini *et al.* 2010); but also emphasise the need for well-designed certification schemes and communication instruments, in order to avoid unclear and confusing messages to consumers.

Eco-labelling schemes are primarily designed as policy tools aimed at signalling the best options available on the market for consumers who want to express their preferences through purchasing choices. Our study clearly shows that these tools are able to fully achieve their main task only if consumers are informed and aware of their meaning, characteristics, requirements, guarantees they provide and so on.

As a consequence, eco-labels can also be usefully exploited by companies as marketing tools, only if supported (and accompanied) by a communication strategy and a complete set of information addressed to consumers on which they can rely as a stimulus and as a guide for their purchasing choices.

Environmental labels and trademarks

In the last few years, the role of trademarks and product labels has grown dramatically in importance in public policies and business strategies aimed at improving environmental safety and efficiency of products and services.

The 1980s were marked by a boom in the variety of labels, trademarks and various symbols or wording used to demonstrate the alleged environmental quality of products. These were virtually all 'self-certified' statements by businesses or, at the best, certifications issued by private organisations or institutes covering specific ecological features of the product ('*single-criterion*' trademarks: recyclable products, chlorofluorocarbon [CFC] gas free…), or in a broader, generic sense, the environmental friendliness of specific product categories ('*single-product*' trademarks: environmentally friendly detergents, natural fibre products, etc.).

These forms of private eco-labelling, which were quite often based on tenuous scientific foundations, spurred on by unrestrained competitive dynamics, reached a level of dissemination that was as far-reaching as it was unexpected given the fledgling demand for so-called 'green' products even in the most advanced countries[6].

This dissemination persuaded policymakers, on the one hand, of the potentiality of the tool to pursue goals of collective interest, and, on the other, applied pressure so that they intervened and established order and instituted rules in the realm of eco-labelling.

From the mid-1980s onwards, numerous countries set up national programmes for ecological labelling in response to the request for clarity and certainty by consumers and businesses that were faced with the increasing confusion reigning in the vast panorama of private trademarks.

The speed with which the markets and businesses had assimilated and commandeered the use of eco-labelling caught the policymakers by surprise and forced them into conferring greater consistency, scientific rigour and certainty on a tool that had been conceived for marketing purposes and had originally had the sole objective of enhancing the product's image (and the reputation of the company) in the name of the environment.

The efforts by the ISO (*International Organization for Standardization*) in this area to regulate and harmonise the situation, which initiated intense activity around environmental standardisation through the work of the TC207 Technical Committee, have constantly renewed interest by companies in trademarks and eco-labels. The publication of the 14020 series standards by the ISO has encouraged the development and distribution of standards, which, according to their declarations, should put consumers in the position of making a better informed and more knowledgeable choice and, as a result, guarantee fair competition between the increasing numbers of manufacturers who are actively committed on this front. These standards make up the main methodological reference grid of any environmental product communications initiative based on voluntary certification. It is worthwhile giving a brief overview of the key indications set forth in the ISO 14020 series standards in order to 'prepare the ground' for a discussion on the certifications of excellence outlined in the following paragraphs.

The ISO 14020 standard is known as the fundamental guiding principles for correct environmental product communication and, for this reason, is considered to be the 'reference framework' for other ISO standards in the same series. Firstly, it is interesting to note that the standard offers a 'catalogue', unchanged up until publication, of possible forms of environmental product communication that can be 'standardised' and therefore, easily regulated by defining methodological requirements and, in some cases, also certified by independent third parties on their accuracy. ISO 14020 collates the different forms of communication that can be standardised under the sole term 'environmental claims'.

According to ISO, the aim of 'environmental claims' is to encourage the development of a more sustainable demand and supply with an environmental profile by communicating verifiable, accurate, non-deceptive information on the environmental aspects of products and services and by stimulating the market through the mechanism of continual improvement.

'*Labels*' (environmental labels), '*claims*' (so-called 'self-declarations' by the manufacturer) and '*declarations*' (or '*eco-profiles*') all fall in the range of the definition of 'environmental claims': alternatively, they are all statements that attempt to communicate the environmental aspects of a product or service to a public of potential consumers and customers.

These statements, irrespective of the form they take, must respond to some guiding principles, among which

- all the 'environmental claims' must be verifiable, accurate, significant and non-deceptive;
- these claims must be based on scientific methodologies with accurate and reproducible results;
- the development of environmental statements must consider all aspects concerning the product's life cycle.

The state of the art ISO standards stemming from 14020 and other voluntary environmental claims cover three types of categories, each one regulated by a specific standard reference, as follows:

- Type I: *eco-labels* (or 'environmental labels') certified in a scheme with independent third party verification (ISO 14024);
- Type II: ecological labels with 'self-declarations' (*environmental claims*) on the environmental features of the product (ISO 14021);
- Type III: environmental product declarations (or *eco-profiles*), which give environmental information on a product, quantified by appropriate indicators built on fixed parameters and verified independently (ISO 14025).

The first examples of national programmes for eco-labelling using *type I eco-labels* started back in the 1970s. The German eco-label Blauer Engel was the very first label to appear in 1978 and the driving force behind the others. Just a decade later, eco-labelling programmes started to develop gradually in many other industrialised countries. Among the first national programmes to be set up along the lines of the German label were: the Canadian Ecologo (1988), the Japanese Ecomark (1991), the White Swan of the Nordic Countries (1989) and the French NF-Environment (1991). Today, virtually all the Organisation for Economic Co-operation and Development (OECD) countries have a public eco-labelling programme and many emerging countries are adopting similar schemes.

The type I eco-labelling programmes have set themselves ambitious, generalised goals: on the one hand, to guarantee reliable information to consumers in as much detail as possible to educate them on the ecological quality of products, raise their awareness on the environment, allow them to make better-informed buying choices and thus, promote the consumption of more eco-friendly products; and on the other hand, to stimulate businesses to make improvements in production from an environmental perspective (especially through eco-efficient innovation by offering them the opportunity to have their product excellence officially recognised). Because of these ambitious objectives, the type I eco-labelling schemes are characterised by a series of requirements aimed at guaranteeing credibility and scientific substantiation. The most important requirement is that in order to obtain the label, the schemes must be represented by quantitative thresholds with regard to the environmental performances of the product or service determined by an LCA study (*Life Cycle Assessment*) and be based on a *multi-criteria* approach (namely, they cover more environmental aspects than all the impacts that can be traced back to the life-cycle of the product or service).

At the beginning of the 1990s, the European Union decided to adopt a scheme to certify the ecological quality of products, known as Ecolabel, which will be discussed in detail later in the chapter.

The *environmental claims (type II)* are 'self-declared' environmental claims by the manufacturer regarding the specific environmental characteristics of its product. These claims cannot be certified by a third party and are not based on pre-set, recognised requirements. The ISO 14021 standard is placed in this category and aims to promote and encourage the harmonisation of so-called 'environmental claims' in order to stop misleading and not adequately guaranteed information from reaching consumers about environmental marketing, which is often at risk. The development and dissemination of the standard, as intended by the ISO, should give consumers a better informed, more educated choice and, as a result, guarantee fair competition among the growing numbers of manufacturers committed to this issue.

In accordance with ISO 14021, the claims can only refer to individual aspects of the product, but must not contain excessively generic or vague terms that could confuse consumers (for example, non-specific claims such as 'safe for the environment', 'environmentally friendly', 'Earth-friendly', 'non-polluting', 'green', 'nature-friendly' and 'ozone-friendly').

A particularly interesting feature of ISO 14021 is the effort to identify the desirable 'requirements' for accurate environmental information and communication of products and services. An example of this is the requirement for 'specificity' of an environmental claim. In short, this means the consumer must be told how to act so that the positive results linked to the choice of an 'ecological' product actually occur. For example, ISO 14021 requires that the manufacturer does not simply define its product as 'designed for disassembling' or 'compostable', but includes instructions on how to respectively disassemble or compost the product.

Some features of the *environmental claims* set forth in ISO 14021 specify that they must be consistent with the context in which the product is manufactured, distributed and consumed: what is the sense of extolling the possibility of recycling a product to the public if a suitable recycling system does not exist? Can the mere possibility of recycling be equated to an environmental benefit in the eyes of consumers? ISO 14021 also highlight how other environmental benefits may be communicated inconsistently with respect to the relevant product category, for example: claiming that a paper product can be recycled does not indicate a consistent advantage in a sector where the majority of alternative products have exactly the same advantage. The standard also warns manufacturers and consumers of possible, ill-concealed inconsistencies in trying to repeat the benefits of a single environmental impact simply by changing the wording.

Lastly, particular attention is being paid by ISO 14021 to the issue of labels and certification and on how they are communicated through *environmental claims*. The effectiveness of certification is closely linked to the credibility, sense of authority and recognition of the awarding Body (take the European Ecolabel, for example): for this reason, the ISO 14021 standard requires that the source of any environmental product certification or claims must always be clearly indicated.

It is worth taking a final look at the issue of logos and symbols that evoke the environmental origins of the product. Generally, they are considered a useful, effective tool, but if they are used, they should have some features in common with the information: namely, they are coherent, easy to understand and recognise. An example concerns all symbols depicting natural images (animals or plants): they should be used only if they are actually linked to the impact of environmental benefit stated by the claim. It is not by chance that the sole symbol, the 'Möbius loop', included in the ISO 14021 standard is very widely used, simple and evocative, symbolising that a product can be recycled or contains recycled material.

Environmental Product Declarations (EPDs) or *Eco-Profiles* are an innovative tool and form part of the so-called type III environmental claims regulated by the ISO 14025 international standard.

This type of 'environmental claim' is illustrated in a brief document that outlines a simple 'profile' of the environmental performance of a product/service and allows objective, comparative and credible data and information to be communicated accordingly. It is important to emphasise that the content of an EPD is for information purposes only it does not, in fact, indicate any requirement for evaluation, preference or minimum levels that the product or service must respect, but simply aims to enable the customer, who is the target of the document, to make an educated choice and be correctly informed when making a purchase.

The main aim of this tool is to highlight the environmental performance of a product/service by increasing visibility and social acceptance, and by encouraging a comparison between products with similar functions. The EPDs allow consumers/intermediary customers of a manufacturer to understand the potential greenhouse gas effect caused by the product they are about to buy and to choose the one that produces less CO_2 emissions.

A strong point of the EPD tool is the opportunity it provides to show that the declaration has been verified and validated by an accredited third party and so, guarantee that the information it contains is complete, comprehensive and true.

Another strong point of the tool is demonstrated by the robust scientific facts on which the information for external communication is based: the environmental performance of a product included in the EPDs should be based on – and guaranteed by – the results of the life cycle analysis (LCA) performed according to the ISO 14040 standards.

ISO 14025 does not simply set forth the features that an EPD must have and the methodological and scientific base on which it is founded; it also defines the requirements that a voluntary EPD programme should comply with in terms of the following: programme management, consultation by interested parties, specific product requirements, choice of product groups to include in the programme itself and functioning of the certification and verifier accreditation process.

The 'Certified Environmental Product Declaration' is one of the first EPD programmes developed in the framework proposed by ISO 14025 and will be discussed in detail later in the chapter.

The extensive use that all types of environmental claims regulated by the ISO make of the LCA approach (for implementing the guiding principles of ISO 14020) affords the opportunity to take a close look at how this essential analysis and assessment tool works by forming the basis of different options for environmental product certification and communication illustrated in this book.

Life Cycle Assessment and the 14040 standard

Over the last few years, different methods have been developed to study and assess a product's environmental impact. The need to create operational tools and management techniques in this field has developed as a result of growing pressure from external stakeholders in the business who increasingly demand guarantees on the environmental friendliness of products. This has stimulated businesses, scientific institutions and standardisation organisations (both national and international) to study, develop and gradually perfect methods that respond to all the requests by the public, authorities, business partners, consumers and, more generally, by all the stakeholders in the company.

The main instrument available to experts carrying out a study that is consistent with the previously mentioned requirements is the method titled 'Life Cycle Assessment' (LCA), namely an assessment of the life cycle. This tool, which was created to prevent these potential problems, focuses on the performance of production systems involving raw materials starting from the moment when they are extracted from the ground (when they are 'snatched' from the environment), through all the conversion processes that they undergo until they 'return to the earth' in the form of waste products. This is why the approach is known as 'from cradle to grave'.

The first life cycle analyses were carried out at the beginning of the 1960s with the aim of measuring emissions, waste, energy consumptions and use of resources associated with product development. From this point onwards, a gradual increase was seen in the use of these techniques encouraged by the positive results produced by their initial application. At the same time, however, the limits of this methodology became clear because the results could not be compared since they had been obtained by different approaches and methods.

In the 1990s, in an effort to close this loophole, both national and international organisations tried to standardise the methods by attempting to rationalise and harmonise the references in this field culminating in the creation of the ISO 14040 family of standards, which were published in 1997.

Today, the ISO 14040 standard is the most important reference for the dissemination of these methodologies. The standard recognises the importance of the LCA tool in identifying the opportunities to improve the environmental aspects of a product in the various stages of its life cycle by pinpointing the most suitable indicators for measuring environmental performance, guiding the design of new products/processes in order to minimise their environmental impact and by supporting the strategic planning of businesses and *policymakers* (ISO, 1996).

It is necessary to point out, however, that ISO 14040 only provides the principles and reference framework for conducting a life cycle analysis along with some general methodological guidance, which is shown in more detail in the complementary ISO 14041, ISO 14042 and ISO 14043 standards relating to the various phases of the LCA[7].

According to the general standard, the life cycle assessment should include the following phases:

1   definition of the objective and field of application for the study;
2   analysis of the inventory;
3   assessment of the impact;
4   interpretation of the results and improvement.

The four phases of the LCA should not be regarded as a fixed, predefined sequence of the methodological steps, but rather as a cycle of interactions with frequent amendments and content revision of each step since every phase is interdependent on the others.

In the *first phase*, the reasons for developing the LCA, the intended use of the results and the type of public targeted are clearly and consistently established with respect to the intended application. In particular, in defining the field of application of the study some elements must be clearly outlined and taken into account, for example: the function of the system produced (or systems in the case of comparative studies[8]); the functional unit; the product system that is the focus of the study; the type of impact, the impact assessment methods and the subsequent interpretation to use; the quality requirements of the initial data, etc.

A fundamental step within this phase is the definition of the *functional unit*, which acts as a reference to link to the input and output flows[9] since it is assumed that the measurements and assessments will be conducted on the basis of the performance of the system being studied.

In other words, the system being studied is the product defined not so much by its physical features as by its function, namely in the service it provides. If the function performed by the coating of a steel product is to protect it from corrosion by atmospheric agents, for example, then the functional unit could be defined as the unit area protected for a fixed length of time.

Table 4.1 contains some examples of possible functional units for different product-systems.

Another fundamental step in conducting an LCA study is the definition of the boundaries of the system being studied – that is the identification of the single operations (units) that make up the process including input and output, which must be included in the study. All the operations or 'process units' within the boundaries of the system are interconnected: they receive input from the units 'upstream' whilst the outputs are formed by the input units 'downstream' according to the process scheme being studied.

The criteria adopted to define the boundaries must always be identified and justified in order to clearly explain the field of application for the study.

The next step in conducting an LCA is the analysis of the *life cycle inventory* (Life Cycle Inventory [LCI]). This phase includes the collection of data and calculation procedures, which allow the types of interaction that the system has with the environment to be quantified; these interactions may be the use of resources and air emissions, water and land drainage associated with the product system (Frankl and Rubik, 2000). The procedure for conducting an inventory analysis is interactive: that is, the data collection gives an increasingly detailed insight into the system and as a result, the need for new data may arise or new requirements or limits concerning the data that has already been collected may be identified. It is must be emphasised how the last few years have been marked by a strong development in commercial and public databases. Both the private sector, which is well aware of the growing importance that the LCA tool is

Table 4.1 Examples of functional units

System	Possible functional units
Production and distribution of electric energy	1 kwh fed into the grid 1 kwh supplied to the user
Production of bottle tops	1 top 1 kg of tops
Production of expanded clay	1 kg of expanded clay 1 m^3 of packaged expanded clay
Provision of hotel services	1 guest 1 room to book

assuming for corporate environmental strategies, and the public sector, with the aim of supporting businesses in its application, have started a process of planning and developing databases to offer companies interested in 'experimenting' with the LCA methodology in their processes/products. In Europe, it is important to note the efforts made by the European Commission's *Joint Research Center* (JCR) in developing a 'network' database and relevant Handbook with the aim of making a series of information gathered from both sector-related databases and in the field available to users on the web. The data gathered during the inventory refers to the use of natural and energy resources, emissions released in the atmosphere and water bodies, as well as solid waste. The input of resource consumption and the output of emissions released into the environment can be attributed to all operations included in the life cycle of the product being examined.

Clearly, the quality of the data collected for the inventory has a strong influence of the significance of the results of the study. In an LCA study, therefore, it is necessary to use as large a percentage of so-called *specific* data as possible, namely data that relate directly to the system under examination or to one that is 'technologically equivalent' (meaning from energy sources, raw material, process phases or similar production facilities).

Flow charts and allocation procedures can be included in the list of tools used to conduct a data collection activity, in addition to the previously mentioned procedures, both of which are becoming increasingly widespread.

Flow charts allow all the process units and interconnected relations making up the system under study to be viewed through an appropriate schematic diagram (see Figure 4.1 for an example).

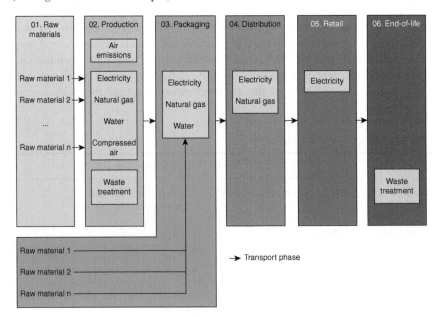

Figure 4.1 Example of flow chart (source: authors' own).

Since the production process and core product can generate numerous co-products or by-products, it may be necessary to define rules to allocate a quota for consumption and impacts on the operations in play to every production output. The requirements for such allocation, known as *allocation methods*, can be condensed in two main groups:

1 allocation based on physical size: consists of a proportional division of the environmental loads based on a physical parameter, such as mass, volume, energy, etc.;
2 economical allocation: consists of a division of environmental loads in proportion to the economic value of the co-products or sub-products. This method should, however, only be used where physical allocation cannot be easily applied.

The *inventory phase* is followed by the assessment of the impact of the life cycle during which the environmental consequences generated by the system under study are analysed. In other words, this phase aims to assess the potential environmental impact caused by the processes, products or activities being studied by using the information collected in the inventory. Furthermore, one or more environmental effects[10] can be associated with every environmental impact, and the person carrying out the study must choose the level of detail and impacts to assess in line with the objectives and the field of application defined during the initial phase of the study. The environmental effects on the other hand can be divided up depending on the level of action: global, regional or local.

Given the subjective elements that mark this phase (notably the choice and assessment of categories of environmental effects); it is necessary to report any assumptions influencing these choices clearly and transparently.

The type of impact categories most commonly used in this phase of the LCA can be listed as follows:

- greenhouse effect;
- acidification;
- eutrophication;
- tropospheric ozone depletivo;
- photochemical smog;
- land occupation.

The ISO 14042 standard covers two phases of impact analysis. The first is mandatory and consists of three sequential activities:

1 the selection of impact categories to study and relevant indicators (acidification $\Rightarrow SO_2$, greenhouse effect $\Rightarrow CO_2$, eutrophication $\Rightarrow NO_3$, ozone depletion $\Rightarrow CFC_{11}$, etc.);
2 the allocation of the inventory results to the selected impact categories (classification);

3   The calculation of the indicators of every impact category (e.g. GWP, etc.) (characterisation).

Classification consists of organising the inventory values of all the gas, liquid and solid emissions generated both directly and indirectly by the operations in question by associating them with different impact categories. *Characterisation*, on the other hand, enables the uniform and quantitative calculation of the contribution of single emissions expressed through category indicators, calculated by using the risk characterisation ratios of every pollutant, which are found in scientific papers (e.g. IPPC [Intergovernmental Panel on Climate Change]; WMO [World Meteorological Organization]; etc.)[11].

The second phase, which is optional, is divided into the following:

- a comparison between indicators that have been calculated and the reference values (normalisation);
- determination of the importance of the single environmental effects (weighting).

These phases are aimed at aggregating the results of the different impact categories by developing a single index expressed as a score, for example, which allows the environmental impact of the system in question to be assessed overall.

During the *final phase* of the life cycle analysis, which is *interpretative*, the results of the previous phases are summarised, analysed, checked and evaluated on the basis of the objective of the study to reach a set of conclusions and recommendations that allow improvements to be made to the environmental performance of the product system being analysed. This phase is aimed, then, at supporting the decisional phase of creating and programming the actions for improvement. The objectives and the goals defined in the initial phase come to fruition in the actions planned subsequent to the interpretation phase. However, this phase may lead to a partial review of the basis of the study (field of application, nature and quality of the data collected), in order to achieve the objective originally established.

The European Ecolabel

The relationship between the company's environmental performance and its competitive capability has evolved dramatically over the last few decades. Increased environmental awareness of many economic and financial corporate stakeholders and, above all, the occurrence of growing trends in emphasis on and belief in 'sustainable' consumption in the market have joined together and superimposed themselves on growing legislative pressure by pushing company owners towards 'accountability' and giving impetus to the gradual inclusion of the 'environmental' variable in competitive strategies.

When this process was in the fledgling stage at the beginning of the 1990s, the European Union decided to exploit the potentiality by setting up a certification scheme for the environmental quality of products, known as Ecolabel. This tool provides that products meeting pre-set ecological requirements may be granted by a label that informs the market about better environmental quality with respect to other products in the same category.

The publication of Regulation no. 880/92/EC, which set up the Ecolabel, was a decisive step in defining an EU environmental policy aimed at enhancing new voluntary thinking based on guarantees (introduced by the fifth and reinforced by the sixth EU Action Programme) and was accompanied by great expectations, fuelled by the potential to stimulate and interest companies that the scheme brought with it. The strength of a voluntary scheme like Ecolabel lies in the fact that it was simultaneously a tool for

- public environmental policy;
- corporate marketing;
- information about and support for consumers' choices.

First of all, Ecolabel gives the public a tool with which to check how green products are, and although it has a limited standing, is characterised by being very accessible and flexible: the adoption is voluntary and the control and inspection mechanisms are not as onerous as those for complying with the law. Moreover, Ecolabel, in addition to being a tool that is immediately effective in disseminating environmental information to already 'aware' consumers, can also be a true 'educational' tool capable of raising social ecological awareness.

Secondly, for businesses, Ecolabel undoubtedly constitutes the best tool for gaining recognition of their commitment to the product and reaping the benefits from this recognition in terms of image and, consequently, competitiveness.

Thirdly, consumers, in addition to gaining access to a reliable source of official information, are able to influence the market by purchasing labeled products and so, industrial manufacturing, thus exercising the right to participate in decisional processes concerning the environment.

There is no contrast between the three aspects of the Ecolabel, which, on the contrary, enhance one another by interacting: the more consumers are informed and aware, the more effective Ecolabel becomes as a corporate marketing tool, the more a company is motivated to participate in the scheme and improve its products and the more the policymakers fulfil their objectives for environmental quality. By initiating a system of eco-labelling, a mechanism is created that can succeed in obtaining active, spontaneous collaboration by leveraging the interests of the different economic operators involved.

A sort of 'virtuous circle' is created since the fulfilment of the objective of each party implies that the interests of the other are also fulfilled.

Competitive dynamics, therefore, have played a fundamental role for the Ecolabel from the very beginning; in fact, only if the scheme were fully accepted by the market (companies and consumers) could it have been successful as an environmental policy as well.

In July 2000, the European Commission adopted Regulation 1980/00 to improve the application of the Ecolabel, which proposes an initial review of the previous Regulation that originally set it up.

Ten years later, the European Commission published the third version of the Regulation on EU 'quality eco-labels' (Regulation 66/2010) in the Official Journal of the European Union L 27 dated 30 January 2010.

The long review process of the scheme by the Commission and Member States was guided by two main objectives. On the one hand, they concentrated on making the Ecolabel more effective both in terms of its possibility to influence the buying choices of consumers and in terms of its capability to improve the environmental performance of those companies choosing it as a marketing tool and more generally, as a production system. On the other hand, in line with the first objective, the review aimed to simplify the way the system functioned, above all by including new groups of products and developing the relevant criteria for allocation of the label.

The Ecolabel brand is a *voluntary, selective* tool with *Europe-wide distribution*. The request for the Ecolabel brand is, in fact, completely voluntary. Manufacturers, importers or distributors can request the Ecolabel once compliance with the criteria of the products or services they intend to supply the market has been verified.

The environmentally friendly label, therefore, is an award of excellence and as such, is only granted to those products that really have low impact on the environment compared to competitors. Take, for example, the fact that to guarantee that the label is really selective, Regulation 66/2010 provides that the criteria on which the label is issued are based on the best products available in the EU market in terms of environmental performance and, above all, must correspond to about 10–20 per cent of the best products on sale at the time the criteria are adopted. Furthermore, the principle of the so-called 'mobile frontier' is valid in applying the Ecolabel, namely, the criteria of the different groups of products are reviewed and made progressively more stringent if deemed necessary and in accordance with European Commission (EC) Decisions, so that excellence is always rewarded and continual improvement in the environmental quality of products is encouraged.

It should be emphasised that, thanks to this approach, the criteria for Ecolabel depict the many facets of benchmarks for excellence, which prove useful even for those companies choosing not to adopt the label, but which still refer to the sustainable design of their products (see Rubik et al., 2008).

Lastly, the strength of the European Ecolabel lies precisely in the size of Europe: the label can be used by the 28 Member States of the EU and by Norway, Iceland and Liechtenstein.

The way the Ecolabel scheme works is quite simple: once a new category of products or services has been identified with the same function and in competition with one another from the consumer's point of view, which can be put forward for labelling (or falls under the Ecolabel Regulation), and after accurately defining which products or services fall within it and which can be excluded, the environmental impact of a typical product with the characteristics of the relevant category is then analysed and assessed. Lastly, the criteria, with which the products or services in the category must comply in order to be awarded the Ecolabel, are defined (and shared within the Community) based on the impacts deemed to be most significant.

The definition of the groups of products and relevant criteria follows a scheme with two different levels of operation: national and EC. The national level is the 'Competent Body' (CB), created by every Member State to ensure that independence and neutrality are guaranteed in defining the criteria that will be applied to the whole of the EU once they have been approved.

The community level is the European Union Eco-labelling Board (EUEB) made up of representatives of competent bodies from all the Member States and from other interested parties. The Commission, Member States, competent bodies and other interested parties, after consulting with the EUEB, can initiate and guide the development and revision of the criteria for the Ecolabel trademark.

The part that initiates and guides the development and revision of the criteria for the Ecolabel trademark must prepare a *preliminary report* containing the following information, for example:

- a quantitative indication of the potential environmental advantages relating to the group of products;
- motivations for choice and framework of the group of products;
- an evaluation of the possible problems related to marketing;
- an analysis of the criteria of other environmental labels;
- current and future potential for market penetration of products with the EU Ecolabel.

After publication of the preliminary report, a *proposal for draft criteria* and a *technical report* are prepared supporting this proposal. Both documents are widely publicised in order to allow all interested parties to express an opinion and make any comments. The final report must contain clear replies to all the comments and proposals indicating whether they have been accepted or discarded with the relevant motivation. Furthermore, a manual is prepared for authorities awarding public contracts providing guidelines on how to use the Ecolabel criteria.

The award procedures for the Ecolabel are also defined on two levels: a national level for the CB carrying out the initial survey and documentation work in response to requests by the interested company and on an EC level.

The Ecolabel trademark can be requested by manufacturers, importers, service providers and wholesalers and retailers. The request must be presented to the CB of the Member State in which the product is manufactured. After checking the product's compliance with the established environmental criteria, the national CB assigns a registration number to the product and communicates its decision to the Commission.

Transparency and the widest possible participation are also ensured by frequently involving stakeholders such as representatives from the industry, commerce, environmentalists and consumers: in fact, international observers are periodically notified about the work of the Commission and the EUEB.

Since Ecolabel is an ISO type I label, the European scheme is founded on a multi-criteria approach in accordance with which the criteria for awarding the label are not based on a single parameter, but rather on a study that analyses the environmental impact of the product/service throughout its lifecycle from raw material extraction through manufacture, distribution and disposal. The need to guarantee credibility, scientific rigour and selectivity in the eyes of the consumer and participant companies has influenced the choice of procedures to assess the environmental impact by means of a comprehensive, detailed methodology on commonly shared views: the so-called LCA. The criteria, with which the products or services in the category must comply in order to be awarded the Ecolabel, are defined (and shared within the Community) based on the impacts deemed to be most significant in the LCA.

As already mentioned, the criteria are periodically reviewed at set times established in advance for every group or group of products in order to adapt to any environmental improvements required by changes in technological, economic or market conditions.

Table 4.2 shows the category of products/services for which the European Ecolabel can be requested and the categories for which criteria will be established in the coming years.

Table 4.2 Validity of the criteria for Ecolabel product groups (December 2014)

Product groups	Criteria status	Reference document	Valid until
CLEANING PRODUCTS			
All-purpose cleaners and sanitary cleaners	In force	Decision of 23/06/2011 (**2011/383/EU**)	28 June 2015
Dishwasher detergent	In force (under revision)	Decision of 28/04/2011 (**2011/263/EU**)	28 April 2015
Industrial and institutional automatic dishwasher detergents	In force	Decision of 14/11/2012 (**2012/720/EU**)	14 November 2016
Hand dishwashing detergent	In force	Decision of 24/06/2011 (**2011/382/EU**)	24 June 2015
Laundry detergent	In force (under revision)	Decision of 28/04/2011 (**2011/264/EU**)	28 April 2015

Product groups	Criteria status	Reference document	Valid until
Industrial and institutional automatic laundry detergents	In force	Decision of 14/11/2012 (**2012/721/EU**)	14 November 2016
Rinse off cosmetic products	In force	Decision of 09/12/2014 (**2014/893/EU**)	9 December 2018
Absorbent hygiene products	In force	Decision of 24/10/2014 (**2014/763/EU**)	24 October 2018

ELECTRONIC EQUIPMENT AND HOUSEHOLD APPLIANCES

Imaging equipment	In forse	Decision of 17/12/2013 (**2013/806/EU**)	17 December 2017
Personal computers	In force (under review)	Decision of 09/06/2011 (**2011/337/EU**)	9 June 2015
Notebook computers	In force (under review)	Decision of 06/06/2011 (**2011/330/EU**)	6 June 2015
Televisions	In force (under review)	Decision of 12/03/2009 (**2009/300/EC**)	31 December 2015
Light sources	In force (under review)	Decision of 06/06/2011 (**2011/331/EU**)	31 December 2015
Water-based heaters	In force	Decision of 28/05/2014 (**2014/314/EU**)	28 May 2018
Heat pumps	In force	Decision of 09/11/2007 (**2007/742/EC**)	31 December 2016

PAPER PRODUCTS

Converted paper	In force	Decision of 02/05/2014 (**2014/256/EU**)	2 May 2017
Newsprint paper	In force	Decision of 12/07/2012 (**2012/448/EU**)	12 July 2015
Copying and graphic paper	In force	Decision of 7/06/2011 (**2011/333/EU**)	07 June 2015
Tissue paper	In force	Decision of 9/07/2009 (**2009/568/EC**)	30 June 2015
Printed paper	In force	Decision of 16/08/2012 (**2012/481/EU**)	16 August 2015

(*Continued*)

Table 4.2 Validity of the criteria for Ecolabel product groups (*Continued*)

Product groups	Criteria status	Reference document	Valid until
HOUSEHOLD AND GARDEN ITEMS			
Bed mattresses	In force	Decision of 23/06/2014 (**2014/391/EU**)	23 June 2018
Sanitary tapware	In force	Decision of 21/05/2013 (**2013/250/EU**)	21 May 2017
Flushing toilets and urinals	In force	Decision of 07/11/2009 (**2013/641/EU**)	07 November 2017
Wooden furniture	In force (under revison)	Decision of 30/11/2009 (**2009/894/EC**)	31 December 2015
Hard covering	In force	Decision of 9/07/2009 (**2009/568/EC**)	30 November 2019
Textile floor covering	In force	Decision of 30/11/2009 (**2009/967/EC**)	31 December 2015
Wooden floor covering	In force (under revison)	Decision of 26/11/2009 (**2010/18/EC**)	31 December 2015
Growing media	In force (under revison)	Decision of 15/11/2006 (**2007/64/EC**)	31 December 2015
Soil improvers	In force (under revison)	Decision of 3/11/2006 (**2006/799/EC**)	31 December 2015
DO IT YOURSELF			
Paints and varnishes	In force	Decision of 28/05/2014 (**2014/312/EU**)	28 May 2018
CLOTHING			
Shoes	In force (under revision)	Decision of 9/07/2009 (**2009/567/EC**)	30 June 2015
Textile products	In force	Decision of 5/06/2014 (**2014/350/EU**)	5 June 2018

Product groups	Criteria status	Reference document	Valid until
TOURISM			
Camping services	In force (under revision)	Decision of 9/07/2009 **(2009/564/EC)**	30 November 2015
Services for tourist reception	In force (under revision)	Decision of 9/07/2009 **(2009/578/EC)**	30 November 2015
LUBRICANTS			
Lubricants	In force (under revision)	Decision of 24/06/2011 **(2011/381/EU)**	24 June 2015

Source: European Commission

An important innovation introduced in the new version of the Regulation is the aim to make the scheme more widely available and attractive for consumers who are increasingly more inclined to look at the different features of a so-called 'ethical' product working together as a whole (and reward their complexity). The Commission tries, in fact, to place other types of criteria that can better satisfy the requirements of more knowledgeable consumers alongside those for awarding the Ecolabel, which are strictly related to the environment.

Among the aspects to consider in the definition of environmental criteria indicated in Article 6, the Regulation, therefore:

- reconfirms the references to aspects linked to the health and safety of consumers and users, already introduced in the previous version of the Ecolabel, but ignored in the development or review of criteria carried out over the years in which it was in force;
- includes principle of reducing animal testing, an aspect that is on the border between issues concerning ethics and respect for the environment;
- emphasises the opportunity to completely integrate social and ethical aspects by referring to relevant international agreements and codes of conduct, such as the ILO conventions (*International Labour Organization*).

If applied effectively, the three guidelines for a more holistic outlook of the guarantees offered by the label, for a perspective of true 'sustainability' could really become very attractive elements to renew interest by consumers.[12]

Lastly, the new Regulation has introduced some important new elements aimed at the harmonisation of the Ecolabel and other eco-labelling programmes set up and managed by the Member States in an attempt to simplify and accelerate the definition of new groups and criteria Europe-wide as well.

Competition between the sole official European scheme and the numerous pre-existing national schemes was at the centre of a debate on the development of the Ecolabel in the EU and, in particular, in some Member States in which, at opposing ends, the scheme is either widespread or barely present depending on whether or not it can co-exist with similar national schemes with which it partially overlaps.

To this purpose, Regulation 66/2010 establishes the following:

- the obligation to consider analogous criteria for similar products covered by other national environmental labels (above all if they fall under the type I classification proposed by the ISO 14024 standard) during the preparation process of criteria for new groups of Ecolabel products;
- the possibility for a Member State to propose the criteria of its own national label through an 'abbreviated' procedure as a base for the development of criteria of a similar group of products in the EC and therefore, to be able to extend its validity Europe-wide;
- the possibility of those Member States with a national label to introduce criteria for groups of products already included in the Ecolabel scheme, but only if they are as stringent as those included in the European scheme (Art. 11).

The intention of the European Commission is for these dispositions to give more consistency to the attempts to harmonise with the national labels and collaborate with the institutions that are responsible for them, but that have not had the results hoped for in the past (Figure 4.2 shows the new EU Ecolabel logo).

Figure 4.2 The European Ecolabel logo (source: Regulation [ec] no 66/2010 – Annex ii).

The Environmental Product Declaration (EPD)

The EPDs are an innovative tool and are part of the so-called type III environmental claims regulated by the international standard ISO 14025.

The EPD is a short document that outlines a simple 'profile' of the environmental performance of a product/service and allows objective, comparable and credible data and information to be communicated. It is important to emphasise that the content of an EPD is for information purposes only since it does not include criteria for assessment, preference or minimum levels that the product or service must respect, but rather the objective to put the client, the target of the document, in the position of being able to make a knowledgeable and well-informed choice at the time of purchase.

The main aim of this tool is to emphasise the environmental performance of a product/service by increasing its visibility and social acceptance and promoting a confrontation between products with the same function. This shows the great potential for consumer goods normally offered to consumers in retail outlets and exhibition spaces, which enable a direct comparison of their features and sometimes even their performances (including environmental performances). Through the EPD, the consumers can learn about the greenhouse effect that may potentially be caused by the product they are about to purchase and choose the one that causes less CO_2 emissions.

In order to enable a fair confrontation between environmental declarations of functionally equivalent products, the products must be classified in clearly defined groups through uniform criteria. One of the strong points of the EPD is that the declaration can be verified and validated by an accredited third party in order to guarantee the completeness, comprehensiveness and truth of the information contained in it. The outcome of the verification and validation activities is the granting of a certification and a label to accompany the EPD.

Another strong point of the tool is the solid scientific base on which the information communicated externally is based: the environmental product performance provided in the EPDs must, in fact, be based on – and guaranteed by – the results of the LCA conducted in accordance with the ISO 14040 standards.

The aim of the EPD according to the ISO 14025 standard is, therefore, to encourage demand and supply for those products and services that cause less impact on the environment and as a result, trigger a mechanism for continual improvement of competitive and environmental performance.

The EPD is a series of quantified environmental data consisting of pre-set categories of parameters based on the LCA although some additional environmental information may be included on aspects that the life cycle analysis method does not envisage (e.g. visual impacts, noise, level of danger and risk analysis, etc.). The EPD also contains information about the correct use of the product and its disposal and quantifies the different impacts of what could happen to the product at the end of its life.

The information published in the EPD must be appropriate for the group of products, the user and presented in standard format.

ISO 14025 does not only establish the features that an EPD must have and the methodological and scientific grounds on which it should be based, but it also defines the requirements that a voluntary EPD programme must adhere to in terms of programme management, consultation by interested parties, specific product requirements, choice of product groups to include in the programme itself and the functioning of the verifiers' certification and accreditation process.

One of the first EPD programmes developed within the framework proposed by ISO 14025 is the 'Certified Environmental Product Declaration'.

Today this programme, which was originally developed in a Member State (Sweden), is the most widely used in the European Union. It was set up in 1997 on the instigation of some industry sectors and the programme is one of the most successful innovations on the international scene of type III environmental declarations including products with EPD certifications in numerous European countries (especially in Italy and Sweden, but also in Belgium, Poland, the Czech Republic and Lithuania) and non-European countries (Japan, South Korea).

Currently the EPD system is governed by a 'competent body' that was originally appointed by the Swedish government to manage the programme *Swedish Environmental Management Council* (SEMC),[13] which as '*program operator*' has gradually allowed representatives from other countries to take part in its decision-making bodies. The main tasks of the SEMC are to develop the requirements of the scheme, define the product groups, develop or approve the Product Category Rules (PCRs) with which to conduct the LCA studies and draft the declarations, coordinate all the parties involved in implementing the programme, register the declarations and promote the system through information campaigns for the target audience (Figure 4.3 shows the EPD logo).

In order to provide some practical guidelines, we can take a look now at how a manufacturer can obtain EPD certification of its products. Any type of organisation situated anywhere in the world intending to develop and use an EPD on the market must, first of all, apply certain 'rules' established by the ISO reference standards and by additional provisions of the international system for conducting a life cycle analysis of its product or service including the '*Product Category Rules*' (PCRs) – which, if not already in existence, are proposed by the same organisation and undergo a rigorous approval process involving public consultation). The PCR are, in fact, an identity document for each single product group to which the manufacturer or service provider must refer in order to produce an EPD that complies with the system. They are developed with the aim of making some common 'rules of the game' available to manufacturers of goods and service providers, so they can clearly identify the functional and performance features

Figure 4.3 EPD logo (source: The International EPD® System).

characterising a product category, define the criteria to use in the LCA study of the products in the category and indicate the type of information that must be included in the EPD. The PCR are proposed by the organisations participating in the EPD process (or by the relevant trade associations) and made available for public consultation to competitors, sector-related associations, consumers and all interested parties before receiving final approval by the operator of the scheme.

The environmental performance guidelines resulting from the LCA must be summarised into an official EPD according to an explanatory diagram including the information such as

- energy consumption (renewable and non-renewable);
- waste generation;
- impact on the main global and regional environmental problems (greenhouse effect, ozone depletion, acidification, etc.);
- correct product use to limit impacts;
- recommendations for correct re-use;
- product and component recovery and recycling, etc.

The EPD is divided into three sections. The first section contains general information about the organisation and the product or service covered by the Declaration. The LCA study results are included in the second section showing the relevant indicators for the consumption of renewable and non-renewable resources, electricity consumption, waste generation and the main categories of environmental impact (e.g. GWP [Global Warming Potential] or ODP [Ozone Depletion Potential]) divided into phases for production and user (unless the PCR for a specific product category calls for quantified performance information of other phases). The third and final section is reserved for additional information that may be of interest to anyone using the tool who, due to methodological limits and settings, cannot be guided by a life cycle assessment (such as indications reserved for users on how to reduce the environmental impact during the product's use and disposal).

The EPD, including any corporate processes behind it guaranteeing credibility and methodological robustness, efficient communication and continual updates, must then be submitted to an *accredited environmental verifier*. Once validation and EPD registration are obtained, the organisation can use this performance 'profile' as a marketing and communications tool, for example, to enhance the environmental benefits of a product/service in comparative advertising with its main competitors.

The product environmental footprint (PEF) and the product carbon footprint

The proliferation of environmental claims in the market and the increase of misleading claims regarding the environmental performance of products has mined the level of trust of consumers towards the environmental information that a producer communicate about own products. This situation pushed the European Commission to establish a common harmonised methodological approach to assess the potential environmental impact of products and services over the entire life-cycle to create a green single market.

The LCA of products and services in compliance with the ISO 14040-14044 standards or the requirements of the ILCD manual (*International Reference Life Cycle Data System*) developed by the European Commission's Joint Research Centre (JRC) has provided an initial, partially shared tool to calculate and communicate potential environmental impacts. However, given the excessive flexibility of the ISO standards, on the one hand, and the wordiness of the ILCD manual on the other, the European Commission has decided to draft a new methodology to regulate the product life cycle analysis.

The Product Environmental Footprint methodology (PEF) is principally aimed at providing the analyst with technical guidelines in as much detail as possible to carry out the LCA, so that studies and results conducted by different analysts on similar products can be compared more easily. In other words, where pre-existing different calculation methods provided a spectrum of alternatives for a certain choice of methodology for carrying out the LCA, the PEF methodology instead aims to provide a single alternative or requirement (or at least to provide other guidance or additional requirements) in order to ensure that PEF studies are carried out in a more robust, consistent, comprehensive and reproducible manner.

Currently, the PEF methodology is included in Annex A of the Commission Recommendation of 9 April 2013 (2013/179/EU) regarding the use of common methodologies to measure and communicate environmental performance during the life cycle of products and organisations.

It provides both general guidelines for calculating the PEF and specific methodological requirements for the definition of rules per product category (hereinafter PEFCR [*Product Environmental Footprint Category Rules*]).

The PEFCRs are a necessary extension of, and complement to, the more general guidance for PEF studies, and are aimed at providing more detailed technical guidelines on how to conduct an environmental impact study for specific product categories. In short, the PEFCRs accompany and complete the general guidelines by providing specific indications for each product category.

As previously explained, the model proposed by the PEF methodology is based on the concept of 'product life cycle'. Just as in the LCA analysis defined in the ISO 14040 series of standards, the life cycle concept takes into consideration the flow of resources and environmental interventions associated with a product from a supply chain perspective. This includes all phases from the procurement of raw materials to manufacturing, distribution, use and end-of-life disposal, as well as all relevant environmental impacts, effects on health and risks associated with the resources and burden on the company.

Even though the PEF methodology was published quite recently (April 2013), it is not an entirely new reference for carrying out assessments on the complete life cycle of products and services since it takes into account recommendations from numerous, widely recognised environmental accounting methods such as the previously mentioned ISO standards (especially ISO 14044:2006) and the ILCD manual (*International Reference Life Cycle Data System*); and also the standards for ecological footprint (Ecological Footprint Standards 2009); the protocol for greenhouse gas (Greenhouse Gas Protocol Product Life Cycle Accounting and Reporting Standard, 2011); the general principles for an environmental communication on mass-market products; and the specifications for the assessment of the life cycle greenhouse gas emissions of goods and services (PAS 2050, 2011).

Before analysing the various methodology phases and requirements, it is advisable to list and briefly assess the principles for supporting robust, consistent, comprehensive and reproducible PEF studies. The five principles as defined in the Recommendation are outlined as follows:

1 *The principle of relevance*: all methods used and data collected for the purpose of quantifying the PEF shall be as relevant to the study as possible;
2 *The principle of completeness*: quantification of the PEF shall include all environmentally relevant material/energy flows and other environmental interventions as required for adherence to the defined system boundaries, the data requirements and the impact assessment methods employed;
3 *The principle of consistency*: strict conformity to this Guide shall be observed in all steps of the PEF study so as to ensure internal consistency and comparability with similar analyses;
4 *The principle of accuracy*: all reasonable efforts shall be taken to reduce uncertainties in product system modelling and the reporting of results;
5 *The principle of transparency*: PEF information shall be disclosed in such a way as to provide intended users with the necessary basis for decision making, and for stakeholders to assess its robustness and reliability.

Unfortunately, it is not always possible to objectively quantify the adherence of a PEF study to these principles. Since PEF methodology complies with the ISO 14040-14044 standards, the phases that make it up are those described by the ISO standards as shown in Figure 4.4.

The *first phase* in a PEF model is the definition of the objectives in which the general context of the study is set. The definition of the objectives is a very important step because it guides all the subsequent methodological choices from the choice of the system boundaries to the requirements for data quality, to the method of analysis impact. It is especially important in this initial phase to identify the possible allocations and the degree of detail and robustness of the analyses.

For the sake of simplicity, the recommendation provides a list of the aspects that need to be taken into account in the goal definition:

• intended application(s);
• reason for carrying out the study and decision context;

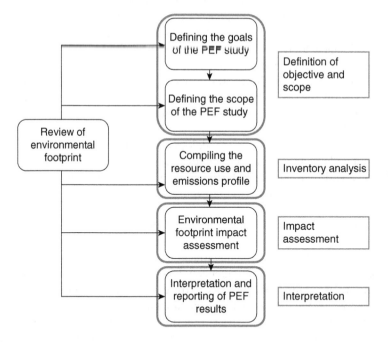

Figure 4.4 PEF phases (source: authors' own).

- target audience;
- whether comparisons and/or comparative assertions are to be disclosed to the public;
- commissioner of the study;
- review procedure (if applicable).

Table 4.3 gives an example taken from the Recommendation to better illustrate the goal definition phase. For each individual aspect, the analyst must provide clear answers that will subsequently influence the construction of the model and any feasible simplifications.

   In the second phase of the study, the assessment model and the relevant analysis criteria are outlined:

- unit of analysis and reference flow;
- system boundaries;
- Environmental Footprint impact categories;
- assumptions and limitations.

Although this phase is already included in the ISO 14040-14044 standards, there are some notable differences between the requirements for ISO, the ILCD manual and the PEF methodology with regards to the definition of the functional unit and the system boundaries.

Table 4.3 Definition of PEF goal

Aspects	Detail
Intended application(s)	Provide product information to customer
Reason for carrying out the study and decision context	Respond to a request from a customer
Comparisons to be disclosed to the public	No, it will be made publicly available, but it is not intended to be used for comparison or comparative assertions
Target audience	External technical audience, business-to-business
Review	Independent external reviewer, Mr. Y
Commissioner of the study	G company limited

Source: European Commission, 2013

The ISO standard simply specifies that the functional unit shall be consistent with the goal and scope of the study be clearly defined, whereas the ILCD manual goes further and specifies that the functional unit must be clearly defined both in terms of quantitative and qualitative aspects. The PEF methodology, however, requires the functional unit of the study to be defined more precisely on various aspects, namely:

- 'what' – the function or service provided;
- 'how much' – the magnitude of the function or service;
- 'how long' – the duration of the service provided or the service life-time;
- 'how well' – the expected level of quality;
- NACE codes.

Table 4.4 shows an example of the functional unit definition and reference flow for a hypothetical LCA study of a T-shirt (taken from the Recommendation).

Another difference is in the identification of the system boundaries, namely in the choice of which parts of the product life cycle and which associated processes belong to the analysed system. The ISO standard emphasises the iterative nature of the system boundary definition process where the initial system boundaries are defined on the basis of goals and objectives of the study whilst the final system boundaries are determined after various initial calculations. The PEF methodology specifies that the system boundaries include all the processes linked to the product supply chain and can be traced both by the 'cradle to grave' approach or otherwise, if specified in PERFCRs.

The processes included in the system boundaries are divided into *foreground* and *background* processes: the former, the 'foreground' processes, are the core processes in the product life cycle for which direct access to information is available;

Table 4.4 Function unit of a T-shirt

What	T-shirt (average for size S, M, L) made from polyester
Quantity	One T-shirt
Duration	For 5 years
Quality level	Wear one time per week and use washing machine at 30 degree for cleaning
Reference Flow	160 g of polyester

Source: European Commission, 2013

the latter, the 'background' processes, are those processes for which direct access to information is not possible.

There are also differences between the ISO standard and the PEF methodology when it comes to the identification of impact categories to consider in the study. Where the ISO standard requires the choice of impact categories, category guidelines and characterisation models to be justified and consistent with the goal and scope of the LCA allocation, but leaves ample room for the analyst to decide which impact categories to consider; the PEF methodology provides a predefined set of impact categories that must be considered (14 in the PEF methodology).

Lastly, another difference between the various guidelines is the 'modelling' approach. The ISO standard provides the principles of how to calculate the environmental burden associated with products and expresses the preference for approaches avoiding allocation for multifunctional processes, whereas the PEF methodology uses elements taken from both attributional and consequential modelling approaches.

In the third phase – *Compiling and Recording the Resource Use and Emissions Profile* – an inventory of all the material/energy resource inputs/outputs and emissions into air, water and soil for the product supply chain is compiled ('Life Cycle Inventory' in the ISO standards). In the PEF methodology it is recommended that the following classification of flows is adopted in the study:

* elementary flows;
* non-elementary or complex flows.

A two-step procedure is recommended for compiling the resource use and emissions profile in the PEF methodology. In the first phase known as screening, generic data is used (or specific if readily available) to populate the resource use and emissions profile and the environmental footprint impact assessment method is applied. The initial phase is an LCA screening and helps identify which flows (elementary and non-elementary) are the most important for the product in question and determine priorities for data collection and the definition of data quality criteria.

In the second phase, the resource use and emissions profile is completed by the best or most up-to-date data collected to ensure that the collected data meet the quality requirements and by the transformation of any remaining non-elementary flows into elementary flows.

Apart from the different name given to the phase (defined as 'inventory', as we have seen, in the ISO standard) and the suggestion of how to collect the data, there is also a notable difference in the assessment of the data quality. In the ISO standard, various data quality requirements are listed (time-related coverage, geographical coverage, technology coverage, precision, completeness, consistency, data sources, uncertainty of the information), but no minimum requirements are specified for the data quality. Moreover, the eight ISO criteria only need to be taken into consideration for comparative assessment. The PEF methodology only defines six requirements for data quality (technological representativeness, geographical representativeness, time-related representativeness, completeness, parameter uncertainty, methodological appropriateness and consistency), but establishes that they must be met by any PEF study intended for external communication.

Furthermore, a semi-quantitative assessment method of data quality is set in the PEF methodology and a minimum requirement of data quality is set for those processes/activities accounting for at least 70 per cent of contributions to each impact category.

Once the resource use and emissions profile has been complied, the *assessment of the environmental footprint impact* takes place (fourth phase) to calculate the environmental performance of the product using the environmental footprint impact categories and model. The PEF impact assessment includes two mandatory phases (classification and characterisation) and two optional steps (normalisation and weighting).

To carry out the impact assessment, the first step is to 'assign' a certain PEF impact category to every input and output flow of the analysed system. Every flow must be analysed to assess whether it has at least one for the pre-defined impact categories by the PEF methodology. A by no mean complete list of the impact categories is as follows: resource depletion, greenhouse effect, ozone depletion, human toxicity, ecotoxicity, formation of photochemical oxidants, acidification and eutrophication. Once the input and output flows from the system have been classified, the contribution of each of these flows to their respective impact categories is calculated and the contributions of the different flows are aggregated within the individual impact categories.

The calculation of the magnitude of the contributions is carried out between the characterisation factors, which are specific for every substance in every impact category. They represent the impact intensity of a single substance relative to a common substance, which may vary from category to category. In addition to the two compulsory phases, which have been described, a normalisation phase (recommended in the PEF studies) and a weighting phase (optional for the PEF studies) can also be performed. Table 4.5 shows an example of data classification in an impact category (in this case, climate change). Classification is the assessment, for each substance, of whether it is caused by a given impact or not. In the example, an assessment is carried out on whether the individual substances cause climate changes and so, carbon dioxide (CO_2) and methane (CH_4) are classified as sources of climate change whilst the other two substances are not considered in the climate change impact category, but will presumably be assessed in other impact categories.

Table 4.6, on the other hand, shows an example of characterisation of substances in an impact category (global warming). This is carried out by creating an impact category indicator, which is the aggregation of the contributions of all the substances classified as having an impact for that category. To calculate the contribution of a substance, the quantity of the substance in the inventory is multiplied by a characterisation factor that allows all the contributions to be aggregated and their effect on the common substance to be shown.

The two mandatory steps produce the results relating to the potential impacts of the product disaggregated by impact categories and in absolute values. In other words, in most cases it will be impossible to objectively assert that one product is

Table 4.5 Classification of substances in the climate change impact category

Substance	Classification
CO_2	Yes
CH_4	Yes
SO_2	No
NO_X	No

Source: European Commission, 2013

Table 4.6 Characterisation of substances in the global warming impact category

Substance	Quantity [kg]	Characterisation factor	kg CO_2eq
CO_2	5,132	1	5.132
CH_4	8.2	25	0.205
SO_2	3.9	0	0
NO_X	26.8	0	0
		Total	5.337

Source: European Commission, 2013

better than another because presumably there will be other impact categories in which product A is better than product B, others in which product B is better that product A and others still in which the performance of the two products is similar or equivalent. The results are shown in different 'formats', that is, each impact category has its own unit of measurement and scale. The spectrum of impact categories gives a complete overview of the potential impacts of the product, but makes it difficult to compare and interpret them.

For the reasons given, in some cases it may be advisable to carry out the normalisation and weighting phases of the results. In the normalisation phase, the results are shown as common values and expressed as dimensionless and normalised. The normalisation factors used enable the magnitude of the contributions of the results of the individual impact category assessment to be calculated and compared to a reference unit, typically the pressure related to that category caused by emissions over one year of a whole country or an average citizen. Consequently, dimensionless results are obtained. If the normalisation of results is carried out in a PEF analysis, the results must be communicated both before and after this phase.

Whilst the normalisation phase is recommended in PEF analyses, weighting is a complementary phase that may support the communication and interpretation of the results. In this phase, the results of the environmental footprint, for example the normalised results, are multiplied by a set of weighting factors that reflect the perceived relative importance of the impact categories considered. The weighted results can then be aggregated in various ways to obtain several aggregated values or a single overall impact indicator.

As already indicated in the ISO standard, the *interpretation phase* (fifth phase) mainly serves the purpose of ensuring the model respects the goals and quality requirements of the study and deriving robust conclusions and recommendations from the analysis. To meet these objectives, the interpretation phase must include the following four steps:

1   assessment of the robustness of the PEF model – it is advisable to carry out checks on completeness, sensitivity and consistency;
2   identification of hotspots – the key elements contributing to the PEF results are identified;
3   estimation of uncertainty – this helps to assess the robustness and applicability of the study results;
4   conclusions, recommendations and limitations.

The ISO standard, however, proposes three steps to meet the objectives: the first step identifies the significant aspects based on the inventory analysis results and the impact analysis; the second step assesses the checks on completeness, sensitivity and consistency; and the third step contains the conclusions, limitations and recommendations.

It is important to emphasise a totally new aspect of the PEF methodology if compared to the previously published guidelines, namely the qualification of the review and reviewer: the ISO standard gave general indications for drafting third party reports and called for a critical review of the study whenever the initial goal was to compare the product with other products on the market. The PEF methodology, however, calls for studies intended for public disclosure to be a reviewed by an independent, qualified, external reviewer (or panel of reviewers). If the study is intended to support a comparative assertion to be disclosed to the public, then is should be based on the relevant PEFCRs and critically reviewed by an external reviewer supported by panel of interested parties. Moreover, the PEF methodology includes minimum requirements to qualify as a reviewer.

The energy labels

One of the main challenges of the twenty-first century is to change people's behaviour in relation to energy consumption. However, there are many obstacles in the way of adopting energy-related behaviour, such as financial, psychological or material ones.

Studies have shown that electricity consumption in private households could be substantially reduced if people paid more attention to unnecessary use of electricity and if such attention were mirrored by a change in everyday behaviour (e.g. Gram-Hanssen et al., 2004). As the International Energy Agency has concluded, there is the need for 'a huge step-change in the attitudes to energy efficiency and consumer purchases by hundreds of millions of people worldwide…' (IEA, 2008).

Moreover, energy-saving behaviours based on a new 'technology choice' (e.g. purchasing of energy efficient appliances) could also generate relevant savings and contribute to the resource efficiency of all economy.

The purchasing of energy savings products determines both an environmental protection and an economic savings for the consumer. This strict linkage is well understood by consumer that if effectively informed, can address his/her purchasing choice towards more energy efficient products.

Starting from these assumptions, European Commission has published, in 1992, the Framework Directive 92/75/CEE on the use of energy label for the main household appliances.[14] The EU energy label is designed to provide consumers with accurate, recognisable and comparable information on domestic household products regarding energy consumption and other essential characteristics. The label is uniform for all products in a given category and consumers can compare easily the characteristics of appliances in a given category such as energy.

The various labels all have more or less the same graphical design: a series of arrows of increasing lengths in different colours. Each arrow is associated with a letter of the alphabet (from A to G). The length of the arrows depends on consumption: for equivalent performance; devices with lower consumption have a shorter arrow whilst those with higher consumption have a longer arrow.

Applying a label indicating energy consumption information is very important because it expresses the energy efficiency for that product and enables consumers to make choices regarding use, need and habits. It also influences production processes since the label tends to favour products with higher energy efficiency and thus, stimulates eco-design aimed at marketing products that gradually absorb less energy.

In 2003, the success of the labelling scheme led the European Union to introduce two new classes for refrigerating appliances, A+ and A++. These new categories were placed on top of the A class to respond to a market-led demand for environmental-friendly products and to incentivise suppliers to develop even more efficient products in this category. Even if the available data are quite old, there is a great expectation of a constant increase of consumer choice towards more efficient energy appliances. For instance, DEFRA has estimated that, from 2005 and 2009, the zero setting of sales of washing machine in energy class B has been achieved.

In 2010, the European Union adopted the new *Framework Directive* 2010/30/ EU, which brought in some important new elements for the energy-labelling system.

The first element concerns the definition of classes for energy efficiency. The labelling system can be broken down into three directives: if a new product consumes less energy than existing ones, the classification is revised to A+ so the least efficient energy class changes to F. If it is revised to A++, then the least efficient energy class changes to E. Lastly, if a new product consumes even less energy, then it will classified as A+++ and the least efficient energy class will be D. The colour scale, from dark green for devices with the highest energy efficiency, to red for those with least efficiency, will be adjusted so that the highest energy efficiency will be dark green and the lowest red.

The second new element concerns the type of products involved. The directive is applied to products that have a significant direct or indirect impact on the consumption of energy, and, if applicable, of other essential resources during their use, as well as additional information for energy-related products, so that end users can choose the most efficient products.

Another energy label was introduced into the European Union in 2001 through the 'Energy Star' programme, which covers the introduction of a voluntary label for high energy efficient office equipment. 'Energy Star' is a voluntary international labelling system for energy efficiency introduced by the American Environmental Protection Agency (EPA) in 1992. The European Community participated in the Energy Star system for office equipment through an agreement with the American government. The programme guarantees that devices bearing the specific logo (a five-pointed star) have reduced energy consumption. Currently computers, monitors, printers, faxes, franking machines, photocopiers, scanners and multifunction devices (such as combined printers and photocopiers) can be labelled. The product specifications are periodically reviewed on the basis of indications by the European Community Energy Star.

Notes

1 http://www.marketingcharts.com/interactive/consumers-recall-green-ads-but-often
 -skeptical-of-them-4343/hurst-media green ad claims-bellevability jpg/.
2 http://adage.com/article/news/survey-finds-consumer-economic-priorities-trump
 -environment/229915/.
3 http://environment.nationalgeographic.com/environment/greendex/.
4 http://www.consumerfocus.org.uk/assets/1/files/2009/06/Green-expectations-single
 -page.pdf.
5 http://www.greenerpackage.com/green_marketing/study_clear_environmental
 _claims_critical_consumer_acceptance.
6 Look no further than the widespread use of labels for natural and biological products
 in the food sector.
7 In particular, this series of ISO standards is broken down as follows: 14040 – Principles
 and Framework; 14041 – Goal and Scope Definition and Inventory Analysis; and
 14042 – Life Cycle Impact Assessment; 14043 – Interpretation.
8 The LCA can, in fact, be used to compare the environmental loads connected to alternative products or processes.
9 The standard defines input flow as material or energy that enters a process unit (the
 material can be raw materials or products); and it defines output flow as the material
 or energy that leaves a process unit (the material can be raw materials, intermediate
 products, products, emissions or wastes).
10 In this context, *impact* means the immediate physical result due to a given operation
 (e.g. the production of CO_2 resulting from combustion processes), whilst *effect* means
 the more general environmental "problem" associated with the impact (e.g. the greenhouse effect due to CO_2 emissions).
11 Given the complexity of the methodological approach and the processing and calculations to carry out, LCAs are normally conducted, starting from the layout of the study
 up until the assessment phase, with the support of specific software including databases
 (more or less complete) of secondary data, which can be used as a replacement when
 data cannot be collected in the field, above all for the life cycles that go beyond the
 company's management control and/or placed in remote geographical locations. The
 most commonly used software, in Italy as well, include: Bousted, Gabi and SimaPro,
 available in continually updated versions.
12 Article 6, in keeping with the objective of increasing the ability of the label to respond
 to the concerns today of community members/consumers, puts 'climate changes' as the
 first environmental aspect to consider when preparing criteria, an important current
 affairs topic and for which the Commission has recently developed and released a specific software to calculate the 'Carbon footprint' within the Ecolabel scheme.
13 Joint enterprise owned by the State, private enterprises and Swedish local
 authorities.
14 The product category of Energy labeling Directive are: lamps; luminaires; household
 air conditioners; household televisions; household tumble driers, household washing
 machines, household dishwashers; household refrigerating appliances; vacuum cleaners; wine storage appliances; space heaters; and water heaters.

References

Ajzen, I. 1988. *Attitudes, Personality and Behavior*. Milton Keynes: Open University Press.
Ajzen, I. 1991. 'The theory of planned behavior'. *Organizational Behavior and Human
 Decision Processes*, 50, 179–211.

Abdul Wahid N., Rahbar E., Shyan T. S., 2011. 'Factors influencing the green purchase behavior of Penang environmental volunteers'. *International Business Management*, 5, 38–49.

Aman A.H.L., Harun A., Hussein Z., 2012. 'The influence of environmental knowledge and concern on green purchase intention the role of attitude as a mediating variable'. *British Journal of Arts and Social Sciences*, 7, 145–167.

Bamberg, S., 2003. 'How does environmental concern influence specific environmentally related behaviors? A new answer to an old question'. *Journal of Environmental Psychology*, 23, 21–32.

Biel A., Thøgersen, J., 2007. 'Activation of social norms in social dilemmas: A review of the evidence and reflections on the implications for environmental behaviour'. *Journal of Economic Psychology*, 28, 93–112.

Biel A., Eek D., Gaärling T., 1999. The importance of fairness for cooperation in public-goods dilemmas. In P. Juslin & H. Montgomery (Eds.), *Judgment and Decision Making*. Hillsdale, NJ: Erlbaum, 245–259.

Blake D.E., 2001. 'Contextual effects of environmental attitudes and behavior'. *Environment and Behavior*, 33, 708–725.

Brécard D., Hlaimi B., Lucas S., Perraudeau Y., Salladarré F., 2009. 'Determinants of demand for green products: an application to eco-label demand for fish in Europe'. *Ecological Economics*, 69, 115–125.

Carrete L., Castaño R., Felix R., Centeno E., González E., 2012. 'Green consumer behavior in an emerging economy: confusion, credibility, and compatibility'. *Journal of Consumer Marketing*, 29, 470–481.

Chen T. B., Chai L. T., 2010. 'Attitude towards the environment and green products: consumers' perspective'. *Management Science and Engineering*, 4, 27–39.

Coleman J., 1990. *Foundations of Social Theory*. Cambridge, MA: Harvard University Press.

Cottrell S., 2002. Predictive model of responsible environmental behaviour: application as a visitor monitoring tool. Monitoring and management of visitor flows in recreational and protected areas, MMV 1 – Proceedings, 129–135.

D'Souza C., Taghian M., Khosla R., 2007. 'Examination of environmental beliefs and its impact on the influence of price, quality and demographic characteristics with respect to green purchase intention'. *Journal of Targeting, Measurement and Analysis for Marketing*, 15, 69–78.

Darnall N., Ponting C., Vazquez-Brust D. A., 2012. Why consumers buy green. In D. A. Vazquez-Brust & J. Sarkis (Eds.), *Green growth: managing the transition to a sustainable economy. Greening of industry networks studies*, Volume 1. New York: Springer.

De Boer J., 2003. 'Sustainability labeling schemes: the logic of their claims and their functions for stakeholders'. *Business Strategy and the Environment*, 12, 254–264.

Eurobarometer. (2011). Attitudes of European citizens towards the environment, Flash Eurobarometer 365. Available from: http://ec.europa.eu/public_opinion/archives/ebs/ebs_365_en.pdf.

Gotschi E., Vogel S., Lindenthal T., Larcher M., 2010. 'The role of knowledge, social norms, and attitudes toward organic products and shopping behavior: survey results from high school students in Vienna'. *The Journal of Environmental Education*, 41, 88–100.

Gram-Hanssen K., Kofod C., Nærvig Petersen K., 2004. Different everyday lives: Different patterns of electricity use. 2004 ACEEE Summer study on energy efficiency in buildings, 1–13.

Grob A., 1995. 'A structural model of environmental attitudes and behaviour'. *Journal of Environmental Psychology*, 15, 209–220.

Guagnano G. A., Stern P. C., Dietz T., 1995. 'Influences on attitude-behavior relationships a natural experiment with curbside recycling'. *Environment and Behavior*, 27, 699–718.

Ha H., Janda S., 2012. 'Predicting consumer intentions to purchase energy-efficient products'. *Journal of Consumer Marketing*, 29, 461–469.

Heberlein T. A., 1972. 'The land ethic realized: Some social psychological explanations for changing environmental attitudes'. *Journal of Social Issues*, 28, 79–87.

Heberlein T. A., Black J. S., 1976. 'Attitudinal specificity and the prediction of behavior in a fjeld setting'. *Journal of Personality and Social Psychology*, 33, 474–479.

Hornik J., Chertan J., Madansky M., Narayana C., 1995. 'Determinants of recycling behavior: a synthesis of research results'. *The Journal of Socio-Economics*, 24, 105–127.

Iraldo F., Testa F., Bartolozzi I., 2013. 'An application of Life Cycle Assessment (LCA) as a green marketing tool for agricultural products: the case of extra virgin olive oil in Val di Cornia, Italy'. *Journal of Environmental Planning & Management*, doi:10.1080/09640568.2012.735991.

Jackson T., 2005. Motivating sustainable consumption: a review of evidence on consumer behaviour and behavioural change: a report to the Sustainable Development Research Network. Centre for Environmental Strategy, University of Surrey.

Kalafatis S.P., Pollard M., East R., Tsogas M.H., 1999. 'Green marketing and Ajzen's theory of planned behavior: a cross-market examination'. *Journal of Consumer Marketing*, 16, 441–460.

Leonidou L.C., Leonidou C.N., Palihawadana D., Hultman M., 2011. 'Evaluating the green advertising practices of international firms: a trend analysis'. *International Marketing Review*, 28, 6–33.

López-Mosquera N., Sánchez M., 2012. 'Theory of Planned Behavior and the Value-Belief-Norm Theory explaining willingness to pay for a suburban park'. *Journal of Environmental Management*, 113, 251–262.

Loureiro M. L., McCluskey J. J., Mittelhammer R. C., 2001. 'Assessing consumer preferences for organic, eco-labeled, and regular apples'. *Journal of Agricultural and Resource Economics*, 26, 404–416.

Martiskainen M., 2007. Affecting consumer behaviour on energy demand. Sussex: SPRU–Science and Technology Policy Research 81.

Moisander J., 2007. 'Motivational complexity of green consumerism'. *International Journal of Consumer Studies*, 31, 404–409.

Mostafa M. M., 2007. 'Gender differences in Egyptian consumers' green purchase behavior: The effects of environmental knowledge, concern and attitude'. *International Journal of Consumer Studies*, 31, 220–229.

Oskamp S., Harrington M., Edwards T., Sherwood P.L., Okuda S.M., Swanson D.L., 1991. 'Factors influencing household recycling behavior'. *Environment and Behavior*, 23, 494–519.

Paco A.F., Raposo M.L., Filho W.L., 2009. 'Identifying the green consumer: a segmentation study'. *Journal of Targeting, Measurement and Analysis for Marketing*, 17, 17–25.

Peattie K., Crane A., 2005. 'Green marketing: legend, myth, farce, or prophesy?' *Qualitative Market Research: An International Journal*, 8, 357–370.

Perrini F., Castaldo S., Misani N., Tencati, A., 2010. 'The impact of corporate social responsibility associations on trust in organic products marketed by mainstream retailers: a study of Italian consumers'. *Business Strategy and the Environment*, 19, 512–526.

Ramayah T., Lee J.W.C., Mohamad O., 2010. 'Green product purchase intention: Some insights from a developing country'. *Resources, Conservation and Recycling*, 54, 1419–1427.

Stern P.C., 2000. 'New environmental theories: toward a coherent theory of environmentally significant behavior'. *Journal of Social Issues*, 56, 407–424.

Testa F., Iraldo F., Tessitore S., Frey M., 2011. 'Strategies and approaches green advertising: an empirical analysis of the Italian context'. *International Journal of Environment and Sustainable Development*, 10, 375–395.

Testa F., Iraldo F., Vaccari A., Ferrari E., 2013. 'Why Eco-labels can be effective marketing tools: evidence from a study on Italian consumers'. *Business Strategy and Environment*, DOI: 10.1002/bse.1821.

Tikka P., Kuitunen M., Tynys, S., 2000. 'Effects of educational background on students' attitudes, activity levels, and knowledge concerning the environment'. *Journal of Environmental Education*, 31, 12–19.

Thøgersen J., 2003. 'Monetary incentives and recycling: Behavioral and psychological reactions to a performance-dependent garbage fee'. Journal of Consumer Policy 26, 197–228.

5 The application of an environmental management system at territorial level

The literature framework in the field of environmental management systems at territorial level

An increasing amount of research indicates that the proximity of economic activities enables higher levels of productivity and innovativeness (Smith, 1994; Bathelt, 1998; Porter, 1998; Bengtsson and Soelvell, 2004).

In recent years, there has been a growing recognition of the idea that clusters of proximate firms play a key role in supporting innovation and wealth creation. For example, some authors (Schmitz and Nadvi, 1999) concluded that clustering helps firms to 'overcome growth constraints and compete in distant markets'. For some scholars, high performing clusters are underpinned by the economic efficiencies they confer on constituent firms, including increased specialisation, reduced transaction costs and enhanced reputation (Aharonson et al., 2007). From this perspective, spatial proximity, in particular, allows firms to take advantage of economies of scale and positive externalities such as an abundance of highly skilled labour, specialised subcontractors and rapid flows of information (Hirschman, 1958; Rosenthal and Strange, 2003).

One may wonder if the higher capability of resilience demonstrated by firms operating in clusters is a limited or negligible phenomenon considering the economy as a whole. This is certainly not the case with the EU: the Cluster Observatory of the European Commission carried out a quantitative analysis of EU-based clusters grounded on a fully comparable methodology. This study shows that clusters are a crucial part of the Union economy: according to this analysis, it can be assumed that roughly 38 per cent of all European employees work in enterprises that form a part of a cluster. Other studies show that in some regions this share reaches over 50 per cent, while in others it drops to 25 per cent (MERIT, 2006).

A peculiarity of the clusters is that the companies in this kind of territorial contexts are mostly Small and Medium Enterprises (SMEs). Quite interestingly, a part of the literature focusing on clusters, in the most recent years has emphasised how this co-operative approach is leading SMEs to gain new competitive edges, thanks to the ability of these territorial aggregations to tackle environmental, social and ethical issues linked to industrial production. In particular, the environmental problem has become, especially for SMEs, a key factor affecting their ability to comply with the law and to respond to consumers' and customers' demand, thus to survive on the market.

There are many studies in the literature that attempt to provide insights into the environmental problems caused (and faced) by SMEs. The ECAP (Environmental Compliance Assistance Programme) by the European Commission (European Commission, 2007), for example, reports that SMEs contribute up to 70 per cent of the industrial pollution in the EU. Other studies concentrate on specific environmental aspects. The Institute of Directors (2006) carried out a survey reporting that SME members involved in sectors such as construction, mining, transport or manufacturing are 'heavily exposed' to environmental regulation.

In light of this empirical evidence, one of the main emerging research questions concerning clusters regards their possible role to support proximate SMEs in managing environmental issues. In other words, the question is: can an SME participating in a cluster rely, for environmental management and innovation, on the same peculiar co-operative dynamics and locally-based resources that have traditionally supported its competition, growth and resilience to economic downturns?

According to empirical evidence and several research studies, networking between SMEs is one of the most important factors to foster environmental management and eco-innovation. Many authors (Hillary 1999; Steger, 2000; Rizzi et al., 2012) emphasise that working together with other 'fellow companies' is a useful and efficient way of adopting eco-innovation, particularly for SMEs, which often suffer from a lack of human, technical and economic resources needed for the application of eco-innovative solutions (Kassinis, 2001). This happens to be particularly effective between organisations operating in the same sector and between organisations operating in the same territorial area.

Moreover, consistently with the Marshallian theory of the 'industrial atmosphere', the high degree of cooperation, engagement and, sometimes, even strategic integration that takes place in the cluster between the SMEs and their social-institutional context, proves to be very effective in promoting eco-innovation, as confirmed by many studies (e.g. Alshuwaikhat and Abubakar, 2007).

The European Commission has underlined the key role of networking for overcoming the barriers to the adoption of eco-management and innovation practices among SMEs (European Commission, 2007). According to this perspective, SMEs operating in a cluster can exploit synergies and gain benefits in several ways: e.g. by identifying and tackling the same environmental aspects (because these originate from similar production processes and technologies), by developing common technological and operational solutions that can be applied to similar production processes and products, as well as by defining collective 'organisational structures' (e.g. cluster organisations) that are suitable for the same kinds of managerial needs and business models. Moreover, there can be synergies both in improving the environmental impacts on the same ecosystem (e.g. using the waste produced by a 'fellow SME' as a secondary raw material, as it happens in industrial ecology), and in interacting and communicating with the same stakeholders (local population, authorities, etc.) (Daddi et al., 2010).

There are cases in which a specific environmental policy has stimulated co-operative behaviour, and even network creation, among SMEs within a cluster, in order to support information exchange and skill sharing and to define and apply common solutions to similar environmental, technical and/or organisational problems, or to share environmental management resources. This has happened particularly with the set of voluntary policy instruments introduced since the early 1990s by the European Commission: the EMAS Regulation, the EU Ecolabel, covenants and voluntary agreements, etc. The EMAS implementation has been strongly enhanced and empowered by way of co-operative formal or informal networks of SMEs, often taking place within the supply chain, e.g. with a larger customer willing to stimulate and support small suppliers in applying, and eventually registering in this scheme (Andreas et al., 2010).

The 'EMAS cluster approach'

On the basis of these premises, a new model for supporting the adoption of voluntary management tools (known as the 'EMAS Cluster Approach') has been developed in the last few years (Battaglia et al., 2010; Von Weltzien and Shankar, 2011).

This 'territorial' approach to Environmental Management originated in the European context at the end of the 1990s (Iraldo, 2002; Battaglia et al., 2008). The first cluster-oriented EMAS experiments revealed the possibility of a new way of applying the scheme requirements (according to Reg. EC/761/2001, modified in Reg. EC/1221/2009) to spatial aggregations of many similar SMEs, strongly innovating what had been, until then, the process of implementing an environmental management system (EMS) only to a single organisation or site. At the beginning, this approach led to the EMAS registration of a productive areas and industrial parks (i.e. groups of companies located in a limited and constrainable area), but it was not applicable, as such, to wider territorial clusters. Only at a later stage, at the end of the 1990s, the EMAS Cluster approach was extended and upgraded to be applicable also to wider contexts, such as industrial districts or even local and regional supply-chains.

This approach fosters a cooperative and integrated environmental management at the cluster level, based on the relations existing between territorial environmental performance and the proximity between firms and other local actors and stakeholders. The methodology underpinning the approach encompasses the implementation of exactly the same steps foreseen by the EMAS Regulation for single companies, but reinterpreted at the cluster level, i.e. by exploiting the 'co-opetition' attitude (i.e. cooperation between firms that also compete) and the potential collaboration between private companies and the other economic and institutional actors.

This wider applicability of EMAS provides the possibility to consider the EU scheme as a new policy tool that is capable of pursuing together and in synergy two goals at different levels: on one hand, fulfilling the environmental managerial needs of the smaller companies and, on the other, responding to the interests of Local Governments to improve the environmental performance of companies under their jurisdiction (Del Brio and Junquera, 2003; Lepoutre and Heene, 2006).

The first need emerges from the fact that, despite their constraints in terms of human, technical and economic resources, the adoption of EMAS represents a relevant opportunity for SMEs facing the competitive challenges induced by the globalisation process and the increased (and increasing) social and market attention on environmental performance (Steger, 2000; Rennings et al., 2005; Barla, 2007; Daddi et al., 2011). The second need, for a new and more effective approach to territorial environmental management, stems from the considerable limits of the traditional policy tools available to Local Governments, such as the Agenda 21 Local processes (Baldizzone, 2000). The EMAS cluster approach can be an answer to this twofold need felt by both the private and the public actors operating in an industrial district, a technological park or any other form of territorial agglomeration.

This approach relies on the possibility that, since the SMEs in a cluster are similar and face the same environmental problems, they can develop and share solutions at the territorial level. For instance, when tackling the key steps of an EMS implementation process, the SMEs located in a cluster could take advantage from defining shared environmental 'targets' and common improvement plans, from identifying the same relevant environmental aspects, as well as by responding to the needs of the same environmental stakeholders, given the same social and institutional 'fabric' with which they interact.

Moreover, the SMEs belonging to a cluster must presumably comply with the same local and sectoral legislation, make business with the same players in the supply-chain (e.g. the raw material suppliers or the technology providers) and face the same environmentally relevant emergency situations. In addition, there are several scale-economies that can result from joint environmental management of the equipment and services shared by the SMEs in the cluster (e.g. water purification systems). Finally, in a cluster there are positive effects resulting from interacting with the citizens as environmental stakeholders, due to the almost total coincidence of companies' personnel with the local community of the cluster.

According to this perspective, a 'territorial' approach based on EMAS has been considered in many EU Member States as an opportunity to integrate industrial, territorial and environmental policies in industrial clusters (Battaglia et al., 2008; Daddi et al., 2012; Battaglia et al., 2010).

This approach has been tested and developed especially in the Member States where EMAS has had greater success: Germany (with the so-called 'Konvoi' approach), Italy (for with the APO 'Ambiti Produttivi Omogenei' scheme, i.e. homogeneous productive contexts), Spain (cooperation in the supply chain, especially in the tourism sector) and Nordic countries (especially in Denmark and Sweden).

A study by IEFE et al. (2006), carried out on behalf of the European Commission to support the revision of EMAS, confirmed the importance of networking. The results of 200 interviews with EMAS registered organisations and other stakeholders showed that

- EMAS is positively affecting environmental management within the supply chains, e.g. 77 per cent of the EMAS registered organisations are supporting their suppliers in the adoption of measures and initiatives for environmental improvement, and 72 per cent declare that the EMS influences their products performance in the supply chain;
- 54 per cent of the interviewees believe that a simplified access to registration for micro enterprises and SMEs, also based on co-operative and networking initiatives, would be a fairly or very important support for EMAS development (another 17 per cent believe that that this would be 'somewhat important'). This percentage is higher if we consider the sub-sample of the small companies (fewer than 50 employees);
- 31 per cent believe that it would be (very or fairly) important to use a 'cluster approach' as a potentially effective support for the diffusion of EMAS among SMEs (an additional 23 per cent think it would be 'somewhat important').

Similarities can be also identified between the EMAS Cluster approach and the Regional Environmental Management Systems (REMS). In the literature, some papers describe REMS application experiences (Welford, 1996; Niutanen and Korhonen, 2003; Welford, 2004). To apply the 'REMS model', there is no specific fixed criterion established as a standard. Despite this, the model works through some principles that can be linked to the requirements of the EMAS cluster approach. For example, the model foresees a wide public-private partnership and the identification of shared local, regional and state priorities, relevant to the partnering organisations (Parrish and Wassersug, 2012).

Recently, an additional experience on EMAS cluster approach has been developed. The 'Move it!' project had the objective to reduce internal and external cost for SMEs to implement EMAS in five European countries (Belgium, Germany, Bulgaria, Cyprus and Estonia), involving 15 touristic clusters. The project involved 144 companies and 110 of them were labeled or recognised by the end of project in June 2012 (Merli et al., 2014).

Finally, a recent paper describes the capacity of EMAS cluster approach to spread the tool not only among industrial companies: the experience involved a cluster of 33 small municipalities (Botta and Comoglio, 2013). The authors observe that 'the cluster approach allowed to analyze in a uniform and comprehensive way the environmental issues of the territory both at cluster and at single municipality level, sharing knowledge and resources among cluster members, creating scale-economies that led to a significant costs reduction and enforcing the position of the municipalities in the relationships with relevant stakeholders'.

Grounding on these experiences, several studies have been performed in the past on cooperative environmental management and voluntary policy instruments adopted in industrial clusters, but very few assessed the effectiveness of these approach. In this article, we aim to evaluate if and how the EMAS cluster approach has been fully effective in improving the environmental performance of companies operating in a cluster. To achieve this goal, we use the evidence collected in the case study of the Lucca paper industry cluster located in the Region of Tuscany in Central Italy.

The application of an environmental management system in industrial clusters

The possibility of using EMSs and associated certification schemes in territorial policies has attracted the attention of international institutions. The OECD Territorial Development Policy Committee has produced a document analysing the ways in which compatibility and synergy between these policy areas can be promoted. The document touches on the potential of the 'territorial management system' approach and emphasises that it could enable

- information flows on cross-linking of competence and expertise in the territory to enrich the potential of local experience in managing different environmental problems;
- the level of coordination and cooperation in implementing local environmental policies to be strengthened through an information exchange between public and private parties in the area allowing them to identify and focus on local priorities;
- any interactions between different environmental media and social and economic activities that are generated and influenced by them to be taken into account;
- a solid base to be offered in negotiations on joint environmental improvement goals with public and private commitment;
- a change in the way competitiveness between territories is handled, to be encouraged by transitioning from competition based mainly on lower production costs due to 'lighter' regulatory environmental pressure to one based on 'environmental quality'.

The size of the cluster area and, above all, the industrial district makes it an excellent candidate for the application of certification tools discussed in this book.

The advantages of the 'cluster' approach

The first legislative input for an 'area' and territorial approach in implementing EMAS came with the Commission Decision 680/2001 (EC) supplementing the EMAS II Regulation, but is no longer in force since it was repealed by Regulation 66/2010.

The Decision defining the 'entities' undergoing registration, introduced the possibility for the first time for 'small enterprises operating in a given large territory and producing the same or similar products or services' to develop and implement the so-called 'territorial environmental programme', namely a general programme implemented by local authorities, industrial associations, chambers of commerce and other stakeholders in the area for environmental improvement of the whole territory. Furthermore, the same point in the Decision indicated that this programme could be based on an initial environment analysis 'of the whole territory' and identified it as 'a very useful preliminary step for organisations in the territory approaching EMAS' by establishing that it must be 'clearly identified, published' and above all, 'accepted by all concerned parties'.

Moreover, the Decision clarified that prior to the environmental programme, the local stakeholders could develop 'a common environmental policy' and 'search for common solutions to their environmental problems', as well as 'participate in local environmental projects, such as Agenda 21 processes'.

Lastly, among the suggestions that the Commission made, one in particular was worthy of note, namely 'setting up a promotion body' to coordinate the proposed territorial programme.

The Decision was subsequently backed by Recommendation 680/2001/EC, which provided a series of interesting guidelines intended for EMAS verifiers operating in SMEs and micro-enterprises, establishing that partnership solutions among micro-enterprises can be accepted to share resources and practical experience in conducting audits or that audits can be conducted by chambers of commerce, trade and craft associations, locally based SME associations or similar, which is clearly intended to further emphasise the importance of intermediary institutions in simplifying the process of adopting the EMAS tool by local SMEs.

A final reference, subsequent to the above-mentioned documents, is Recommendation EC 532 of 10 July 2003 for the choice and use of environmental performance indicators regarding the EMAS Regulation. This Recommendation advocates the basic principle of comparing data to form indicators and in order to comply with this principle, organisations are invited to use generate indicators for comparison consistently to avoid the comparison of 'apples and pears'.

From this point of view, the Recommendation recognises the specific importance of the role of trade and professional associations and local or regional administrations (as well as national ones, of course) in setting these standards. Organisations, as stated in the Recommendation, should be aware of these benchmarks and choose their indicators to allow direct comparison of their data with them. So, the opportunity was confirmed for significant local stakeholders to contribute significantly in an important activity regarding EMSs: the measurement and monitoring of data relating to environmental aspects considered crucial in the organisation's operations.

Since SMEs in a uniform production system have similar characteristics and probably deal with the same environmental problems, they can exploit the advantages of identifying shared environmental targets, environmental significance of the same environmental aspects and interaction with the same social and institutional framework. The SMEs belonging to the same territorial system should, therefore, comply with the same environmental regulation, interact with the same supply chain and tackle the same environmental emergencies. For this reason, it should be possible to coordinate environmental management between different organisations (both private and public) leading to an improvement in performance and a reduction in the costs and expenses of environmental management for all the organisations.

Significant economies of scale can be derived, for example, from sharing the environmental management of equipment and environmental services by enterprises in an industrial district, as well as the positive effects of interaction with the community (due to the large numbers of local community members employed by companies in the same district) and the knock-on effect caused by the integrated management of the supply chain through the influence that bigger companies can exercise on smaller, less structured companies.

The operational phases for EMS application by clusters

The first goal in a cluster wanting to apply an Environmental Application System is to determine in exactly which area it will be applied. This phase is exactly the same as the definition of the field of application of an EMS within an organisation. It is, above all, necessary to clearly indicate which organisations fall into the uniform production process and what areas of activity and/or production chains are involved.

The operational steps required are the following:

1   to nominate a Promotion Committee: this party will have the goal of setting up a single governing body to manage cluster policies developed in applying the EMS;
2   to draft an environmental policy: which is not only very important in establishing broad principles shared by the stakeholders in the cluster, but also in determining the modus operandi for subsequent activities;
3   to prepare an Environmental Cluster Analysis: to be used as an operational document by the Promotion Committee in the subsequent phases (especially in the Programming phase) with particular attention on the parts of the Analysis document that can be shared with organisations in the cluster;
4   to draft a Cluster Improvement Programme;
5   to initiate internal and external communications initiatives.

1. Creating a Promotion Committee

The first, preparatory step for an EMS cluster approach concerns the creation of a Promotion Committee that can animate and coordinate all the activities concerning the management of environmental problems in the area occupied by the cluster, prioritise any interventions or actions required and the relevant implementation methods. In order to grant the Promotion Committee the necessary authorisation to carry out activities governing the entire process, the nomination must be approved by an official agreement and formalised by all the members. Moreover, in order to ensure the effectiveness of the actions that the Committee will have to carry out, it is recommended that the following three principles are met in full:

a   *Representativeness of the Promotion Committee*: the Promotion Committee must represent the main public and private interests within the industrial district and directly involve both parties with a collective interest in environmental protection (government institutions) and the main representatives of the manufacturing sector operating in the industrial area. The participants in the Promotion Committee should be able to involve and activate other parties, which although outside the Committee, are deemed essential for the implementation of the planned environmental improvement actions; the methods of achieving this involvement must be formally documented.

b   *Functioning of the Promotion Committee*: the modus operandi of the Committee should be clearly defined with particular reference to the methods of nominating the participants and the terms of their office, the methods for organising meetings and resolutions, as well as minutes of any decisions taken. The resolutions should be confirmed by a unanimous vote or approved by the majority of the participants in the Promotion Committee, or at least for

- approval of the Cluster Environmental Policy
- approval of the Cluster Environmental Programme
- approval of the set of indicators to monitor from within the cluster
- approval of the external communications tool

c   *Functions of the Promotion Committee*: the Promotion Committee must be able to

- identify any actions required to improve the conditions of main environmental hotspots;
- look for resources and directly implement any actions called for whenever members of the Committee are exclusively involved in them;
- mobilise and involve other parties whenever the actions required do not exclusively involve members of the Promotion Committee and support them in the search for resources needed to implement whatever has been planned;
- directly carry out the operational activities linked to applying EMAS in the cluster, including:

  - The implementation of the Cluster Environmental Review;
  - The definition and dissemination of the Cluster Environmental Policy and Programme;
  - The identification of the most suitable external communications tool for the specific production and territorial context, drafting and distribution of the tool.

2. Drafting a Cluster Environmental Policy

In order for the Environmental Policy of the district to be considered truly representative of all local interests, it must be drafted and approved by the Promotion

Committee and signed by all its members; the date of approval must be specified and written on the document.

The Cluster Environmental Policy must establish the guiding principles and general priorities for any actions to adopt in the future in the reference territory.

The Policy is the reference framework for the environmental policies, which can be drafted by all the organisations operating in the cluster and for establishing and reviewing the Cluster Environmental Programme by the Promotion Committee. From this point of view, this document takes precedence over the documents that are created from it by the individual organisations; it should be distributed among all the stakeholders of the Promotion Committee and made available to anyone requesting it in accordance with the current EMAS Regulation.

The Cluster Environmental Policy should ensure the following:

- formal adherence by all interested parties and in particular, that all local parties with control and influence over future programming of the environmental performance are involved;

Box 5.1 Example of possible commitments included in a Cluster Environmental Policy

The Cluster Promotion Committee, as a whole, is committed to the following:

- *defining and implementing improvements on environmental aspects and cluster problems deemed significant in the Initial Review using the cluster environmental management tools;*
- *stimulating and supporting initiatives by other parties in the cluster to improve environmental performance, particularly of the most significant environmental aspects and territorial problems;*
- *distributing the environmental management tools provided by the Promotion Committee among all the cluster organisations to facilitate the management of their environmental aspects and encourage prevention of pollution;*
- *encouraging verification and management of regulatory conformity and compliance with the obligations established for the different types of cluster organisations by providing support to identify, update and manage these obligations;*
- *encouraging continual improvement of the environmental performance of the cluster measured by monitoring an indicator system for environmental quality and the performance of the local production system;*
- *disseminating the voluntary concept of environmental management and, in particular, participation in EMAS or the European Ecolabel by companies in the industrial cluster and all the other organisations operating in the territory in question;*
- *providing information on the environmental quality of the territory and the development of the state variables deemed significant for monitoring the environmental performance;*
- *promoting transparency and open communications towards other institutions and authorities operating in the territory, towards the community and all the social stakeholders about actions taken to protect the environment and the evolution of environmental performance.*

- the duration of the agreement is consistent with the time required to achieve the pre-established general objectives;
- roles and responsibilities are correctly identified and provisos exist to maintain them (through any legally binding agreement or else that they are explicitly mentioned in the agreement);
- appropriate human and financial resources are identified for the activities that the Promotion Committee/Manager must carry out, as indicated in the agreement, or by quoting the source in which the information can be found.

3. Carrying out a Cluster Environmental Review

The Cluster Environmental Review must be carried out and periodically updated by the Promotion Committee (with the support of the most suitable technical personnel) on a time schedule and/or requirements agreed by all the members. It must be a tool that can be used by individual companies operating within the cluster to aid them in identifying their respective significant environmental aspects; in order to achieve this, the Review must meet at least two of the following requirements:

- the ability to identify the main environmental hotspots in the cluster and define the link between these and the direct or indirect pressures applied by the given sector;
- the ability to provide methodological and quantitative indications (for example on the average performance of the sector, or better, of the district or area identified as the benchmark territory) for every organisation that decides to undertake the pathway to EMAS registration so that these indications can be used to define the initial individual environmental reviews.

Moreover, it is also advisable to carry out two types of analyses: an analysis of the hotspots in the main production areas/supply chains; an analysis of the territory affected by the aspects and impacts and the contributions to these impacts by the organisations. A subsequent assessment then follows to establish how critical these levels are by analysing the determinants, environmental pressures, conditions of the local environment and impacts and responses implemented in the uniform production area. The environmental analysis must be periodically updated by the Promotion Committee.

In order to ensure fulfilment of the above-mentioned principles, the Cluster Environmental Review must, for example, contain the following information:

a   an overall description of the cluster both from a physical point of view (geomorphological and lithological features, the territorial layout and relevant hotspots) and from a social and production point of view (resident population and their location, features of the specific industrial and production framework, types of collective services and plants available in the territory with an environmental impact);

b   a survey of the environmental problems of the area carried out by identifying and describing the different physical elements (air, water, soil and subsoil, etc.) and a quantification and assessment of their environmental conditions (carried out using carefully selected indicators);

c   a survey of the specific sector carried out by a careful reconstruction of the production process and relations between the specific sector and the processes before and after this process, which identifies, describes, quantifies and assesses any environmental aspects and impacts directly or indirectly connected to each phase of the process;

d   an overview of any initiatives developed in the past and any responses implemented in the cluster by various institutional and private parties.

In carrying out the above-mentioned actions, the Promotion Committee should bear in mind two aspects that are essential for an effective approach in applying an EMS to the cluster:

1   on the one hand, when selecting which environmental performance indicators to use (both in the territory and in the sector), the Promotion Committee, where possible, should adopt any requirements and suggestions outlined by *Core Performance Indicators* in the EMAS III Regulation and any future *Reference Documents* (where they are available for the specific cluster sector);

2   on the other hand, when assessing the requirements of the environmental problems of the territory and the environmental aspects of the specific sector, the Promotion Committee should bear in mind the opinions of the interested parties, especially any opinions expressed by local residents. Both direct methods (e.g. questionnaires and interviews carried out directly with the residents) and indirect methods (e.g. survey of number and type of environmental complaints presented to the controlling and governing bodies) can be employed to gather the opinions of interested parties.

4. Preparation of a Cluster Environmental Programme

The Environmental Programme is a very important document managed directly or indirectly by the Promotion Committee to improve the cluster.

It is necessary to adopt the objectives and programmes shared among the parties adhering to the project. In particular, the roles and responsibilities for implementing the programmes belonging to public and private parties must be apportioned. It must be clear to the different individual organisations operating within the cluster in which objective they can participate and contribute to.

Furthermore, the environmental programme must be drafted in accordance with the EMAS Regulation or the ISO 14001 standard (identification of personnel in charge, resources, timeframes, monitoring indicators, etc.) and an adequate system must be put in place to periodically check on its progress, as well as any corrective actions in case of failure to meet the goals or if new critical situations arise.

In view of the importance of the document, the Cluster Environmental Programme should be drafted and approved by a unanimous vote or by the majority of Promotion Committee members whilst ensuring that every single action is also approved by the local stakeholders who are directly responsible for them; the

Programme will be reviewed and updated according to a pre-set schedule (a yearly basis would be considered reasonable).

In order to make it easier for organisations in the cluster to share the Cluster Environmental Programme (and possibly adhere to it), it must also be clearly identified and summarised in a document containing the following information:

- a description of the *general objectives* for improvement and demonstration of their consistency with the guiding principles previously indicated in the Cluster Environmental Policy;
- the identification of *specific targets*, where possible, quantified and measured, relevant to the various general objectives;
- an indication of the environmental aspect and/or problem of the area to which each objective and target refers, illustrating what contribution the fulfillment of the target would guarantee in improving those aspects;
- a description of the actions and *sub-actions* required to pursue a given objective;
- the identification of any *resources* already available to carry out the actions and sub-actions and/or an estimate of any resources needed, but not yet available, as well as the identification of possible financial sources;
- a definition of the *deadlines* by which to complete any projects (expected actions and interventions) and any pre-set targets;
- an indication, for each objective and associated project, of the *indicators* needed to assess their completion;
- the identification of the parties in the cluster (both members of the Promotion Committee and third parties) involved in carrying out each project and, among these, the identification of the party/parties in charge of meeting each objective.

An example of the Territorial Environmental Programme is shown in Table 5.1.

In order to ensure that the Environmental Programme becomes an effective tool for the cluster, the projects and actions in it should be completed through one or more formal acts (e.g. programme agreements, memoranda of understanding, environmental programmes for individual organisations with EMAS registration, planning by public administration…) that may concern only some of the participants in the Promotion Committee or involve third parties with which the Promotion Committee shares the implementation of specific activities.

There is one final reference left to discuss which concerns the suggestion of integrating improvement plans outlined by other local government plans into the Cluster Programme, such as those in the Local Agenda 21 process or outlined for specific projects funded on a national or international scale.

5. Definition of an external communications system

The Promotion Committee must ensure a link and communications to the stakeholders in the area. In particular, the Promotion Committee, in full compliance

Table 5.1 Extract from the Territorial Environmental Programme of the Promotion Committee for the Paper District of Capannori (Italy)

Objective	Goal	Deadline	Actions	Indicator	Resources	Overseen by
Reduction in subsidence	Reduction of ground water withdrawal from well fields in Pollino: 200 L/s; Reduction of ground water withdrawal for household drinking water from well fields in Pagnanico: 40 l/s	31/12/2008	Water supply from the river Serchio for household drinking water and for agricultural and industrial use: construction of a new pipe line to supply at least 400 l/s from the river Serchio; construction of a water purification plant for public supply: 200L/s	% reduction, l/sec, m³/year	10,000,000 (33% Ministry of the Environment, 33% Tuscany Region, 34% Acque S.P.A.)	Acque S.P.A.
Intensification and enhancement of the "Tubone" project, to reduce and recover water in production processes – Voluntary Agreement 7 May 2004, Supplementary Agreement for the protection of water resources	Reduction of ground water withdrawal up to max. estimated use for industry: 210 /s (art. 12 Programme Agreement)	31/12/2012				Industrial Associations, Paper companies
	Reduction of ground water withdrawal for household drinking water from well fields in Cerbaie: 500 L/s	31/12/2012				Acque S.P.A.

with the spirit of the EMAS Regulation, must periodically communicate both to the organisations within the cluster and all the interested parties:

- the outcome of the environmental analysis;
- the environmental programme and its progress;
- the results achieved;
- the point of reference for additional information.

In addition to the above-mentioned mandatory steps, the Position provides that the Promotion Committee can undertake a series of support activities for the cluster organisations, which are defined as 'simplifications' or 'synergies'.

In addition to an Annual Communications Plan, the Promotion Committee also needs to set up one or more active tools for communicating with the public (e.g. a web site, environmental report, information desk, etc.) to pursue, by way of example, the following goals:

- to give a report on the current status of the activities developed by the Promotion Committee in order to check that the objectives and environmental goals defined in the programming phase have been reached, and the actual use and effective benefit of any tools implemented by the cluster organisations;
- to provide the residential and stakeholder community, encompassing civil society and the economic system, with evidence of improvement in the environmental performance within the cluster, measured by the quantification and progress of the indicators selected in the Analysis phase and representative of the territorial benchmark;
- to communicate to the cluster organisations (both public and private) the quantity and type of tools that the Promotion Committee has made available to the cluster and thus, promoting a simplified process for participation by individual organisations in EMAS;
- to provide the individual organisations in the district with an additional 'tool' to use in drafting their own Environmental Declarations and conclude the process of adhering to EMAS or ISO 14001.

Simplifications and synergies: Collective activities and resources defined by the Promotion Committee for individual organisations

In an attempt to encourage and simplify the process of adhering to the EMS by individual organisations, the cluster approach indicates that the Promotion Committee must define and carry out additional activities to substitute the individual obligations in the Management System of the individual organisations in the area.

If the motivation behind a cluster approach is mainly to stimulate and enable participation in the voluntary scheme by individual organisations operating within the area, then the implementation process is duty bound to implement a series of initiatives supporting environmental management of individual organisations aiming to achieve precisely this. In light of this, the members of the Promotion Committee should prioritise the activities that they intend to promote within the cluster on the grounds that these initiatives are both economically practical and actually beneficial to the organisations concerned.

By way of example, a list of management, technical and organisational type activities is shown below, which could be provided by the Promotion Committee over time as support for the individual organisations in the area (both public and private, for production and services) to enable them to improve their environmental performance and limit the impacts deriving from their activities.

In this respect, it is plausible that the Promotion Committee could

1   implement tools to

    a   facilitate legislative updates and planning of regulatory deadlines by organisations within the cluster (especially those belonging to the specific sector) to support them in managing and ensuring legal compliance;

    b   support organisations in developing their EMSs by providing them with

        • indications on operational requirements to adopt in developing procedures to manage any environmental aspects considered to be significant;

        • diagrams and models for creating management procedures, environmental management manuals and the Environmental Declaration;

        • liaison tools between the various organisations operating in the area for managing specific environmental problems that could be detected in the area, especially when responding to emergencies whose effects might extend beyond the company's boundaries or when developing operational coordination systems between community environmental management service providers and users of these services.

    c   support individual organisations in the cluster to look for, identify and possibly obtain economic, technical and human resources required to implement their EMS or at least, to contribute to the fulfilment of one or more improvement objectives within the Cluster Environmental Programme;

    d   support individual organisations in developing training initiatives for their personnel by providing appropriate guidelines or other forms of knowledge sharing;

    e   support individual organisations in conducting internal audits to verify the effectiveness of the EMSs (check lists, questionnaires and verification protocols).

2   more directly, develop initiatives to

    a   plan and carry out or, alternatively, promote and encourage the organisation of training activities to implement locally by acknowledging the training requirements of the cluster organisations and defining their possible content;

b create periodic coordination meetings (and the sharing of resources and tools developed for the cluster) with the Environmental Managers and/ or Management Representatives of the companies registered to EMAS and/or certified to ISO 14001 in the area or, at least, interested in developing and adopting these tools;

c define and periodically update environmental performance indicators regarding the environmental aspects of the sector and any territorial problems deemed significant; the set of chosen indicators should be documented and the sources of the quantitative information contained in them clearly identified. The chosen indicators should allow (whenever possible):

- comparisons with legal limit or quality standards to be made;
- comparisons to be made over time;
- comparisons with similar regions and sectors.

Furthermore, the indicators measuring the specific sector performance should be a useful benchmark for individual companies intending to measure the effectiveness of their specific performance (especially the *Core Performance Indicators* set forth in EMAS III).

In addition to the above-mentioned initiatives, there are also ones about how to conduct a programmed audit of the EMS defined for the cluster with the following objectives:

- to assess the efficiency and effectiveness of the cluster environmental management tools, especially their ability to affirm the principles of environmental improvement defined in the Cluster Environmental Policy and the pursuit of the objectives and goals established in the Environmental Programme;
- to use the results that emerge during the audit to review the initiatives promoted within the cluster.

In order to meet these objectives, the following types of audits could at least be conducted for the cluster:

- an audit of the steps carried out to implement environmental management (starting from the Analysis and Policy up to the communal resources and shared tools for environmental management made available to the individual organisations) to check their effectiveness and the progress status of the objectives and goals;
- an audit on the effectiveness of the tools made available by the individual organisations in the cluster, carried out both directly in the organisations that have decided to adopt them (by on-site checks) and indirectly by monitoring the benefits perceived by the organisations themselves.

These audits could be carried out by parties suitably qualified by the Promotion Committee ensuring the objectivity and impartiality of the verification process.

The sector-related analysis of the pathway of the Tannery District in Tuscany

In the early 2000s, two local organisations, in particular, the Tannery Association of Santa Croce sull'Arno and the Tannery Consortium of Ponte a Egola (along with a few other associations in the same category in the Tuscany area) decided to promote a pathway for EMAS registration covering the whole district.

The territorial approach adopted on this pathway meant that voluntary environmental certification could be promoted among the SMEs, which had already started the process with the support of analytical and management tools made available by the district EMAS. It was here that the first EMAS registrations in the world of two tanneries occurred.

The area earmarked for the Cluster includes the four main municipalities in the district, situated between the province of Florence and Pisa, with a population of 76,175 encompassing nearly all the tanneries in the Tuscany Region.

The area is situated in the plains of Valdarno inferiore. The heart of this area, covering about 233 km², is the district of Santa Croce sull'Arno, which takes in the largest number of companies operating in this sector, namely tanneries and third party companies. The tannery sector employs about 10,000 workers in this area in a total of about 540 local companies broken down as follows:

- 284 tanneries/leather factories;
- 126 third party processing companies for the soaking phase;
- 130 third party processing companies minus the soaking phase.

There are various areas of environmental and scenic importance in the area (protected areas, rivers and agricultural land), which extend across the area of Padule di Fucecchio, Colline delle Cerbaie and the hills of S. Miniato, taking in a territory that reaches as far as Padule di Bientina, Valdinievole and the Circondario Empolese Valdelsa.

The approach adopted by the Promotion Committee of the Distretto Conciario Toscano (Tuscany Tannery District) to carry out the environmental analysis of the specific sector is particularly interesting.

A special work group including some members of the Promotion Committee and technical partners was set up to identify and assess the environmental aspects of the companies in the tannery sector situated in the four municipalities of the benchmark territory. The aim of the group was to calculate, for each environmental aspect, environmental performance indicators representing the actual conditions of the companies in the Tuscany Tannery District. Subsequently, a series of requirements for levels of significance was stipulated and shared by the entire Promotion Committee, which meant that, once they were applied, the main environmental aspects caused by the production cycle under examination could be identified.

A detailed questionnaire was sent to all the companies forming the Tannery Association of Santa Croce and the Tannery Consortium of Ponte a Egola in order to obtain preliminary data typical for all the tanneries in the district.

The sample turned out to be typical for the entire leather production area made up, on average, of 80 per cent hide manufacturers and 20 per cent leather manufactures. Within the leather production, the breakdown of production type for the area shows that: about 45 per cent carry out chrome tanning, 35 per cent vegetable tanning and 20 per cent mixed tanning.

The preparation of the questionnaires taken among sample companies in the area meant that a series of environmental indicators were developed that described, for each environmental aspect examined, the situation of the two types of processing examined.

Tables 5.2 and 5.3 show two examples of average indicators calculated on typical environmental aspects for tanneries both as an illustration of the average performance trends for the area and as a benchmark (numeric and methodological) for the organisations in the area wanting to participate in the pathway to voluntary environmental certification.

A series of assessment criteria for the level of significance has, therefore, been applied to the environmental performance indicators calculated with reference to each of the environmental aspects.

Table 5.2 Average indicators calculated on typical environmental aspects for tanneries: Energy consumptions

Energy consumption	Hide production		Leather production	
Electricity	2003	2.74 kWh / m² of hide	2003	0.71 kWh / kg of leather
	2004	2.51 kWh / m² of hide	2004	0.87 kWh / kg of leather
	2008	**2.90 kWh / m² of hide**	**2008**	**0.87 kWh / kg of leather**
Methane	2003	0.837 m³ / m² of hide	2003	0.14 m³ / kg of leather
	2004	0.836 m³ / m² of hide	2004	0.18 m³ / kg of leather
	2008	**0.77 m³ / m² of hide**	**2008**	**0.15 m³ / kg of leather**
Diesel	2003	0.018 l / m² of hide	2003	0.0049 l / kg of leather
	2004	0.011 l / m² of hide	2004	0.0067 l / kg of leather
	2008	**0.023 l / m² of hide**	**2008**	**0.005 l / kg of leather**

Table 5.3 Average indicators calculated on typical environmental aspects for tanneries: Air emissions

Emission factor VOC (g / m²)	Tuscany area
2004	157.2 g / m²
2008	**95.5 g / m²**

These criteria were aimed at assessing the environmental aspect originating in the tannery sector by looking at its entity compared with similar situations. The chosen significance criteria are

- *the presence of legal limits:* on the basis of this requirement, a different value of significance is attributed depending on whether there is a legal limit or not for the environmental aspects being examined;
- *intertemporal trend indicator* of the environmental aspects being examined: a value was attributed depending on the trend over time for those environmental aspects for which data is available over several years;
- *comparison with international benchmarks:* the indicator identified in the project was compared to other indicators in the tannery sector reported in studies and international reports that will act as a benchmark for comparison to establish the significance of the indicators from the Santa Croce sector. The benchmark used was Bref, or the 'Reference Document', which contains a description of the BAT (Best Available Techniques) and the relevant emission values for the tannery sector. This document is published by the EC and is included in the framework of the European directive IPPC/IED (Integrated Pollution Prevention and Control);
- *comparison with national benchmarks:* the indicator identified in the project was compared with other indicators in the tannery sector reported in studies and national reports such as the 2008 environmental report for UNIC (Unione nazionale Industria Conciaria – National Union Tannery Industry).

In order to carry out a comparative assessment of the level of significance, for every requirement a value between a minimum of one and a maximum of three was attributed, where three represents the worst-case scenario. Subsequently a weighted average was calculated from all the assigned averages until a single value was obtained representing the level of significance of the aspect under examination.

We can now take a look at the methods of applying the above-mentioned criteria and calculating the level of significance.

Presence of legal limits:

- Value 1: if there is no legal limit for the environmental aspect being considered;
- Value 3: if there is a legal limit for the environmental aspect being considered.

Intertemporal trend:

- Value 1: if there is a reduction exceeding 5 per cent over the previous year for the indicator referring to two consecutive years;

- Value 2: if the reduction is basically stable for the indicator referring to two consecutive years (±5 per cent over the previous year);
- Value 3: if there is an increase of more than 5 per cent over the previous year for the indicator referring to two consecutive years;

International benchmark (BREF for the sector)

- Value 1: if the indicator calculated in the project is more than 5 per cent lower than the Bref indicator;
- Value 2: if the indicator calculated in the project is basically stable (±5 per cent) in comparison with the Bref indicator;
- Value 3: if the indicator calculated in the project is more than 5 per cent over the Bref indicator.

National benchmark (UNIC Environmental Report)

- Value 1: if the indicator calculated in the project is more than 5 per cent lower than the indicator reported in the UNIC Environmental Report;
- Value 2: if the indicator calculated in the project is basically stable (±5 per cent) in comparison with the indicator reported in the UNIC Environmental Report;
- Value 3: if the indicator calculated in the project is more than 5 per cent over the indicator reported in the UNIC Environmental Report.

Once the values associated with the indicated requirements have been obtained for every environmental aspect (in each of the areas being studied and for all types of processing), the final value is then calculated for each one through a weighted average such as the one described in the following formula:

$$V = [(\text{Trend})*0.25] + [(\text{Legal Limit})*0.25] + [(\text{Bref})*0.25] \\ + [(\text{UNIC Report})*0.25]$$

The result was still a value V between 1 (minimum) and 3 (maximum) against which:

- $1 < V < 1.66$: insignificant environmental aspect;
- $1.66 < V < 2.33$: environmental aspect of average significance;
- $2.33 < V < 3$: Significant environmental aspect

Tables 5.4 and 5.5 show the final results of the overall assessment in two subsectors: hide and leather.

The conclusion based on the result of the assessment is that water in general is a priority for action for the area.

A final mention should be dedicated to the perspective chosen by the Promotion Committee to examine, as mentioned, the issues relating to environmental impacts in the supply chain by being among the first areas in Italy to

Table 5.4 Level of significance assessment: Leather production

Leather production	CRITERIA				Result
	Presence Regulatory Limit	Trend	Bref	Unic Report 2008	
AIR EMISSIONS	3	2	n.a.	1	**2**
ENERGY	1	1.33	n.a.	n.a.	**1.16**
WATER CONSUMPTIONS	3	1	n.a.	n.a.	**2**
WATER EMISSIONS	3	1.66	n.a.	n.a.	**2.34**
WASTE	1	2	2	n.a.	**1.63**
CONSUMPTION AUXILIARY MATERIALS	1	2	n.a.	n.a.	**1.5**

Table 5.5 Level of significance assessment: Hide production

Hide Production	CRITERIA				Result
	Presence Regulatory Limit	Trend	Bref	Unic Report 2008	
AIR EMISSIONS	3	1.66	n.a.	1.66[1]	**2.18**
ENERGY	1	2	1	1.5	**1.37**
WATER CONSUMPTIONS	3	2	1	1	**1.75**
WATER EMISSIONS	3	1.66	n.a.	n.a.	**2.34**
WASTE	1	3	1	3	**2**
CONSUMPTION AUXILIARY MATERIALS	1	2	2	3	**2**

develop the application of a life cycle analysis to two kinds of typical products for the area (leather and hide). This choice was basically driven by the desire to experiment with management and communications tools that could better exploit the environmental performance of the area's product in the market in conjunction with its excellence guaranteed by traditional methods of production and the origins of the product (and the relevant trademarks). To this end, over the last few years, the area has initiated the calculation of an average area LCA (Life Cycle Assessment) directing the strategic choices of the Promotion Committee towards a future preparation of an area PEF (Product Environmental Footprint) in accordance with the EC methodology set forth in recommendation 179/2013.

Certification of local authorities: the specific features of applying management systems in public administration

In the last years we observed a fast increase of the number of ISO 14001 certifications and EMAS registrations obtained by enterprises in the industrial sector. However, more and more EU public authorities are adopting an EMS.

The application of EMSs by public institutions (and local authorities in particular) has been broadly developed both on a theoretical (Von Malmborg, 2003) and on an operational level, through many international projects regarding both EMAS Regulation and the standard ISO 14001 (Union of Baltic Cities, 2004).

Generally, literature review as well as most of the experiences developed by local authorities in the EU (Von Malmborg, 2003; Lozano and Vallés, 2007; Emilsson and Hjelm, 2007) show the success of the EMS in improving municipalities' environmental performance, both in general terms and in specific environmental spheres.

From a more detailed perspective, improvements often regard waste management, indeed an increased separate waste collection rather than a decrease in production. Other significant improvements, often registered among local authorities, concern the use of resources and better environmental conditions on the governed territorial area (Barret, 1995; Habib and Ismaila, 2007).

Relevant literature emphasises that public administrations, like any other organisation, produce environmental impacts linked to their structures and to the supply of given public services. The key point is that such bodies do have decision powers concerning land use, planning and management on their own territory: in other words, they can influence, through the planning and control (and the proper implementation) of administrative functions, the activities and behaviours of the 'society' being governed (companies and citizens) (Ridolfi et al., 2008).

Industrial organisations implementing an EMS are mainly concerned with the control of environmental aspects generated by the production activities (Yasuhumi and Eric, 2008). Like all organisations, public institutions have similar 'direct' aspects, generating impacts on the environment, but they mostly have major 'indirect' environmental impacts arising from the way they deliver their services and exert their land planning and control powers (Von Malmborg, 2003; Emilsson and Hjelm, 2007).

Generally speaking, adopting EMAS in public administrations today is seen as an extremely important scheme in many European countries, including Italy, because it is the sector with the greatest number of registrations, with over 160 institutions registered.

From its very first version in 1996, the ISO 14001 standard was open to all organisations, not just those in the industrial sector (although emphasis on the importance of indirect environmental aspects was only introduced in the 2004 version). It has also achieved high numbers of applications in public administration; the values are quite low since the sector is in eleventh place for number of certifications, but in absolute terms, they are much greater as there are now over 500 public administrations with certification.

It is quite clear that the application of EMAS and ISO 14001 in public administrations is very different from that in an industrial setting both in terms of objectives and operational solutions.

In particular, a closer look at local authorities, whether in the form of a small municipality or an entire region, shows how ISO 14001 and EMAS can take on a role that goes beyond one of a simple management mechanism to become a true tool for governance.

It became clear from the first experimental application in municipalities and provinces how the EMS could prove to be a useful tool for administrations in managing the consequences of policy decisions in the territory in terms of control, communications and transparency. EMAS is an ideal way of integrating any voluntary and institutional tools that a local administration may have, a sort of 'container' of initiatives for the environmental sustainability of the Institution and the territory under its administration.

In order to analyse which operational solutions for applying EMAS and ISO 14001 are better suited to public administration, it is a good idea to take a look at some of the features that define this type of organisation.

Local authorities are characterised by the institutional role-play in governing the territory. They are, in fact, responsible for land use and urban planning, economic and financial programming, regulatory interventions in the territory, the execution of public works and infrastructures, as well as ensuring many public services and monitoring activities within the territory. A local authority, therefore, can be regarded both as a market regulator (since it is in the position to create suitable conditions for promoting sustainable products, services and activities) and also a direct consumer of goods and services (since it can promote the production of 'green' products and services, for example, by adopting Green Procurement or including environmental clauses in public contracts).

Another important reason for applying an EMS to a local authority is the opportunity to create local conventions or policy agreements with different higher or lower level institutions in the territory.

While this leads to an assessment of the possible benefits of a development pathway to sustainability, it is important not to lose sight of some basic considerations that clearly show that administrative limits do not coincide with physical thresholds and therefore, in order for a territorial management policy to be effective, it must be applied uniformly and consistently in the local area, even if by parties with totally different responsibilities.

When planning environmental improvements, therefore, it is advisable for all local authorities in the same territory to be involved in the decisional processes.

If an EMS is being applied to a public administration, there are certain problems and specific elements that must be taken into account when preparing the initial environmental analysis and creating the system in general. These can be listed to highlight where necessary the main differences with respect to a more conventional application in an industrial setting:

- It is important to remember that the institution operates on two different decisional levels, one political and the other technical and administrative. The political authorities are represented by the Mayor/President, Council and Committee whilst the administrative authorities are represented by the Secretary, Director General, Managers of sectors/services and officials;
- In contrast to organisational charts for private companies, the different functions in a public institution are regulated by different, less obvious hierarchies;
- Communications are often regulated by 'institutional' channels and therefore are much more rigid and formal than for businesses;
- Structures and infrastructures (e.g. roads, schools, etc.) are part of institutions and therefore, impacts resulting from administrative activities and the use and maintenance of the above-mentioned structures have to analysed differently;
- Generally speaking, the management of movable and immovable property implies that direct impacts will occur on the environment (e.g. water and electricity consumption, emissions in air and water, waste production) whilst the main indirect consequences are linked to the running of the territory, such as planning (territorial and by sector), environmental control (e.g. authorisation for discharges, emissions etc.) and economic programming, to name just a few;
- Local authorities can be responsible for the indirect management of other organisations and/or structures through shareholding or institutional affiliations (e.g. schools, parks, mountain communities);
- Local public services (e.g. waste and water management, etc.) are usually carried out by operators in which the local authority has a shareholding. Moreover, this kind of service is decided by the local authority, which usually owns the networks;
- Local authorities generally contract out or award concessions for managing goods and services; preliminary investigations into assessment procedures for environmental impact, identification of suitable sites for setting up waste treatment and disposal plants;
- Some local authorities are in charge of environmental control, which covers many different sectors (e.g. authorisation for public and industrial sewer waste, census of contaminated sites that need to be reclaimed, authorisation for emissions into the atmosphere, etc.);
- Relations with other authorities can occur on different levels regarding the same portion of land administered by authorities of different size (e.g. Municipality and Region) and the same responsibility, which must be carried out in conjunction with other authorities (e.g. environmental control agreed between various authorities);

- The emergencies management is referred to both accidents in actual physical structures (e.g. fires, explosions, damage to pipelines and leakages, etc.) as well as emergencies in the territory for which the Authority is responsible (e.g. landslides, floods, earthquakes, forest fires).

Given the complexity of the organisation of local authorities, it is possible for just a part of the organisation to undergo registration/certification (for example, a single Service/Department), basically to allow the EMS to be adopted gradually and to then progressively extend it to all authorities.

The specific features characterise the approach to environmental certification by public administrations can be looked at from various angles in terms of:

- motivation and incentives for adopting the scheme;
- obstacles and barriers to adopting and implementing the scheme;
- the benefits associated with environmental certification.

Motivation and incentives for adopting EMAS by local authorities

According to the relevant literature, the decision of public institutions to adopt an EMS is closely related to their nature and functions, e.g. the role they play in being an example for the communities they govern (firms and citizens) and their need to obtain and maintain their consensus (political consensus above all, within a broader framework of stakeholders' relations) (Ernoul, 2009). These motivations are often very different by the reasons of the adoption of EMS from industrial organisations (Burstroem, 2000; Zutshi and Sohal, 2004; Gavronski et al., 2008).

The most common drivers spurring PAs to implement an EMS can be summarised as follows:

- 'environmental and management performance improvement': the aim is to achieve better environmental and organisational/managerial capabilities. Among the reasons that motivate public institutions to implement an (certified) EMS, the aim of improving environmental and land-use policies' effectiveness emerges as the most important. Providing administrators with practical tools to support their decision making process also plays a relevant role;
- 'stakeholders' and local community's relations improvement': the focus is on improving transparency and credibility towards stakeholders. Demonstrable environmental awareness and competence can also increase the authority's standing with various stakeholders groups and improve public institution's image and communication;
- 'territorial image's improvement': EMAS registration and ISO14001 certification are often seen by local authorities as an opportunity to promote the attractiveness of the governed territorial area, both for business and tourism purposes. The opportunity to obtain an environmental certification is particularly relevant for PAs governing touristic areas. A survey investigated the

experiences in EMAS implementation by the municipalities belonging to the area that hosted the Winter Olympic Games in 2006 (Venturello, 2005). When asked about the main drivers that spurred them to implement EMAS, all local authorities involved (8 municipalities and a 'Mountain District', a superior-level authority with a co-ordination role) mentioned the possibility to improve the image and attractiveness of the territory, in order to maximise the benefits that the Olympic event may produce over time, in terms of increase in the population, employment and added value produced;

- 'consistency with their role as public institution with environmental objectives': e.g. giving a coherent message about environmental responsibility and behaviour to the local community;
- 'leading by example': e.g. promoting EMSs for SMEs and/or demonstration and example for local enterprises.

Additional drivers could include 'a push by local community members', 'improving access to public and EU funding', 'fulfilling environmental commitments' and 'complying with legislation'.

The findings of the EVER study further support evidence emerging from literature: the main drivers identified refer to 'political consensus' (50 per cent of the PAs interviewed) and to 'local stakeholders and community's relations' improvement' (43 per cent) (IEFE et al., 2006).

Obstacles and barriers to adopting environmental management systems

All the studies and research projects dealing with EMS implementation by public institutions illustrate the barriers tackled in the implementation of this management tool (Lozano and Vallés, 2007). Some of the main barriers that have been highlighted can be summarised as follows:

- lack of time, human resources, skills and competences;
- difficulties in achieving staff involvement and motivation;
- budget constraints: when resources are limited, EMS has to compete with many other local government priorities. Although the process may reveal areas where the authority could save money, the initial costs could be substantial when the authority is under financial pressure;
- lack of political support and commitment: EMS requires changes in the policy agenda, but a major hindrance refers to maintaining the environment as a top priority on this agenda after the initial certification process. This is sometimes tackled by the lack of awareness among elected members and officers;
- technical difficulties linked to the understanding and, especially, to the implementation of the EMS requirements.

As regards barriers in maintaining the EMS over time, it has to be firstly noted that public institutions generally are not keen on dropping out, as their institutional role implies a somehow 'irreversible' commitment to the principles underpinning EMS. However, according to literature, a lack of recognition by public institutions (mainly superior administrations) and lack of external feedbacks act as relevant barriers to EMS effectiveness after the initial certification.

In the already mentioned EVER study, the 'lack of human resources, competence and external incentives', 'costs of registration' and 'difficulties in achieving and maintaining legal compliance' were not considered as important barriers. The difficulties related to the roles of the verifier and of the Competent Body were not rated as substantial hindrances within EMS adoption, either.

The benefits associated with environmental certification

Relevant literature emphasises that the benefits arising to public institutions extend beyond improving the environmental performance. As regards internal benefits, many studies (Burstroem, 2000; Hertin et al., 2008) highlight the following improvements:

- 'better management of performance' – EMS spurs a systematic approach to management, improving the overall organisational efficiency of local authorities, through a rationalisation and a more structured knowledge of internal activities (better coordination, internal communication, planning of processes and activities). Significant improvements also regard compliance with legislation and better management control, by adding information on PA's environmental performance to the decision making process;
- 'economic savings' – EMS is able to bear financial savings through a more eco-efficient operational management (by improving recycling performance, reducing energy consumption, increasing income generated from sale of recovered waste as a raw material, etc.). However, while some of these benefits arise quickly and require no additional expenditure (simply implying changes in work instructions, training and personnel behaviour), there's a limit from the savings that can be generated from such changes, after which savings can only be realised through investments in new processes and services. Hence, it is important to gain savings early in the EMS process, to justify increased capital investment for the environmental program to then realise long-term savings.

Other benefits mentioned include 'continuous improvement', 'staff motivation' and 'securing funding'.

As regards external benefits, literature review pointed out the specificities characterising the implementation of the pattern within public administrations, mainly from two points of view:

1 'competitiveness' – PAs deliver services, and so should be seen as organisations competing on such issues as 'customer satisfaction' for 'market share'. According to literature, local authorities that are ISO 14001-certified or EMAS-registered do benefit from a competitive edge over those who do not.

This is particularly relevant for the perceived 'quality' and the attractiveness of a territory (e.g. EMS capability to attract investments and tourists, recruiting and retain quality staff, attract and retain self-sufficient residents);

2   'political consensus and dialogue with local stakeholders/community' – As reported by many studies, a certified EMS is able to increase opportunities for effective communication within local community and stakeholders, to enhance transparency and credibility and improve the image of the institution (Studer et al., 2008).

According to many public administrations, EMSs (especially EMAS) tend to improve dialogue with the local community and are considered an effective 'consensus building' tool (as regards in particular better relations with social stakeholders and better cooperation with local industries and environmental NGOs).

On the contrary, a relevant part of the literature (e.g. IEFE et al., 2006) pointed out that today registered PAs are not fully exploiting all the communication opportunities that are offered especially by EMAS, in the relations with stakeholder and local communities, mainly because of the difficulties faced in effectively communicating with their territory. As to EMAS, for example, there is a strong agreement on the limitations of the Environmental Statement (the document that is conceived to inform the stakeholders) in its current full format as a communication tool.

Besides organisational and stakeholders' relations improvements, the other most important benefits perceived by PAs are those related to 'economic efficiency' (e.g. cost savings through decrease in resource use, material reuse and recycling and through waste reduction) (IEFE et al., 2006).

References

Aharonson, B.S., Baum, J.A. and Feldman, M.P., 2007. 'Desperately seeking spillovers? Increasing returns, industrial organization and the location of new entrants in geographic and technological space'. *Industrial and Corporate Change*, 16, 89–130.

Alshuwaikhat, H. M., Abubakar, I., 2007. 'Towards a Sustainable Urban Environmental Management Approach (SUEMA): Incorporating environmental management with Strategic Environmental Assessment (SEA)'. *Journal of Environmental Planning and Management*, 50, 257–270.

Andreas, B. Eisingerich, S., Bell, J. and Tracey, P., 2010. 'How can clusters sustain performance? The role of network strength, network openness, and environmental uncertainty'. *Research Policy*, 39, 239–253.

Baldizzone, G., 2000. 'L'Agenda 21 come strumento cardine delle politiche di sviluppo sostenibile.' *Ambiente e Sviluppo*, 5, 6–18.

Barla, P., 2007. 'ISO certification and environmental performance in Quebec's pulp and paper industry'. *Journal of Environmental Economics and Management*, 53, 291–306.

Barret, B.F.D., 1995. 'From environmental auditing to integrated environmental management: local government experience in the United Kingdom and Japan'. *Journal of Environmental Planning and Management*, 38, 307–331.

Bathelt, H., 1998. 'Regionales Wachstum in vernetzten Strukturen: Konzeptioneller Überblick und kritische Bewertung des Phänomens,Drittes Italien'. *Die Erde*, 129, 247–271.

Battaglia M., Daddi, T. and Ridolfi, R., 2008. 'Environmental Territorial Management: A New Approach for Industrial Clusters, in Robert H. Theobald (Eds.), Environmental Management: 105–120. New York: Nova Publisher.

Battaglia, M., Bianchi, L., Frey, M. and Iraldo, F., 2010. 'An innovative model to promote CSR among SMEs operating in industrial clusters: evidence from an EU project'. *Corporate Social Responsibility and Environmental Management*, 17, 133–141.

Bengtsson, M. and Soelvell, O., 2004. 'Climate of competition, clusters and innovative performance'. *Scandinavian Journal of Management*, 20, 225–244.

Botta, S., Comoglio, C., 2013 'Implementing environmental management systems in a cluster of municipalities: a case study.' *American Journal of Environmental Science* 9: 410–423.

Burstroem, F., 2000. 'Environmental management systems and co-operation in municipalities'. *Local Environment*, 5, 271–284.

Daddi T., Magistrelli M., Frey M. and Iraldo F., 2011. 'Do Environmental Management Systems improve environmental performance? Empirical evidence from Italian companies'. *Environment, Development and Sustainability*, 13, 845–862.

Daddi T., Testa F. and Iraldo F., 2010. 'A cluster-based approach as an effective way to implement the ECAP (Environmental Compliance Action Program): evidence from some good practices'. *Local Environment*, 15(1), 73–82.

Daddi T., Tessitore, S., Frey, M., 2012. 'Eco-innovation and competitiveness in industrial Clusters'. *International Journal of Technology Management*, 58, 49–63.

Del Brío, J.A. and Junquera, B., 2003. 'A review of the literature on environmental innovation management in SMEs: implications for public policies'. *Technovation*, 23, 939–948.

Emilsson, S. and Hjelm, O., 2007. 'Managing indirect environmental impact within local authorities' standardized environmental management systems'. *Local Environment*, 12, 73–86.

Ernoul, L., 2009. 'Residents' perception of tourist development and the environment: a study from Morocco'. *International Journal of Sustainable Development World Ecology*, 16, 228–233.

European Commission, 2007. Small clean and competitive – a programme to help small and medium sized enterprises comply with environmental legislation [online]. Communication from the Commission to the Council, the European Parliament, the European Economic and Social Committee and the Committee of Regions, COM (2007)379 final. Available from: http://ec.europa.eu/environment/sme/programme /programme_en.htm.

Gavronski, I., Ferrer, G., Ely Laureano, P., 2008. 'ISO 14001 certification in Brazil: motivations and benefits'. *Journal of Cleaner Production*, 16, 87–94.

Habib, M.A. and Ismaila, A., 2007. 'Towards a Sustainable Urban Environmental Management Approach (SUEMA): incorporating environmental management with Strategic Environmental Assessment (SEA)'. *Journal of Environmental Planning and Management*, 50, 257–270.

Hertin, J., et al., 2008. 'Are EMS environmentally effective? The link between environmental management systems and environmental performance in European companies'. *Journal of Environmental Planning and Management*, 51, 259–283.

Hillary, R. 1999. *Evaluation of Study Reports on the Barriers, Opportunities and Drivers for Small and Medium Sized Enterprises in the Adoption of Environmental Management Systems*. London: Routledge.

Hirschman, A.O., 1958. *The Strategy of Economic Development*. New Haven: Yale University Press.

IEFE, Adelphi Consult, IOEW, SPRU, Valor & Tinge, 2006: EVER: Evaluation of eco-label and EMAS for their Revision – Research findings, Final report to the European Commission – Part I–II, DG Environment European Community; Brussels. Available from www.europa.eu.int/comm/environment/emas.

Institute of Directors. 2006. *The Business of the Environment: Policy and Opportunities.* London: IOD.

Iraldo, F., 2002. *Ambiente, impresa e distretti industriali.* Milano: Franco Angeli.

Kassinis, G., I., 2001. 'Location, Networks and Firm Environmental Management Practices.' *Journal of Environmental Management and Planning,* 44, 815–832.

Lepoutre, J. and Heene, A., 2006. 'Investigating the impact of firm size on Small Business Social Responsibility: A critical review'. *Journal of Business Ethics,* 67: 257–273.

Lozano, M. and Valle´s, J., 2007. 'An analysis of the implementation of an environmental management system in a local public administration'. *Journal of Environmental Management,* 82, 495–511.

MERIT – Maastricht Economic and social Research and training centre on Innovation and Technology, 2006. 2006 European Regional Innovation Scoreboard. Maastricht: MERIT.

Merli, R., Preziosi, M., Massa, I., 'EMAS regulation in Italian clusters: investigating the involvement of local stakeholders'. *Sustainability,* Vol. 6, 2014, 4537–4557.

Parrish, J., Wassersug, S., 2012. The Virginia Regional Environmental Management System Partnership. 'Partnership benefits and examples of success', Global Environment & Technology Foundation, 2012. Available at: http://www.cscaweb.org/EMS/sector_team/support_files/case_studies/VREMS%20benefit%20flyer.pdf.

Porter, M.E., 1998. *On Competition.* Boston: Harvard Business School Press.

Rennings, K., Ziegler, A., Ankele, K. and Hoffmann, E., 2005. 'The influence of different characteristics of the EU environmental management and auditing scheme on technical environmental innovations and economic performance'. *Ecological Economics,* 57, 45–59.

Ridolfi, R., et al., 2008. 'The application of environmental certification to the province of Siena'. *Journal of Environmental Management,* 86, 390–395.

Rizzi, F., Bartolozzi, I., Borghini, A. and Frey, M., 2012. 'Environmental Management of End of Life Products: Nine Factors of Sustainability in Collaborative Networks'. *Business Strategy and the Environment,* DOI: 10.1002/bse.1766.

Rosenthal, S.S. and Strange, W.C., 2003. 'Geography, industrial organization, and agglomeration'. *Review of Economics and Statistics,* 85, 377–393.

Schmitz, H. and Nadvi, K. 1999. 'Clustering and industrialization: introduction'. *World Development,* 29, 1885–1903.

Smith, R. and Van de Ven, A., 1994. 'Developmental processes of cooperative interorganisational relationships'. *Academy of Management Review,* 19, 90–118.

Steger, U. 2000. 'Environmental Management Systems: Empirical Evidence and Further Perspectives'. *European Management Journal,* 18, 23–37.

Studer, S., et al., 2008. 'SMEs and voluntary environmental initiatives: a study of stakeholders' perspectives in Hong Kong'. *Journal of Environmental Planning and Management,* 51, 285–301.

Union of Baltic Cities, 2004. EMAS – peer review for the cities, final technical report [online]. European Commission. Available from: http://ec.europa.eu/environment/emas/local/pdf/emascities_en.pdf [accessed 24 September 2009].

Venturello, I., 2005. EMAS registration within local authorities: the case of Olympic municipalities. Thesis (Masters). Sant'Anna School of Advanced Studies.

Von Malmborg, F., 2003. 'Environmental management systems: what is in it for local authorities?' *Journal of Environmental Policy & Planning,* 5, 3–21.

Von Weltzien Høivik, H. and Shankar, D., 2011. 'How Can SMEs in a Cluster Respond to Global Demands for Corporate Responsibility?' *Journal of Business Ethics,* 101, 175–195.

Yasuhumi, M. and Eric, W.W., 2008. 'The ISO 14001 environmental management standard in Japan: results from a national survey of facilities in four industries'. *Journal of Environmental Planning and Management,* 51, 421–445.

Zutshi, A. and Sohal, A., 2004. 'Environmental management system adoption by Australasian organizations: part 1: reasons, benefits and impediments'. *Technovation,* 24, 335–357.

Index

Abbott Laboratories, 85–88
absenteeism, 10
absorber elements, 31
Accreditation Body, 28
accuracy principle, 171
active business, 16
adaptive business, 15
adaptive model, 16
advertising, green, 146–48
allocation procedures, 156–57
Ambiti Produttivi Omogenei (APO)
    scheme, 187
anticipative context, 15, 16
asymmetrical information, 146
Attitude Behaviour Context (ABC)
    theory, 145
audit, *see* environmental audit
audit cycle, 114, 116–17
audit plan, 117, 119
audit programme, 117, 118
audit report, 121
auditors, competencies for, 114–16

Bhopal, 2
Blauer Engel, 150
brand image, 10
BRAVE study, 59
Brazil, 60
buffalo extinction, 1
business competitiveness: definition of,
    7; dimensions of, 7–8; environmental
    management and, 6–10; environmental
    practices and, 9; key variables affecting,
    8; levels of, 7–8; measurement of, 8–9
business models, 15–16

Canada, 60
Canadian Ecologo, 150

capitalism, birth of, 1
carbon emission certifications, 29–32
carbon footprint, 24, 169–78
ceremonial behaviours, 5
Certified Environmental Product
    Declaration, 152
Chalcolithic period, 1
Chernobyl, 2
cherry picking, 22
China, 62
Chinese organisations, drivers for adoption
    in, 58, 60
clean technologies, 14
climate change, 2, 144; carbon emission
    certifications, 29–32; impact, 176
Cluster Environmental Policy, 192–94
Cluster Observatory, 184
clustering, 184–85; advantages of, 189–91;
    collective activities and resources,
    198–200; EMAS Cluster Approach,
    186–89; industrial clusters, 189–206;
    operational phases for EMS application,
    191–98; Tuscany Tannery District,
    201–06
coercive mechanisms, 5
command and control measures, 13
Commission Decision, 189–90
communication processes, 89, 105–08,
    131–32, 136, 138–39, 196–99
Community Regulation, 26–27
Competent Body, 28, 65, 161, 168
competitive advantage, 2, 5, 6, 12,
    211–12; Ecolabels and, 44–46; of
    environmental certification, 40–47
competitive success, 8
competitiveness, *see* business
    competitiveness
complaints collection system, 108

type I eco-labels, 150–51
type III environmental claims, 167

United States: conservation movement in, 1–2; Industrial Revolution in, 1

validation mechanism, 137
Value-Belief-Norm (VBN) theory, 145

values, 145
verification, 137

WEPA-Lucca, 124–30
White Swan, 150
work methods: analysis, 80–81; defining and implementing, 97–101; documentation of, 99–101